Gregory Maertz

LITERATURE AND THE CULT OF PERSONALITY

Essays on Goethe and His Influence

Gregory Maertz

LITERATURE AND THE CULT OF PERSONALITY

Essays on Goethe and His Influence

ibidem-Verlag
Stuttgart

Bibliografische Information der Deutschen Nationalbibliothek
Die Deutsche Nationalbibliothek verzeichnet diese Publikation in der Deutschen Nationalbibliografie; detaillierte bibliografische Daten sind im Internet über http://dnb.d-nb.de abrufbar.

Bibliographic information published by the Deutsche Nationalbibliothek
Die Deutsche Nationalbibliothek lists this publication in the Deutsche Nationalbibliografie; detailed bibliographic data are available in the Internet at http://dnb.d-nb.de.

Cover picture: Portrait of Johann Wolfgang von Goethe by Friedrich Bury (1763–1823).
Source: Klassik Stiftung Weimar.

∞

Gedruckt auf alterungsbeständigem, säurefreien Papier
Printed on acid-free paper

ISBN-13: 978-3-8382-0981-4

© *ibidem*-Verlag
Stuttgart 2017

Alle Rechte vorbehalten

Das Werk einschließlich aller seiner Teile ist urheberrechtlich geschützt. Jede Verwertung außerhalb der engen Grenzen des Urheberrechtsgesetzes ist ohne Zustimmung des Verlages unzulässig und strafbar. Dies gilt insbesondere für Vervielfältigungen, Übersetzungen, Mikroverfilmungen und elektronische Speicherformen sowie die Einspeicherung und Verarbeitung in elektronischen Systemen.

All rights reserved. No part of this publication may be reproduced, stored in or introduced into a retrieval system, or transmitted, in any form, or by any means (electronic, mechanical, photocopying, recording or otherwise) without the prior written permission of the publisher. Any person who does any unauthorized act in relation to this publication may be liable to criminal prosecution and civil claims for damages.

Printed in the EU

Contents

Contents V

Acknowledgements VII

Preface IX

Prelude
Literature and the Cult of Personality:
On Goethe's Influence in Britain 1

Chapter One
Goethe and the Generation of 1789:
Cultural Mediation and Literary Enfranchisement 27

Chapter Two
Goethe, the Reception of Kant,
and the Romantic Culture War in Britain 57

Chapter Three
The Accidental Intermediary: Henry Crabb Robinson
and the Translation of Goethe's Poetry 77

Interlude One
Goethe and the Romantic Idealization of the Artist 99

Chapter Four
Resistance and Concealment:
Goethe and the Canonical British Romantic Poets 115

Chapter Five
Thomas Carlyle and the *Imitatio* Goethe 139

Interlude Two
Cultural Identity and the Transmission of Goethe
in New England 161

Chapter Six
The Failure of Romanticism and the Triumph of Realism in *Middlemarch*: Goethe and the Literary Formation of George Eliot 173

Postlude
De-mythologizing Goethe: George Saintsbury and the Assertion of British Cultural Autonomy 189

Bibliography 205

Notes 223

Index 265

Acknowledgements

> "Besuch im Goethehaus.... Der Kustos fordert uns zur Eintragung ins Fremdenbuch auf.... Wie ich hinzutrete, finde ich beim Blättern meinen Namen schon mit grosser ungefüger Kinderschrift verzeichnet."
>
> Walter Benjamin[1]

My research and writing on Goethe and his critics was aided by the following grants and fellowships for which I am grateful: a John D. and Rose H. Jackson Fellowship at the Beinecke Library; a NEMLA Summer Fellowship at the Houghton Library; an ACLS Travel Grant to the Niedersächsische Staats- und Universitätsbibliothek at the Georg-August-Universität Göttingen and to the Goethe- und Schiller-Archiv in Weimar; a Kate B. and Hall J. Peterson Fellowship at the American Antiquarian Society; Membership at the Institute for Advanced Study in Princeton; an NEH Fellowship for University Teachers; a Stipendium from the Gerda Henkel Stiftung; a National Humanities Center NEH Fellowship; an ACLS Senior Fellowship; a Visiting Research Professorship in the Department of Germanic Languages and Literature at Duke University; and research leave awarded by St. John's University, my home institution.

Matthew Feldman took a special interest in seeing that this book was published. For his generous encouragement, I could not be more thankful. I am also indebted to Bella Muccari for her expert proofreading and for so much more. In addition, I wish to express my thanks for the assistance of Valerie Lange and Florian Bölter at ibidem as well as that of Lana Umali and Antonio Fontana at St. John's. My work on this book has been fortunate to enjoy the support of colleagues in the English Department and elsewhere at St. John's, such as C. Scott Combs, Jeffrey Fagen, Amy Gansell, Amy King, John Lowney, Kathleen Lubey, Steve Mentz, and Stephen Sicari. Other names are reference points for the journeys and conversations that propelled the writing of this book: James G. Basker, George Bridge, Frederick Burwick, Caroline H. Cooney, Kevin L. Cope, William C. Donahue, Florence Dore, Kata Gellen, Gerald Gillespie, Ruth V.

Gross, Sabine Hake, Geoffrey Harpham, Robin Hemley, Martyn and Jessie Imrie, Martin Kagel, Wynfrid Kriegleder, Timothy Lenoir, Michael McKeon, Elizabeth Mansfield, Jakob Norberg, Thomas Pfau, Barry V. Qualls, Ruben D. Quintero, Jeffrey Sammons, Jane Sharp, Erik Tonning, Kevin Van Anglen, Heinrich von Staden, and Frederick Wegener. Unless otherwise indicated, the translations in the text and notes are my own.

The publication of this book commemorates the mentorship of Erich Heller and Lilian R. Furst during my student days at Northwestern and Harvard. As refugees from Hitler's Europe, they converted me to the understanding that the life of the mind was first and foremost a German-speaking territory. This book also pays homage to my teachers at Harvard—Walter Jackson Bate, Jerome H. Buckley, James Engell, and David Perkins—whose generosity of spirit, if not their superior learning, I have tried to emulate in my own career.

Highgales, Gravir, The Isle of Lewis

Preface

> "Every Goethe text, however divergent from the others, bears the mark of his unique and overwhelming personality, which cannot be evaded..."
>
> Harold Bloom[1]

This book argues that the fabrication of Johann Wolfgang von Goethe, the German poet and polymath, as an Anglo-American sage and literary icon was the product of a cult of personality that lay at the center of nineteenth-century intellectual politics. A reconstruction of the culture wars fought over Goethe's authority in Britain and the United States, a previously hidden chapter in the intellectual history of the period ranging from the late eighteenth century to the threshold of Modernism, is thus the focus of *Literature and the Cult of Personality*. Marginal as well as canonical writers and critics participated in this process, and the essays that follow offer insight into the mediation activities of Thomas Holcroft, Henry Crabb Robinson, Lord Byron and Percy Bysshe Shelley, Thomas Carlyle, the cream of New England intelligentsia, and George Eliot. For women writers and Jacobins as well as Dissenters, Scots, and Americans, transmitting the works of Goethe to an English-speaking audience emerges as an empowering paradigm of literary development according to which "re-writers" became original writers through an apprenticeship of translation and reviewing.

At the center of this process stands the figure of Carlyle who simultaneously serves as the chief advocate for and embodies the beau idéal of Goethean *Bildung* or self-realization in Britain. Approaching mid-century, Carlyle's emphasis on the person of the poet rather than the poetic text—and thus the construction of the Goethean cult of personality—continues and exfoliates in the writings of Carlyle's epigones and imitators. By reading Goethe's life experiences and personality as exemplary and worthy of emulation, Carlyle established a pattern that will dominate British and American cultural life throughout the last decades of the nineteenth century. Initially limited to Goethe and German literature, Anglo-American enthusiasm for the German intellect eventually encompasses aesthetics, philosophy, theology, and science.

The voices of Goethe's opponents—critics writing for *The Anti-Jacobin Review* as well as more prominent figures such as William Taylor, Samuel Taylor Coleridge, William Wordsworth, Thomas De Quincey, William Hazlitt, and George Saintsbury—are equally well represented in this book. Anticipating the opposition to high theory in the modern academy and the personal attacks on the émigré scholar Paul De Man, who, like Goethe, once served as the mouthpiece of an authoritarian regime, Goethe's British and American antagonists in the Romantic and Victorian eras, typically cultural nationalists with an inward-looking conservative agenda, seek to construct, preserve, and defend a myth of the self-sufficiency of British literature.

In the diverse and fascinating body of critical writing and translations examined in this book textual exegesis plays an unexpectedly minor role; in its place a full-blown cult of personality materializes along with a blueprint for an ideology of hero-worship that becomes more fully mapped out in the cultural and political life of twentieth-century Europe and early twenty-first century America.

Prelude
Literature and the Cult of Personality:
On Goethe's Influence in Britain

> "Überhaupt, der persönliche Charakter des Schriftstellers bringt seine Bedeutung beim Publikum hervor, nicht die Künste seines Talents."
>
> Johann Wolfgang von Goethe[1]

> "This new generation shared a culture which, largely thanks to Samuel Taylor Coleridge and Thomas Carlyle, was almost as much German in its origins as it was English."
>
> Rosemary Ashton[2]

In a letter dated 20 July 1827 Goethe responds to a new English-language biography of Schiller sent to him by the young Thomas Carlyle: "Der Koran sagt: 'Gott hat jedem Volke einen Propheten gegeben in seiner eignen Sprache.' So ist Jeder Übersetzer ein Prophet seinem Volke" [The Koran says: 'God has given every people a prophet in their own language.' Thus each translator is a prophet to his people].[3] In this memorable tribute to the young Scottish author, who had "learned from the Germans to represent literature as the new liturgy,"[4] Goethe offers an assessment of the privileged status of cultural intermediaries in the age he declared was that of *Weltliteratur* [world literature]. Until Goethe's death five years later Carlyle played the combined roles of *Dolmetscher* [interpreter], *Übersetzer* [translator], and *Vermittler* [mediator] of German culture in Britain with unflagging zeal. Recognized by Goethe as successor in this endeavor to Walter Scott (1771–1832), he introduced an exegesis of Goethe's strong personality that made a lasting impression on the intellectual life of mid- to late nineteenth-century Britain and America. The main vehicle for this subversive force was a diverse body of writing, including critical essays, translations, and prefaces that appeared during the most formative decade of Carlyle's career, 1822 to 1832.

Klaus Doderer has argued that Carlyle's cumulative critique of Goethe led to a "Vertiefung und eine neue Wendung" [an intensification and a new departure] in the reception of German thought and literature in Britain. "Obwohl gerade Carlyle die *German Romance* schrieb und Novalis sehr liebte" [although Carlyle published *German Romance* and very much admired Novalis], he nonetheless put Goethe squarely in the foreground of his meditations on literature, not merely as Germany's but also as Europe's leading poet and critic of comprehensive authority. Accompanying the resulting tendency to consider literature, in Doderer's phrase, "als moralisches Erziehungsmittel" [as a medium of ethical formation], Carlyle placed new emphasis on the "Dichterperson" [the person of the poet] rather than "Dichtung" [poetry].[5] In focusing on the author rather than the work, Carlyle was building upon Germaine de Staël's suggestive approach in *De l'Allemagne* [*On Germany*] (1813) and anticipating Heinrich Heine's portrayal of Goethe's imperial persona in *Die Romantische Schule* [*The Romantic School*] (1832–1835). As much as these assessments might differ in emphasis and specific detail, all three critics identified Goethe as the dominant cultural phenomenon of the time. Moreover, the technique employed by all three critics consists of a fusion of biography and practical criticism. Staël's and Carlyle's interest in Goethe reveal the impact of interpreting Goethe on the formation of national cultural identity in France and Britain. The naming of a foreign writer as the cultural hero in two national literary traditions more mature and advanced than Germany's reflects the astonishing permeability of national and cultural boundaries in the early decades of the nineteenth century.[6]

Carlyle also presaged Wilhelm Dilthey's method in *Das Erlebnis und die Dichtung* [*Experience and Poetry*] (1905), one of the foundation texts of modern literary hermeneutics. As with Staël (1766–1817) and Heine (1796–1856), both Carlyle (1795–1881) and Dilthey (1833–1911) derived their concepts of the imagination, literariness, authorship, and the function of criticism from an examination of Goethe's life and works; both critics reached the conclusion that Goethe, perhaps alone of all classic European writers, pursued a life so soaked with meaning that his lived experiences demand to be interpreted for their semaphoric value. It is as if the writer's life and work formed a palimpsestic unity. The following passage from the second chapter of Dilthey's book, "Die dichterische Phantasie Goethes" ["The Poetic Imagination of Goethe"], suggests intriguing parallels with Carlyle's approach in his reverential essays of 1832, "Goethe" and "Goethe's Works":

> Poesie ist Darstellung und Ausdruck des Lebens. Sie drückt das Erlebnis aus, und sie stellt die äußere Wirklichkeit des Lebens dar.... Hieraus erklärt sich, was uns ein lyrisches Gedicht oder eine Erzählung sehen läßt–und was für sie nicht existiert. Die Lebenswerte stehen aber in Beziehungen zueinander, die in dem Zusammenhang des Lebens selbst gegründet sind, und diese geben Personen, Dingen, Situationen, Begebenheiten ihre Bedeutung. So wendet sich der Dichter dem Bedeutsamen zu.... Da ist es nun die erste und entscheidende Eigenschaft des Dichtung Goethes, daß sie aus einer außerordentlichen Energie des Erlebens erwächst.... Seine Stimmungen schaffen alles Wirkliche um, seine Leidenschaften steigern Bedeutung und Gestalt von Situationen und Dingen ins Ungemeine, und sein rastloser Gestaltungsdrang wandelt alles um sich in Form und Gebilde.[7]

Upon closer examination the comparison with Dilthey seems especially fitting. Indeed, according to Rudolf A. Makreel, Dilthey's view of literature is biographical "not in the sense of manifesting personal mannerisms, but of revealing a unity of style which derives from the total being of the poet—a being that comprehends more than private states of mind."[8] Biography as an expression of the organic fusion of style and personality also underlies Carlyle's hermeneutic as applied to the German author: "Goethe's poetry is no separate faculty, no mental handicraft, but the voice of the whole harmonious manhood; nay, it is the very harmony, the living and lifegiving harmony of that rich manhood which forms his poetry."[9]

It is a curious feature of the history of the transmission of foreign cultures that in Britain, Goethe's reputation was not, in contrast to the scene in Russia or France, formed by appropriating or resisting such major texts as *Die Leiden des jungen Werthers* (1774), *Faust* (1808 and 1832), and *Torquato Tasso* (1790). Rather, Goethe's reputation in Britain grew out of the controversy surrounding his personality, ethics, and character. From the publication of the first English translation of *Werther* in 1780 to the appearance of Carlyle's translation of

Wilhelm Meister in 1824, the criticism of Goethe in Britain and North America was inflected by a series of conflicting interpretations focused not on readings of these and other works—at least not in the sense indicated by Coleridge's "practical criticism"—but, quite differently, on what George Saintsbury, in his reappraisal of Goethe's impact on Victorian critics, derided as "anthropological" interpretations or pre-Freudian probings of the authorial psyche as well as moral judgments which were inferred from the text and then projected back onto the author. A process that Saintsbury complains, had the effect of overshadowing the textual features of the literary work.[10]

The biographical impulse in Carlyle's criticism was in fact assimilated from Goethe's own reflections on literature and his practice. In *Gespräche mit Goethe* [*Conversations with Goethe*] (1836 and 1848), for example, Eckermann notes the poet's assertion that

> "Allerdings," sagte Goethe, "ist in der Kunst und Poesie die Persönlichkeit alles; allein hat es doch unter den Kritikern und Kunstrichtern der neuesten Zeit schwache Personagen gegeben, die dieses nicht zugestehen, und die eine große Persönlichkeit bei einem Werke der Poesie oder Kunst nur als eine Art von geringer Zugabe wollten betrachtet wissen. Aber freilich, um eine große Persönlichkeit zu empfinden und zu ehren, muß man auch wiederum selber etwas sein. Alle, die dem Euripides das Erhabene abgesprochen, waren arme Heringe und einer solchen Erhebung nicht fähig; oder sie waren unverschämte Charlatane, die durch Anmaßlichkeit in den Augen einer schwachen Welt mehr aus sich machen wollten und auch wirklich machten, als sie waren."[11]

In fact, Goethe's remarks on literature almost invariably lead to speculations on the psychology or personality traits of leading authors. An example of this approach is recorded by Eckermann as a memorable characterization of Dante on 3 December 1824:

> Übrigens sprach Goethe von Dante mit aller Ehrfurcht, wobei es mir merkwürdig war, daß ihm das Wort *Talent* nicht genügte, sondern daß er ihn eine *Natur* nannte, als womit er ein Umfassenderes, Ahnungsvolleres, tiefer und weiter um sich Blickendes ausdrücken zu wollen schien.[12]

Among contemporary poets Goethe admired Byron more than any other and in all of his recorded discussions of this prodigious talent, Goethe's emphasis is, rarely if ever, on the special qualities of the Briton's works, but more on the force and distinctiveness of his personality. On 24 February 1825 Goethe cited Byron's importance as the major argument in favor of learning English:

> "Er ist ein großes Talent, ein *geborenes*, und die eigentlich poetische Kraft ist mir bei niemand größer vorgekommen, als bei ihm. In Auffassung des Äußeren und klarem Durchblick verganger Zustände ist er eben so groß wie Shakespeare."[13]

Indeed, a perusal of the *Gespräche mit Goethe*, the collected *Briefe*, and all of Goethe's criticism confirms that he only rarely discusses a specific work and its literary characteristics; instead, his interest in the writer's personality nearly always supersedes textual analysis or an explicit discussion of aesthetic qualities. Thus not only does Goethe validate a critical method or hermeneutic based on reading authorial personality, deciphering the allegorical value of his personal history emerges as one of the chief organizing principles in the cultural life of nineteenth-century Europe. The critical response to Goethe displayed in the work of Staël and Hippolyte Taine (1828–1893) of France, Heine and other writers associated with the *Jungdeutschland* ["Young Germany"] literary movement, and Carlyle and his disciples in Britain, suggests Goethe's pertinent impact on European intellectuals.

Goethe, who is credited with opening "a new world to him,"[14] is the subject of Carlyle's first significant appearance in print in April 1822, an article on *Faust* published in the *Edinburgh Review*. While this modest little piece was not included in the first edition of Carlyle's complete works, it marked the beginning of his involvement with Goethe and German culture as critic, translator, and editor, and it reveals that at the outset of his career he tied his literary fortunes to the mediation of Goethe in the English-speaking world. Moreover, on this foundation Carlyle staked his first claim to speak with cultural authority and it is clear that his mature views on art, society, economics, and politics were formed in the crucible of his critique of Goethe and German literature. The process of substituting an emphasis on biography for interpretation of the literary work culminates in Carlyle's five major statements on Goethe—the "Translator's

Preface to the First Edition of *Meister's Apprenticeship*" (1824), "Goethe's Helena" (1828), "Goethe" (1828), "Death of Goethe" (1832), and "Goethe's Works" (1832). Textual exegesis plays an unexpectedly minor role in Carlyle's assessment of Goethe; in its place we find the outline of a full-blown cult of personality and a blueprint for the ideology of hero-worship and submission to authority that is more fully mapped out in such later major works as *On Heroes and Hero-Worship* (1841), *Oliver Cromwell's Letters and Speeches* (1845), and *The History of Frederick the Great* (1858, 1862, 1864, 1865).

As the product of a strict nonconforming religious upbringing Carlyle was initially repelled by what critics before him had depicted as Goethe's tendency to condone or represent licentious behavior in his writings. Even his close identification with Goethe from 1822 to 1832 was initially qualified by feelings of ambivalence and even of disgust.[15] Resistance to Goethe from 1822 to 1823 was replaced by sympathy from 1828 to 1832 but only after Carlyle had interpolated his own idiosyncratic, self-reflexive interpretation, according to which Goethe's writings embody the drama of

> a mind working itself into clearer and clearer freedom; gaining a more and more perfect dominion of its world. The pestilential fever of Skepticism runs through its stages; but happily it ends . . . in clearer, henceforth invulnerable health.[16]

Once Goethe's biography had been configured according to Carlyle's plot of redemption—and references in his writings to relevant experiences were identified as pivotal—the process of reading his works triggered a rapturous conversion experience: "The sight of such a man" was to Carlyle "a Gospel of Gospels," which "literally" offered preservation "from destruction outward and inward." Goethe, he averred, was the first person who had "travelled the steep rocky road" of self-discovery which he, too, had known, and Goethe thenceforth was to be known as "the first of the moderns."[17] Formerly, as Carlyle confessed in a letter to Goethe, he, too, had been "an Unbeliever . . . storm-tossed in my imagination; a man divided from men; exasperated, wretched, driven almost to despair." But Goethe had restored his faith in "the Mercy and Beauty of which it is the Symbol" and helped him attain "to new thoughts, and a composure which I should once have considered as impossible."[18] Thus Goethe played a key role in the development of what W. H. Bruford calls Carlyle's "humanistic religion" and laid the foundations for the cult of personality surrounding Goethe.[19]

There were, of course, contemporary precedents and parallels for Carlyle's valorizaton of Goethe's cultural authority in Britain. Obviously, none was more important than Staël's *De l'Allemagne*. Her identification of Goethe as a "living classic" seemed to confirm that a "modern" could indeed be the equal of the "ancients." Despite bad country roads and a shortage of decent inns, Staël joined the procession of foreign visitors flocking to Weimar, which featured perhaps the most remarkable concentration of literary celebrities in Europe.[20] But even after a long journey her personal interviews with Goethe and Schiller could not alter her ideologically distorted interpretation of German culture.[21] Subjected to strict censorship in Paris, *De l'Allemagne* was first published in London in 1813. It has been credited with disclosing a contemporary snapshot of the real Germany for the first time to "die ganze Welt" [the entire world].[22] Carlyle found in Staël's idealized vision of German culture a readily available alternative to the Enlightenment aesthetic consensus associated with the elites of Paris and London from whom he felt alienated. And Carlyle was not alone in coming under the spell of Staël's portrayal of Germany as the land of poets and thinkers; this picture of German culture dominated British perspectives throughout the nineteenth century and gave impetus to the transformation of Goethe from a foreign reprobate to universal cultural hero.[23] At a time when Goethe's writings fell short of the popularity shared by those of Kotzebue, Schiller, and Wieland, Staël made the bold claim that Goethe, and not the work of his more accessible and successful contemporaries, "réunit tout ce qui distingué l'esprit allemand" [unites all that distinguishes the German mind] and possessed "les traits principaux du génie allemand" [the chief characteristics of the German genius].[24]

Described by Heine as a "coterie book" and a "kind of salon," in which a cacophony of voices may be heard crying out from its pages, *De l'Allemagne* is, indeed a new kind of criticism. René Wellek believed that "the book cannot be judged primarily as a work of literary criticism. It is the picture of a whole nation, a sketch of national psychology and society, and also something of a personal travel book," and he compared *De l'Allemagne* to Tacitus's *Germania* in its propagandistic intent:

> The French were shown the picture of a good, since pious nation of thinkers and poets with few political ambitions and little national feeling: an idyll which already had been refuted by the history of the years between the writing [in 1810] and publication [in France] during the 1814 occupation of Paris by the Allies].

This idealized image of Germany "lingered on in France till" the Franco-Prussian War of 1870, despite the attacks mounted by Heine and others.[25] Staël's admirers in Britain and America sustained her authority as a cultural guide. Carlyle's translation of Jean Paul's review of *De l'Allemagne* is divided over two issues of *Fraser's Magazine*, Numbers 1 and 4 (1830). As he notes in the translator's Preface: "Students of German literature will be curious to see such a critic as Mme de Staël adequately criticized . . . and what worth the best of [German writers] acknowledge in their chief eulogist and indicator among foreigners."[26] This review and its translation are signs that the authority exercised by Staël's utterly biased and thoroughly inaccurate presentation of German culture was transplanted beyond the national, social, political, and aesthetic contexts of its origins. As a result of this process her interpretation acquired new meaning. Jerome J. McGann has argued, "meaning, in a literary event, is a function not of" the text itself but rather the text's "historical relations with its readers and interpreters."[27] Indeed, Lilian R. Furst indicated that the book's main source of interest is to be found in its "creative distortions."[28]

That Carlyle should have looked abroad for literary predecessors and models for his own criticism is symptomatic of his marginalized status in late Romantic Britain, a condition that was shared by the culturally marginalized exiles Staël, who composed *De l'Allemagne* in Switzerland, and Heine, whose *Die Romantische Schule* was produced in Paris. As a Scot who was brought up in a Calvinist sect and lived and worked as a writer in an isolated village Carlyle was at least twice-alienated from mainstream British literary culture: "My case is this: I comport myself wholly like an alien,—like a man who is not in his own country; whose own country lies perhaps a century or two distant." In his adopted language he once described himself as "an *abgerissenes Glied*, a limb torn from the family of Man."[29] Years later, even after Carlyle was celebrated as a sage among writers living in London, he confided to Anthony Froude (1818–1894) that his work had been produced by "a wild man, a man disunited from the fellowship of the world he lives in."[30]

Carlyle's alienation from the dominant cultural institutions of Britain was experienced by other contemporaries, whose own literary careers were launched in unconventional paths of mediating mostly foreign cultural artifacts. Indeed, the reception of German thought and literature in Britain from the seventeenth through the nineteenth centuries was largely the work of culturally ambitious outsiders—Dissenters, women, and Scots—for whom access to the majority culture was impeded by gender, class, or ethnic identity and by the absence of empowering institutional affiliations with prestigious public schools or with Oxford or Cambridge University. In addition to Carlyle, this group includes William Taylor, Mary Wollstonecraft, Thomas Holcroft, Walter Scott, R. P. Gillies, J. G. Lockhart, Henry Crabb Robinson, Sarah Austin, and Marian Evans (George Eliot). All of these writers preceded the publication of their original work with the translation and criticism of German texts. Such labors reflected their lower-caste status within the majority culture, since it was left to them to mediate the perceived transgressive moral and political elements in German literature before these texts were suitable as commodities for domestic cultural consumption. These mediating activities embodied the shaman's traditional function of going-out-of-the-self and leaving-the-familiar in an effort to embrace the foreign and the other. Serving as a meditative link or bridge, however, risked political defilement of the intermediary and brought suspicion upon him or her by critics associated with defending the nationalist status quo.

Carlyle endorsed and then appropriated Staël's vision of German literature (which emphasized *Sturm-und-Drang* heroic individualism and sublimity) because it offered a vehicle of self-cultivation and spiritual fulfillment that surpassed what could be accomplished by the neoclassical aesthetic consensus. Heine, by contrast, finds these very same qualities—especially hero worship—dangerous because they contradict the egalitarian values enshrined by the French Revolution. In his view there was a direct correspondence and a reciprocal relationship between "the lack of political freedom in Germany" and the cultural dominance enjoyed by Goethe's aesthetic "indifference." Peter Uwe Hohendahl's description of Heine's treatise could also be applied to *De l'Allemagne* and Carlyle's essays on Goethe. He argues that *Die Romantische Schule* "combines in a highly unorthodox manner personal characteristics, descriptions of works, satire, historical commentary, and critique of ideology." What Heine calls "this constant assertion of my personality" in his satire, which also breaks through in Staël's highly idiosyncratic interpretations and in Carlyle's worshipful essays (and is denoted by his baroque style), is considered "the most suitable means of encouraging self-evaluation from the reader."[31]

All three critics' readings of Goethe are based on an interpretation of his personality. While he is actually the one literary figure linking the *Sturm und Drang*, Classicism, and Romanticism, Goethe's mere presence seems to have so distracted Staël that she, as Furst observed, "hardly touches the fringe of German Romanticism" proper in her evaluation of the state of German literature.[32] Heine condemns Goethe for the "zweideutige Rolle" [ambivalent role] he played in the cultural politics of the late eighteenth and early nineteenth century: "Offen gestanden, Goethe hat damals eine sehr zweideutige Rolle gespielt und man kann ihn nicht unbedingt loben." [Speaking frankly, at that time Goethe's contribution was extremely equivocal and is not deserving of unqualified praise.]³³ To the disappointment of Heine and other liberals, Goethe was thoroughly the product as well as the proponent of aristocratic culture. Moreover, Goethe is responsible for condoning the formation of a cult of personality that, as Heine notes, surrounded him like a cloud of incense and adversely influenced Germany's younger poets, including the Schlegel brothers, who counted among Goethe's most dedicated followers. In Heine's colorful retelling of their initial meeting in Weimar, we read that Goethe "so barsch die Schlegel aus dem Tempel jagte und . . . begründete er seine Alleinherschaft in der deutschen Literatur" [brusquely drove the Schlegel brothers from the temple . . . and established his autocratic reign in German literature]. Throughout their conversation "man sprach nicht mehr von Romantik und klassischer Poesie, sondern von Goethe und wieder von Goethe" [one spoke no more of Romanticism or classical poetry, but of Goethe and again of Goethe].³⁴

The same could be said of Carlyle after he got over his infatuation with the sublimity of Schiller and the arabesques of Jean Paul. It has often been remarked that the European mind in the modern age "spricht Deutsch." Goethe's impact on Carlyle reflects the initial phase of this tendency and is a factor of overwhelming importance in his own intellectual development. The extent of this influence is apparent from the outset of Carlyle's career. The major essays and translations published from 1822 to 1832 promote the *Dichterfurst* as a viable leader of British culture. Carlyle's objective in this body of writing is to instigate Britain's breakthrough into a broader cultural compass and to emulate the cosmopolitanism that Goethe himself embodied and propagated. Goethe's reputation in early nineteenth-century Britain is not as he reveals indicative of his true worth. Unlike August von Kotzebue (1761–1819) and other objects of transient literary fashion in London, Goethe is to be revered as a living classic, a writer who possesses "some touches of that old divine spirit" and is worthy of comparison with "the masters of Italian painting, and the fathers of Poetry in England." Goethe represents that singular example of a writer who is "what Philosophy can call a Man," and his writings serve as an expression of "the voice of [his] whole harmonious manhood.... [I]t is the very harmony, the living and life-giving harmony of that rich manhood which forms his poetry."[35]

Carlyle's preoccupation with Goethe's "manhood" or humanity reflects a signal tendency of much nineteenth-century literary criticism: the pursuit of a critical agenda combining ethics and aesthetics through biography. This propensity reaches its culmination in the cultural criticism and historical writings of Carlyle's disciples Froude, Charles Kingsley (1819–1875), and Leslie Stephen (1832–1904). Carlyle puts the matter concisely: "All good men may be called poets in act, or in word; all good poets are so in both." By equating moral and literary excellence, Carlyle identifies Goethe as the "Teacher and exemplar of his age," whose writings embody "the beautiful, religious Wisdom . . . which is proper to his time . . . [and] which may still . . . speak to the whole soul" because in addition to

> his natural gifts, he has cultivated himself and his art, he has now studied how to live and to write, with a fidelity, an unwearied earnestness, of which there is not [or no] other living instance; of which among British poets especially, Wordsworth alone offers any resemblance.[36]

The emphasis placed by Staël on Goethe's genius and the comprehensive greatness of his personality suggests a framework for Carlyle's own interpretative strategy that unfolds in the four major essays. He simply transposes Staël's influential reading of Goethe from an overtly political to a quasi-theological key. Thus Goethe emerges from Carlyle's reading as far more than a dominant cultural figure; his works reveal a divine presence immanent in the world, a *deus absconditus*, a god in the guise of a poet, whose appearance inaugurates a new epoch of faith in a post-Enlightenment world grown weary of doubt and relativism. Carlyle's identification of Goethe as "the Strong One of his time,"[37] exerting religious, ethical, and cultural authority, received corroboration from Matthew Arnold in terms that are so strikingly similar that it is well-worth quoting at length:

> when Goethe came, Europe had lost her basis of spiritual life; she had to find it again; Goethe's task was,—the inevitable task for the modern poet henceforth is . . . to interpret human life afresh, and to supply a new spiritual basis to it . . . . . Goethe is the greatest poet of modern times, not because he is one of the half-dozen human beings who in the history of our race have shown the most signal gift for poetry, but because, having a very considerable gift for poetry, he was at the same time, in the width, depth, and richness of his criticism of life, by far our greatest modern man.[38]

If Goethe served as Arnold's most eminent example of cosmopolitan literary culture, it was Carlyle's efforts as a *Vermittler* of German literature that stimulated Goethe's expression of a coming multicultural utopia of *Weltliteratur*. Concerning the broad intercultural value of translation, in a letter dated 1 January 1828 Goethe asks Carlyle's opinion of Charles de Voeux's English translation of his own *Torquato Tasso* (1827):

> Nun aber möcht' ich von Ihnen wissen, in wiefern dieser Tasso als Englisch gelten kann. Sie werden mich höchlich verbinden, wenn Sie mich hierüber aufklären und erleuchten; den eben diese Bezüge vom Originale zur Übersetzung sind es ja, welche die Verhältnisse von Nation zu Nation am allersdeutlichsten aussprechen, und die man zu Förderung der vor- und obwaltenden allgemeinen Weltliteratur vorzüglich zu kennen und zu beurtheilen hat.[39]

Starting with his early critical writings and translations, Carlyle established a pattern of cultural emulation of German writers that has continued into the present time and is especially noticeable in the prestige enjoyed by Karl Marx, Friedrich Nietzsche, Sigmund Freud, Martin Heidegger, Theodor Adorno, Walter Benjamin, and Jürgen Habermas in Anglo-American academic circles. When viewed as a contribution to intellectual history, Carlyle's essays on Goethe are comparable to T. S. Eliot's reassessment of the cultural significance of the Metaphysical Poets. But the focus on Goethe and other German writers—Schiller, Wieland, Jean Paul, Novalis, and Friederich Schlegel—suggests that Carlyle's critical essays are unique among the works of major British critics from after the time of Dryden until the late nineteenth century. As a coherent, sustained critique of an entire tradition, only Johnson's *Lives of the Most Eminent English Poets* (1779–1781) approaches Carlyle's essays both in scope and in method, which is best described as a fusion of biography and practical criticism. Indeed, Carlyle's guiding conviction that biography provides the most authentic basis for literary criticism—"Would that I saw the Poet and knew him [I] could then fully understand him!"[40]—anticipated Dilthey's psycho-biographical hermeneutic in *Das Erlebnis und die Dichtung*, Freud's investigations of the psychology of artists and writers, and, in the post-war era, the biographical approaches in the work of W. J. Bate, Harold Bloom, John Bowlby, Joseph Frank, William St. Clair, Claire Tomalin, among others.[41]

Carlyle first came to the general attention of the British reading public with his translation of *Wilhelm Meister's Apprenticeship* (1824) and this text played a key role in situating Goethe on Britain's intellectual horizon. Indeed, prior to its publication and the appearance of Carlyle's essays on Goethe (1828–1832), the canonical niche that Goethe would occupy beside Dante and Shakespeare as a representative European poet was not yet established, nor conceivable. Carlyle, however, singlehandedly created a template for the reception of Goethe. This combined speculation on the links between aesthetics and ethics with homilies on the indispensability of great men. In additional essays on Schiller, Jean Paul, Novalis, and other German writers, Carlyle anticipates the enthusiastic appropriation of German culture throughout nineteenth-century Europe in the later nineteenth century. Echoing Carlyle's intuition of the centrality of German thought in forming the modern mind, Taine insisted that "l'Allemagne a produit toutes les idées de notre âge historique" [Germany has produced all the ideas of our historical epoch].[42] Taken as a body of critical writing Carlyle's essays provide much more than a rebuttal to the less gifted William Taylor or to ideologically antagonistic critics such as the antiquarian poet George Ellis (1753–1815) and the critic John Hookam Frere (1769–1846) who wrote for the Tory newspaper the *Anti-Jacobin*; they also comprise a fulfillment of Coleridge's envisioned "history of Belles Lettres in Germany" that he wished to combine with "a biographical and critical analysis" of

"Goethe as poet and philosopher" plus an additional component unplanned by Coleridge: a consideration of the relevance of German culture for post-Romantic Britain, a theme that would recur in Carlyle's writing and conversation to the end of his life.[43] Despite insisting upon a caveat concerning Carlyle's "avowed tendency towards 'philosophical' rather than 'formal' criticism," even the usually skeptical George Saintsbury concedes that "altogether there are few things in English Criticism better worth reading, marking, and learning than the literary parts of these earlier volumes of Essays."[44]

In spite of such heart-felt conviction, voices of dissent regarding Goethe's influence open and close the nineteenth century. Coleridge denounced Goethe's works of imagination as "utterly unprincipled" and Saintsbury, in his massive revisionist literary history, compared Goethe's reputation as a critic to a "stale superstition." Goethe's neglect of purely literary criteria spurred Saintsbury to subject the legacy of Romanticism to a proto-modernist reevaluation, according to which an overriding concern for personality, moral conduct, and character is paramount. In rejecting Goethe's emphasis on the role of the author's personality, Saintsbury refashioned the predominantly ethical or social-cultural function of criticism, which was almost universally adopted by Victorian critics. This is the nativity of Modernism. Coleridge's main objection to Goethe was likewise based on a concern for morality. In a remark made to Henry Crabb Robinson in 1810, Coleridge "conceded to Goethe universal talent, but felt a want of moral life to be the defect of his poetry." Some time later Coleridge elaborated on this position in conversation with Wordsworth. In denying "merit to Goethe's *Torquato Tasso*," he expressed "the improbability of being a good poet without being a good man."[45] It becomes apparent in further conversations with Crabb Robinson that Coleridge's attitude towards Goethe was capable of a certain degree of modification. The appearance of a complete edition of *Faust* compelled him to acknowledge "the genius of Goethe in a manner he never did before." And yet, as in the past, "the want of religion and enthusiasm in Goethe" remains "in Coleridge's mind an irreparable defect." In addition, he found fault with the beginning of *Faust* and with what he describes as the inadequately developed character of Mephistopheles. As for the protagonist of the drama, Coleridge found that "the character of Faust is not *motivirt* [motivated]" because Goethe fails to offer a convincing explanation for the "state of mind which led to the catastrophe." But Crabb Robinson knew Coleridge well enough to remark on his plan to write "a new Faust" that "he would never get out of vague conceptions—he would lose himself in dreams."[46]

As we shall see in Chapter Four, Coleridge's enthusiasm for Goethe during the mid-1810s, like his interest in Schiller during the previous decade, did not endure. Inexplicably, his attitude toward Goethe slipped back into a familiar mood of moral uneasiness.

Twenty years previously Crabb Robinson had published a series of essays that represented the first coherent effort by a British writer to evaluate and to translate Goethe's lyric poetry and epigrams.[47] At the same time he made the first tentative strides toward an interpretation of Goethe as a cultural authority of pan-European significance. He was, moreover, aware of the symbolic quality with which the events in a poet's life are invested. He recognized that in such matters there is always an appeal open to nature, which is ultimately the bond between "Dichtung" and "Wahrheit," poetry and truth: "in a truly great man everything is important." And the greatness of Goethe has to do with his concern for realism: "Goethe has done more than any man to bring back the public taste to works of imagination—a faculty which does not refuse all alliance with frightful realities, but which refines and idealizes them."[48] The first in his generation to perceive the broader importance of Goethe, Crabb Robinson prefigured Carlyle's extension of Goethe's influence from art to ethics. Twenty years later, in his essays for the *Edinburgh Review*, Goethe is described as a prophet and medium through which supernatural revelation in the modern world has taken place.

Carlyle found the British Romantics on the whole deficient in the philosophical vision and moral seriousness that he felt were necessary if poets were to bring about a new cultural dispensation. Scott's "deep recognition of the Past" is deemed superficial because it lacks a philosophical foundation and he is parodied as "the great *Restaurateur* of Europe." Byron is ridiculed as "a Dandy of Sorrows," and Wordsworth is dismissed as "genuine but a small diluted man." Hazlitt is rejected because he "has discovered nothing; been able to believe nothing." Coleridge's "cardinal sin" is a lack of will power:

> He has no resolution.... The conversation of the man is much as I anticipated— a forest of thoughts.... But there is no method in his talk... he is like the hulk of a huge ship—his masts and sails and rudder have rotted quite away.[49]

What is lacking, then, in Britain is a "modern spiritseer," a genius with the "spiritual eye" to discern the potential for the aestheticization of modern life. Goethe, whom he designates as just such a genius, "had opened a new world to him" and countered the loss of a spiritual center in his existence. Thus Goethe's writings represent

> a mind working itself into clearer and clearer freedom; gaining a more and more perfect dominion of its world. The pestilential fever of Skepticism runs through its stages; but happily it ends . . . in clearer, henceforth invulnerable health.[50]

Carlyle's assertion that "Biography is the only History" reflects how, in an age in which literature has usurped functions once served exclusively by religion, the lives of the poets—and of Goethe in particular—become as important as Acts of Apostles and Lives of the Saints were in ages of faith.[51]

In opposition to "these hard unbelieving utilitarian days" Carlyle was convinced that Goethe's writings "reveal to us glimpses of the Unseen but not unreal world, so that the Actual and the Ideal may again meet together, and clear knowledge be again wedded to Religion in the life and business of men." Carlyle admits that his critique of Goethe is intuitive, irrational, unscientific, and wholly "interested" in nature, even though he insists "the merits and characteristics of a poet are not to be set forth by logic," but rather "by personal, and by deep and careful inspection of his works." Understanding is gained through an exertion of imagination, sympathy, and openness of mind, without which it is impossible to "transfer ourselves in any measure into [the author's] peculiar point of vision."[52]

The openness and objectivity that are, for Carlyle, the first duties of the critic are once again to be inferred from Goethe's personality. Indeed, "clearness of sight" is "the foundation of all talent," to which "all other gifts are superadded,"[53] and the superior "Spiritual Endowment" of Goethe and Shakespeare is derived from this "utmost Clearness" and an "all-piercing faculty of Vision":

> For Goethe, as for Shakespeare, the world lies all translucent, all *fusible* we might call it, encircled with WONDER; the Natural is in reality the Supernatural, for to the seer's eyes both become one. What are the *Hamlets* and *Tempests*, the *Fausts* and *Mignons*, but glimpses accorded us into the translucent, wonder-encircled world; revelations of the mystery of all mysteries, Man's life as it actually is?[54]

The writings of Goethe and Shakespeare are vital because they were formed in a process that started from within and moved outwards to the surface manifestations of reality. As a result, those "Macbeths and Falstaffs . . . these Fausts and Philinas have a verisimilitude and life that separates them from all other fictions of later ages."[55] Decisive in this judgment is the perception of Goethe's "sincerity," which here takes on overtones of Hazlitt's "gusto" or Keatsean intensity, as Arnold, aged twenty-five, makes clear in a letter to his mother. He contrasts this quality in Goethe with what he finds in Wordsworth:

> I have been returning to Goethe's life and think higher of him than ever. His thorough sincerity—writing about nothing he had not experienced—is in modern literature almost unrivaled. Wordsworth resembles him in this respect; but the difference between the range of their two experiences is immense and not in the Englishman's favor.[56]

As we have seen, this position is opposed to Heine's view of Goethe, whose indifference to politics is contrasted unfavorably with Schiller's sympathy with the revolutionary spirit of the age as revealed in his sensational play, *Die Räuber* [*The Robbers*] (1781). In the essay "State of German Literature" Carlyle nonetheless stresses Goethe's engagement with the material world and concrete human existence. Indeed, Goethe's greatness is found in his adaptation of "the actual aspects of life" to literature; this "realism" shows us that "the end of Poetry is higher; she must dwell in Reality and become manifest to men in the forms among which they live and move." In Goethe's works "the nineteenth century stands before us, in all its contradiction and perplexity; barren, mean, and baleful, as we have known it; yet here no longer mean or barren, but enameled into beauty in the poet's spirit."[57] The mind of the German poet is governed by an almost instinctive harmonizing impulse that nullifies superficial differences in the act of penetrating to the common core of phenomena. He is "the Uniter and Reconciler" of "the inward spiritual chaos" of "the most distracted and divided age . . . since the introduction of the Christian Religion." Through the "melodious reverence" and "deep, all-pervading Faith" informing his aesthetic vision, Goethe "was to close the Abyss out of which such manifold destruction, moral, intellectual, social, was proceeding."[58] In consideration, then, of the poet's role as a catalyst for the birth of a new phase of cultural achievement, "his Spiritual History" is thus designated as "the ideal emblem of all true men's in these days; the goal of Manhood, which he attained, men too in our degree have to aim . . . in the dim weltering chaos rejoice to find a paved way."[59] Because Goethe set the individual standard of achievement his homeland—Staël makes the same claim in *De l'Allemagne*—he "is to be the leader of spiritual Europe." This is the main emphasis of Carlyle's critique; his essays on Goethe seek to elucidate the "deep movement agitating the universal mind of Germany," whose reverberations can be felt across Europe and thus inspire conflicting interpretations of this phenomenon in Britain and on the Continent.[60]

In the essays "Goethe" and "Goethe's Works," which appeared in the *Edinburgh Review* in 1832, the year of Goethe's death, Carlyle seeks to redress the errors of his predecessors in Britain as well as Germany and properly to introduce Goethe as "a world-changer, and benignant spiritual revolutionist."[61] Critics before Carlyle had invoked pallid clichés in place of genuine psychological profiles of Goethe, which led to a failure to appreciate his "real poetic worth" and his importance to "his own people and to us."[62] Correcting this mistake, Carlyle takes the full measure of Goethe's humanity; the fundamental question underlying his inquiry thus concerns the connection between the writer's personality and his works: "What manner of man is this? How shall we even see him? What is his spiritual structure, what at least are the outward form and features of his mind?"[63] Carlyle's approach to Goethe reflects an adjustment in the function of the biographical impulse in criticism from a preoccupation with major life experiences to an interest in charting the relationship between psychology and literary expression.

As a consequence of Carlyle's critical method, Goethe is endowed with a religious, oracular significance. He has earned this distinction by appearing to have tamed and reconciled, as evidenced in his writings, "the inward spiritual chaos of the age."[64] Because the poet has, according to Carlyle's explication, endured the perplexities inherent in modern life, he "has also mastered these, he is above them, and has shown others how to rise above them."[65] The other decisive characteristic, which Carlyle considers the true "test for the culture of a poet," is Goethe's sincerity, a quality which may be measured by an author's readiness to reveal himself fully in his work. Carlyle's hermeneutic approach was therefore derived chiefly from those works which embody Goethe's renowned confessional impulse, such as *Götz von Berlichingen* (1773), *Die Leiden des jungen Werthers* [*The Sufferings of Young Werther*] and *Faust*. The passage in *Dichtung und Wahrheit* [*Poetry and Truth*] from which Carlyle takes his cue reads: "Alles, was daher von mir bekannt geworden, sind nur Bruchstücke einer großen Konfeßion, welche vollständig zu machen dieses Büchlein ein gewagter Versuch ist" [Everything, therefore, that I have published previously, consists of fragments of a great confession; and this little book is an attempt which I have ventured on to render it complete]."[66] These lines inspired Carlyle's longing for direct, unmediated contact with Goethe and they correspond, in large part, to Coleridge's definitions of poetry and the poet in *Biographia Literaria*: "What is poetry? is nearly the same question with, what is a poet? that the answer to the one is involved in the solution of the other. For it is a distinction resulting from the poetic genius itself."[67]

In the "Translator's Preface to the First Edition of *Meister's Apprenticeship*" Carlyle offers a reading of the early works *Götz* and *Werther* which emphasizes Goethe's centrality to contemporary Britain:

> [I]t would be difficult to name two books which have exercised a deeper influence on the subsequent literature of Europe.... Skeptical sentimentality, view-hunting, love, friendship, suicide, and desperation became the staple of literary ware.[68]

Moreover, the highest importance is assigned to these works because of their role in awakening the historical consciousness of the nineteenth century and in revealing what would presently be recognized as typically modern forms of experience, especially the "feelings that arise from passion incapable of being converted into action."[69] Carlyle deduces from his examination of Goethe's life experiences that he, too, had been driven to despair through "Unrest" and "Discontent" and that *Werther* gives voice to "the cry of that dim, rooted pain, under which all thoughtful men of a certain age were languishing."[70] Affirming Goethe's cultural authority as an expression of his capacity for redemptive suffering, Carlyle identifies the novel as the product of auto-therapy; it is identified as "a symptom, indeed a cause, of his now having got delivered from such melancholy."[71] The salutary effect of *Werther* is contrasted with Byron's "life-weariness, his moody melancholy, and mad stormful indignation."[72] Not discounting Byron's affinity with the *Sturm-und-Drang* phase of Goethe's career—"Byron was our English Sentimentalist and Power-man," Carlyle nonetheless pits the health he construes from Goethe's efforts at self-healing against what he calls the pathological, "spasmodic Byronism" of the age.[73] In a well-known passage in *Sartor Resartus* Carlyle encodes his cultural bias toward Germany and combines it with a rejection of the lingering Age of Reason eudaemonism that he associates with contemporary British culture:

> It is only with Renunciation (*Entsagen*) that life, properly speaking, can be said to begin.... What act of Legislature was there that thou shouldst be HAPPY? ... Art thou nothing other than a Vulture, then, that fliest through the Universe

seeking after somewhat to eat: shrieking dolefully because carrion enough is not given thee? Close thy Byron; open thy *Goethe*.[74]

The pattern of Goethe's authorial development that Carlyle infers from his reading of *Werther* and other early works is appropriated for *Sartor Resartus* (1833–1834/1836), the faux biography of the "Clothes Philosopher" Diogenes Teufelsdröckh [Devil's Shit]. Besides functioning as a caricature of a German idealist philosopher, the novel also functions as a satire on the fictionalized editor as a mediator of German culture. Much of the dramatic interest in the novel is located in the implied symmetry between the protagonist's psyche and the spiritual condition of Europe. Carlyle simultaneously ventriloquizes Goethe's depression in *Werther* and his own personal crisis regarding faith and authority. In Froude's *Life of Carlyle* (1884) the contours of this spiritual crisis are distorted through the use of grandiose comparisons:

> Thus to poverty and dyspepsia there had been added the struggle which is always hardest in the noble mind, which Job had known, and David, and Solomon, and Aeschylus, and Shakespeare, and Goethe. Where are the tokens of His presence? where are the signs of His coming? Is there, in this universe of things, any moral Providence at all?[75]

The teleology of Teufelsdröckh's spiritual growth in *Sartor Resartus*—from the "Everlasting No" through the "Centre of Indifference" to the "Everlasting Yes"—mirrors the triadic structure of Carlyle's construction of the inner biography of Goethe. He identifies the three major phases of Goethe's development with *Werther*, *Wilhelm Meister*, and the *West-östlicher Divan* [*West-Eastern Diwan*] (1819). As previously noted, *Werther* embodies "a poetic structure of the World's Despair." *Wilhelm Meister*, by contrast, belongs to "the second and sounder period of Goethe's life" and the at times bafflingly circuitous plot heralds "a free recognition of Life, in its depth, variety and majesty. Anarchy has become Peace; the once gloomy and perturbed spirit is now serene, cheerfully vigorous . . . . For he has conquered his unbelief; the Ideal has been built on the Actual, [it] no longer floats vaguely in darkness and regions of dreams, but rests on light, on the firm ground of human interest and business."[76]

While the Romantics, especially Coleridge, Byron, and Shelley, expressed a special affinity for *Faust*, the next generation felt a deeper bond with *Wilhelm Meister* (usually in Carlyle's translation). Perhaps an unlikely candidate for the British literary canon, Carlyle's *Meister* nonetheless appealed to Victorian readers by suggesting links between the growth of aesthetic sensibility and ethical self-awareness. But there is a key absence in the text that Carlyle notices; there is "as yet no Divinity . . . recognized here." Only in the masterly exercise in cross-cultural exchange—between West and East, Germany and the Middle East, and Christian and Muslim—of Goethe's last years, the *West-östlicher Divan*, does Carlyle perceive that he expresses anything like transcendental faith. It is in the imitation of Persian poems that a "melodious reverence becomes triumphant; a deep, all-pervading Faith, with mild voice, grave as gay."[77]

In "Goethe's Works" Carlyle responds to the critics of *Wilhelm Meister* in Britain and Germany, including De Quincey and Novalis, who derided the form of the novel and its morality. Despite its structural deviation from neoclassical unity, he praises the novel as "one of the most perfect pieces of composition that Goethe has ever produced . . . [which] coheres beautifully within itself . . . [giving] us the notion of a *completed fragment*." Goethe's fusion of allegory and realism, wisdom literature and the lyric, reminds Carlyle of Spenser's *The Faerie Queene* (1590, 1596) but *Wilhelm Meister* differs in presuming to offer its plot as an allegory of the nineteenth century and therefore contains "a picture full of the expressiveness, of what men are striving for, and ought to strive for, in these actual days."[78] The rootedness of *Wilhelm Meister* in verisimilitude serves as a counterweight to the "wild suicidal Night-thoughts of *Werther*," the signature work of Goethe's youth.[79] The appearance of the later novel indicates to Carlyle "that a great change had taken place in the moral disposition of the man; a change from inward imprisonment, doubt and discontent into freedom, belief and clear activity."[80] He credits Goethe with having gone further than "any other man in his age" in breaking through paralysis-inducing speculation and demonstrating the possibility of engaging in meaningful action in the modern world. Such is the importance of Goethe's achievement that he "conquers heaven for us."[81]

Carlyle reflects on Goethe's achievement in the realistic mode and suggests that his realism has a "supernatural" quality because of its "figurativeness," that is, Goethe's

> singularly emblematic intellect; his perpetual never-failing tendency to transform into shape, into life . . . the opinion, the feeling that may dwell in him. Goethe's figurativeness . . . manifests itself as the constructing of the inward elements of a thought, as the vital elements of it.

As Keats noted concerning Shakespeare that he "led a life of Allegory: his works are the comments on it,"[82] this "emblematic" faculty is, according to Carlyle, "the very essence of Goethe's intellect."[83] Allegory is, of course, also central to Carlyle's first work of original "writing" as opposed to his previous labors of "re-writing." In *Sartor Resartus* the concept of "Natural Supernaturalism" presupposes that the universe itself is a symbol. It is alternatively "the God-like rendered visible" and "the living visible Garment of God." For Carlyle, it is in the nature of "the Symbol proper" that "there is ever some embodiment and revelation of the Infinite; the Infinite is made to blend itself with the Finite, to stand visible attained there." Since it is "in and through symbols" that the individual human being "lives, works, and has his being," Carlyle suggests that everyone, not simply poets and artists, gains their identity as a symbol-maker, *homo eidolons*. The poet's function differs only in that he exploits the bivalent nature of the symbol itself, in which "there is concealment and yet revelation."[84]

The other decisive characteristic of Goethe's mind, which Carlyle considers the "test of the culture of a Poet," is once again his sincerity and, closely related to this, his penchant for self-revelation. This explains Carlyle's interest in those works that seem to provide the most direct expression of Goethe's personality. Consistent with his position that the "wisdom" that these texts contain is of greater value than their status as works of literature, Carlyle's assessment of works other than *Werther* and *Wilhelm Meister* is at times cursory. Of "Wild, apocalyptic" *Faust,* Carlyle remarks that it evokes "a death-song of departing worlds." Although he notes the essentially "anthropomorphic character" of the classical, "Pagan" phase in Goethe's career, he expresses no real sympathy for the masterpiece of this period, *Iphigenie auf Tauris* [*Iphigenia in Tauris*] (1779). By contrast, Carlyle waxes enthusiastic over the "old Ethic tone" of the *Venetianische Epigramme* [*Venetian Epigrams*] (1790–1796), which he describes, anticipating Nietzsche's characteristic diction, as both "musical" and "joyfully strong."[85] But Carlyle is clearly more interested in offering an interpretation of these verses that is consistent with the cult of personality he has derived from his reading of Goethe's works than he is in analyzing the texts as literary artifacts.

At mid-century, the construction of the cult of personality surrounding Goethe continues and exfoliates in the writings of critics such as Arnold, G. H. Lewes, F. D. Maurice, and Walter Pater. At first restricted to Goethe and German literature, British enthusiasm for German culture eventually comes to encompass aesthetics, philosophy, historiography, theology, and, perhaps most important of all, natural science. Carlyle's critique of Goethe, in which the German poet is identified as the prophet of a new aesthetic, philosophical, and moral dispensation, engendered this decades-long process of cultural appropriation. Thus, beginning with Carlyle's essays in the 1820s, responding to Goethe becomes one of the chief organizing principles in the intellectual life of nineteenth-century Britain.

Chapter One
Goethe and the Generation of 1789: Cultural Mediation and Literary Enfranchisement

"When one hasn't had a good father, it is necessary to invent one."
Harold Bloom[1]

"The great significance of Goethe in the history of the European mind lies in the fact that he is the last great poet who lived and worked in a continual effort to save the life of poetry and the poetry of life."
Erich Heller[2]

The essential bond between the transmission of German culture in Britain and the emergence of leading voices of Dissent, radical politics, and feminism in the late eighteenth century has not yet been fully articulated.[3] Similarly, what has also not been fully acknowledged is the prosthetic ligature between the translation and criticism of German literature, on the one hand, and the appearance of original works by radical authors, on the other. With this connection Thomas Holcroft's efforts, as an intermediary between British and German culture, throw into sharp relief the reciprocal relationship between the mediation of German culture in Britain and the rise of Jacobinism—Romanticism in process—that we find on the margins of mainstream British literary culture. While Holcroft's novels have received a good deal of scholarly attention,[4] his achievement as a transmitter of German culture has been largely overshadowed by the work of more prominent intermediaries among the radical *habitués* of Joseph Johnson's bookshop—William Taylor, Henry Fuseli, and Mary Wollstonecraft—all of whom were associated with William Godwin in one way or another. For instance, Godwin shared Taylor's upbringing in a Dissenting household and Norwich roots; Holcroft was his best friend, Wollstonecraft was his wife, and, in addition to friends, he shared with Fuseli the experience of having originally trained for the clergy. But on account of the scope of his translations—what he called "this just and necessary sufferance"[5]—which included the work of such major figures as Goethe, Johann Kaspar Lavater (1741–1801), Friedrich II (Frederick the Great) (1721–1786), and Friedrich Leopold Graf zu Stolberg-Stolberg (1750–1819) in travel writing, poetry, memoirs, and plays—the case of Holcroft discloses to a greater degree the connections between the transmission of German culture and radical politics in Britain.[6]

An examination of this affinity reveals that the turn to German literature among proponents of radical reform answered a deep-seated need in the culture of political and religious Dissent for a breakthrough from insularity into cosmopolitanism, for growth and development achieved along an axis of confrontation between the familiar and the foreign, the self and the other. The response to German culture as an opening up to otherness and an alternative to native sources of self-formation emerged as an ideological litmus test for radical or reform-minded intellectuals seeking access to British literary and academic institutions.[7] The texts generated as a response to German culture—translations and criticism—must be seen as acts of interpretation that inevitably encode authorial biases reflecting political, class, generational, and religious identities. For members of the Godwin Circle the appropriation of German culture replaced the Oxbridge or public school education based on Latin and Greek that had been denied them on account of gender, class or religion. While the identification of spiritual growth with the study of German culture is inseparable from the quest for cultural authority, the attraction of German culture also consisted in its scientific-critical orientation and a dynamic configuration of humanism based on historicity, psychology, and subjective emotion that contrasted with more static characterizations of human nature, perception, and experience associated with the Enlightenment. Embracing review criticism and biography, translations and compilations (of *belles lettres* as well as scientific and philosophical tracts, history and biography), loose adaptations and instances of outright plagiarism, the texts transmitted comprise a diverse body of literary activity that made German texts accessible through modification by such contingent qualities as taste, idiosyncrasy, and even inaccurate or misleading interpretations. As women, Dissenters, radicals, and other members of culturally dispossessed groups, the writers involved in the transmission of German culture at this time occupied the periphery of mainstream literary circles in Britain and their ideological preoccupations (sympathy with the aims of the French Revolution, the expansion of the franchise, legal and economic reform, and the removal of social and political barriers to dissenters and women) are reflected in their mediation activities.

For Holcroft and his fellow intermediaries in the Godwin Circle, Taylor, Fuseli, and Wollstonecraft, the "domestication" of German culture was a means of acquiring cultural capital from an indifferent, even hostile dominant culture and its publishing institutions—booksellers, rival authors, journal and newspaper editors, government censors, and the reading public formed by them—by creating independent institutions in a kind of dissident parallel universe. Translating Goethe and his contemporaries in Germany thus served as an empowering platform for the assertion of an alternative set of political and aesthetic values that challenged the dominant culture. Reviewing ("pre-writing") and translating ("re-writing") German authors provided a means of gaining literary enfranchisement and offered a paradigm of literary development according to which "re-writers" become original writers following an apprenticeship of translation and reviewing. Indeed, ventriloquizing or "re-writing" is a vehicle that facilitates original writing, and for the generation of 1789 in Britain conscious imitation is a key process by which literary identity is formed. At the same time the texts that were produced as an expression of Goethean emulation serve as forms of indirect but nonetheless subversive self-expression. Official censors and compliantly self-censoring booksellers and publishers tolerated levels of "subversion" in translated foreign works that would not have been acceptable in English language original books. And texts associated with political radicalism were also invariably deemed aesthetically and ethically radical. The emergence in late eighteenth-century Britain of hermeneutic vehicles for the transmission of German culture may be likened to what André Malraux in *Les voix du silence* [*The*

Voices of Silence] (1951) termed a "conquest," an "annexation," and a "possession" of otherness and it is certainly a crucial period in the history of British culture when the interpretation and transmission of a foreign literary tradition takes on political and cultural significance. Translating and reviewing German texts was, for Taylor, Fuseli, Wollstonecraft, and Holcroft, an expression of sympathy for the aims of the French Revolution as well as the experience of inner emigration and political marginalization.[8]

The social, political, fictive, and mediative writings of the Godwin circle replicate an intricate web of interrelated and interdependent voices, a region of the mind which is situated on the margins of all these disciplines, at their junctures and points of intersection. Entering this polyphonic borderland we are in an advantageous position from which to approach Holcroft's literary career, especially his contributions to the transmission of German culture in Britain. Dismissed even by many recent critics as the creator of a minor subgenre, "novels of purpose," perhaps in order to distinguish his work from the less overtly ideological novels of the canon, Holcroft's best novels—*Anna St. Ives* (1792) and *Hugh Trevor* (begun in 1794)—had either appeared or were well under way at the time of his arrest in 1794. However subversively one might read canonical Gothic novels such as Ann Radcliffe's *The Mysteries of Udolpho* (1794) and M. G. Lewis's *The Monk* (1796), Holcroft's novels unabashedly espoused a radical political agenda. For Holcroft fictional discourse was merely another means of giving voice to the ideological struggle taking place between monarchist Britain and revolutionary France. Employing the black and white ideological palette of propaganda literature, his protagonists persistently advocate the adoption of a new moral code and predict the inevitable triumph of a revolutionary social and political program that will reeducate and thus recreate the human race along wholly new lines. Published a few months before Godwin's *Enquiry Concerning Political Justice* (1793), *Anna St. Ives* anticipates in detail many of the arguments presented in Godwin's widely influential treatise, a coincidence explained in large part by the daily discussions between the two writers that took place as both works were in progress. As Godwin put it in a letter to Hazlitt, "the principles afterwards developed in my *Political Justice* were the almost constant topic of conversation between Holcroft and myself."[9]

Identified by Godwin as one of his four principle "oral educators,"[10] Holcroft's worldview was largely shaped by the leading writers of Continental Deism—Antoine François Prévost (1697–1763), Jean-Jacques Rousseau (1712–1778), Denis Diderot (1713–1784), Louis-Sébastien Mercier (1740–1814), Christoph Martin Wieland (1733–1813), and, of course, Voltaire (1694–1778)—and he is chiefly remembered today as one of the twelve British radicals who were indicted for high treason in 1794. This group, which included John Horne Tooke (1736–1812) and Thomas Hardy (1736–1832), a shoemaker, an autodidact like Holcroft, and founder of the London Corresponding Society, was swept up in the government's campaign to eviscerate the reform movement, a process that began with the trial and conviction—in absentia—of Thomas Paine (1737–1809) for seditious libel in 1792. It is interesting to note that Godwin's suppressed preface to the original edition of *Caleb Williams*, in which he declares emphatically that it is a novel about injustice, is in fact dated the day of Hardy's arrest, on 12 May 1794. As he remarks in a note appended to the second edition published in 1795: "terror was the order of the day; and it was feared that even the humble novelist might be shown to be constructively a traitor."[11] Godwin's response to the arrest of his colleagues in the reform movement did not end with his examination of "Things As They Are" with respect to "the modes of domestic and unrecorded despotism by which man becomes the destroyer of man."[12] Demonstrating unexpected nimbleness for a mind unfairly seen by posterity as somewhat plodding and discursive rather than agile and intuitive, Godwin turned from allegorical treatment of the government's monopoly of power in *Caleb Williams* to direct confrontation with the judicial system in a heroic feat of political journalism. Without accepting his claim to the lion's share of the credit for the full acquittal of Hardy, Tooke, and Holcroft, we still might agree with Marilyn Butler that the public outcry that greeted Godwin's pamphlet, *Cursory Strictures on the Charge Delivered by Lord*

Chief Justice Eyre to the Grand Jury, October 2, 1794, evidence that "the defence of liberty could still, given the occasion and the rhetorician, outweigh fears for property, and muster in the opposition some sense of a common cause."[13]

With the acquittal of his friends, 1794 constituted the *annus mirabilis* of the British reform movement and the high-water mark of Godwin's fame and influence. During this brief period he published *Political Justice, Caleb Williams*, and his best political journalism. But even feats of superhuman willpower constituted mere stopgap measures, not anything approximating a permanent victory in the struggle against the forces of reaction in Britain. Against a backdrop of commercial blockade and then actual war with France, public support for reform fluctuated with the rise and fall of economic conditions. Popular sympathy for the aims of the French Revolution waned as revulsion spread at the bloodbath of the Terror. In contrast to the fickleness of popular enthusiasm for reform, the government's campaign against dissent was unrelenting. The forces of reaction might receive a temporary setback, but they could not be held indefinitely at bay. A counter-revolution was in the offing that would rollback all the apparent progress signaled by the uncensored publication of *Political Justice* and the release of Hardy, Tooke, and Holcroft. Signs of the changing times included prominent satirist James Gillray's caricature of Godwin, Holcroft and Paine, and public attacks on the "new philosophy" by such former allies as Coleridge in his public lectures and Dr. Samuel Parr in his "Spital Sermon" of 1801. A savage parody of Godwin's 1799 novel, *St. Leon*, appeared anonymously in 1800 as *St Godwin: A Tale of the Sixteenth, Seventeenth, and Eighteenth Century*.[14] While Godwin vigilantly fought his detractors in the press and in private conversations, he saw his literary reputation suffer irrevocable eclipse. In the next decade the leading voice of the radical reform movement was stilled and his energies were channeled into the production of children's books under the imprint of Mary Jane Godwin's "Juvenile Library."

Holcroft evaded the hangman's noose and transportation to Australia's Botany Bay—the fate of those convicted of treason—only to endure the figurative death of his literary voice in the ensuing years of harsh political repression and media censorship. Indeed, his declining fortunes as a playwright paralleled the trajectory of the public's declining tolerance for ideological theater with its *de rigueur* attacks on established authority and upper class privilege. An example of the social criticism to which theater audiences suddenly reacted with howls and catcalls is found in the following speech (in Act V, Scene 4) by the protagonist in Holcroft's drama *Love's Frailties* (1794): "I was bred to the most useless and often the most worthless of all professions; that of a gentleman."[15] If Holcroft and his fellow advocates of reform were to remain faithful to their "religion" as defined in *The Rights of Man* as "do[ing] good," the price paid for such altruism was growing cultural marginalization.

Denied access to the booksellers and theater managers who had previously published and produced his novels and plays, Holcroft turned to translation for the second time in his career, albeit with greater urgency than before. Half a dozen years earlier, following his first trip to France, where he was befriended by the revolutionary journalist Nicholas Bonneville (1760–1828) and the dramatist Mercier, Holcroft had translated a number of texts, including Pierre Beaumarchais's *The Marriage of Figaro* (1785), several novels by the Madame de Genlis (1746–1830), and the *Posthumous Works of Frederick the Great* (13 volumes, 1789) translated from the first French edition. The profits earned from this work allowed Holcroft to retire permanently from the stage where, according to accounts of fellow actors, he had displayed at best an indifferent talent. This phase of translation coincided, of course, with an upsurge in public interest and demand for foreign texts and Holcroft's work at this time was undertaken with no higher motive than to boil the pot as he sought to re-establish himself as a writer of original texts. For obvious reasons, however, the market for French literature declined in the later 1790s and Holcroft was forced to find an alternate source for texts to translate. This new source he would find in German literature—partly as a result of contact with and encouragement received from the dramatist Friedrich Gottlieb Klopstock (1724–1803), the Homeric translator Johann Heinrich Voss (1751–1826), the traveler Stolberg, and other prominent liberal German writers whom he met while living in political exile. But this time around financial pressure, while still a factor in his decision, was not the driving force behind his turn to the translation of German texts. Isolated from the cultural institutions and the literary market place that owed their existence to the State's sufferance or support, his career as a writer, his sense of identity and his economic security, followed the same trajectory as that of his fellow Jacobins and reformers. Declining to allow his intellect to languish, translation became Holcroft's chief creative and ideological outlet during the period of exile and cultural isolation from 1799 to 1803.

Prior to the treason trial in 1794 and the suppression of reform activity, Holcroft had been a prolific and fairly successful author of comedies, light opera, and other pieces for the stage that regularly were performed at Covent Garden. His greatest successes—pieces that ran into several editions—were, like his imitation of Beaumarchais's *Figaro*, often adaptations of French and German works and include plays with such titles as *The School for Arrogance* (two editions in 1791), *The Road to Ruin* (nine editions in 1792), *The Deserted Daughter* (four editions in 1795), *He's Much to Blame* (four editions in 1798). But he is certainly best known for his novels—*Alwyn* (1780), *Anna St. Ives* (1792), *Hugh Trevor* (1794–1797), *Memoirs of Bryan Perdue* (1805)—and this is also the segment of his corpus the most extensively investigated by scholars.[16] Holcroft's novels show how he progressed from being an advocate of free thought to an architect of revolutionary society. The preface to *Bryan Perdue* reflects his stance: "Whenever I have undertaken to write a novel, I have proposed to myself a specific moral purpose."[17] The topical interest aroused by Holcroft's novels prompted their almost immediate translation on the Continent. In 1792, a German translation of *Anna St. Ives* was published in Berlin by Karl Philipp Moritz and a French edition appeared in Paris in 1798. The appeal of these novels to foreign readers indicates the occurrence of ideological cross-pollination as well as the reciprocal flow of revolutionary ideology from a beleaguered outpost of reform in Britain to France and Germany, where sympathy for radical alterations to the social fabric, combined with the growing fervor of nationalism, was undiminished. At home, however, the situation could not have formed a sharper contrast with the Continent. Following the trial, though exonerated but still considered by many as an enemy of the state, Holcroft's published work could only appear under pseudonyms. As a result, his position as a writer, his sense of identity, and his economic security could not have been more tenuous. In the *Reflections on the Revolution in France* (1790) Burke describes the crucial interdependence between a nation's culture and the State on the one hand, and the maintenance of a theological framework that gives the State its power and *raison d'être*, on the other:

> Nothing is more certain, than that our manners, our civilization, and all good things which are connected with manners and with civilization, have, in this European world of ours, depended for ages on two principles; and were indeed the result of both combined; I mean the spirit of a gentlemen, and the spirit of religion.[18]

In this passage Burke seems to anticipate the position adumbrated by Matthew Arnold in *Culture and Anarchy* (1869) on the relationship between the maintenance of social order and the hegemony of state-sponsored culture:

> [A] State in which law is authoritative and sovereign . . . is requisite if man is to bring to maturity anything precious and lasting . . . . The very framework and exterior order of the State . . . [is] sacred; and culture is the most resolute enemy of anarchy, because of the great hopes and designs for the State which culture teaches us to nourish.[19]

The implications for Holcroft's career are fairly clear: in writing plays and novels that violate generic norms and audience expectations and objectify a critical stance vis-à-vis state authority, he rejects the categorical imperative as stated by Edward Said: "to be for and in culture is to be in and for a State in a compellingly loyal way."[20] The result of such flagrant subversion of the State's artistic agenda is cultural disenfranchisement, figurative homelessness, marginalization in the canon, and, ultimately, the silencing of the authorial voice, which amounts to a kind of death. Ventriloquism, or displacing one's voice in translation, becomes the renegade writer's last resort to avoid the complete extinction of literary identity.

The flowering of *Weltliteratur*, which Goethe thought was heralded by the transmission activities of Carlyle, can in fact be seen as the fulfillment of a process that began with the founding of the Royal Society in 1663.[21] Throughout the first century of its existence the Society's composition denoted the permeable borders between the two cultures and anticipated the cultural and economic exchanges made possible by the founding of the modern European Union. Indeed, by 1770 at least 120 Germans had been elected to membership in the Society, including Theodore Haak (1605–1690), the first German translator of *Paradise Lost*, Heinrich Oldenburg (1619–1677), the editor of *The Philosophical Transactions* (which was later renamed *Transactions of the Royal Society*), cartographer Philipp Heinrich Zollmann (c. 1690–1748), the first person to occupy the office of the Society's Foreign Secretary, and familiar Enlightenment figures such as the philosopher Gottfried Wilhelm Leibniz (1646–1716), the mathematician Christian Wolff (1679–1754), the physiologist Albrecht von Haller (1708–1777), the physicist Daniel Gabriel Fahrenheit (1686–1736), and the astronomer and composer Sir William Herschel (1738–1822). Other instances of contemporary Anglo-German cultural exchange were facilitated by the large number of German musicians, artists, and scholars who resided in Britain throughout the eighteenth century but whose impact on the cultural life of the island nation has been largely overshadowed by the gigantic presence of the German-born composer Georg Friedrich Händel (1685–1759).[22] Nonetheless, several of their names will be familiar to historians of science, theater, music, and the fine arts: Johann Christoph Pepusch (1667–1752), one of the founders of the "Accademy of Ancient Music" in 1710; John Ernest Galliard (1687–1747), the composer of music for several of Colley Cibber's (1671–1757) masques and pantomimes and also for John Gay's *Beggar's Opera* (1728); John James Heidegger (1666–1749), who, along with Händel, founded the Royal Academy of Music in 1729 and was a friend of Henry Fielding (1707–1754) and Alexander Pope (1688–1744), though Pope could not resist immortalizing his reputed ugliness in the *Dunciad*, Book V, lines 243–244: "And lo, her bird (a monster of a fowl)/ Something betwixt a Heideggre and owl"). Other prominent German musicians active in England included Johann Friedrich Lampe (1703–1751), Carl Friedrich Abel (1723–1787), and Johann Christian Bach (1735–1782), the eleventh and youngest son of Johann Sebastian Bach (1685–1750), who organized Wolfgang Amadeus Mozart's concerts in London and arranged for the introduction of the prodigy at court in 1764. Native German-speaking artists active in Britain numbered the portraitist Sir Godfrey Kneller (1646–1723), the botanical painter Georg Dionysius Ehret (1708–1770), and the influential artist and critic Henry Fuseli (1741–1825), of whom, according to Gilchrist, "Blake . . . was wont to declare, 'This country must advance two centuries in civilisation before it can appreciate him.'"[23]

Any survey of cultural contacts between Britain and Germany in the early eighteenth century would be incomplete without noting the thriving two-way trade in secular and sacred literary texts during this period.[24] German hymns and poems were widely circulated through skillful translations in Methodist circles. One specific example is *A Collection of German Hymns* published by John Wesley in 1742. The great number of lyrics and hymns by Nikolaus Ludwig, Reichsgraf Zinzendorf und Pottendorf (1700–1760) in this and other hymn books indicates the intimacy of the bond between English Methodism and German Pietism, which suggests that the rise of British Romanticism was inextricably linked to the fusion of dissenting religion, radical politics, the rise of female authorship, and the mediation of German culture.

The popularity and impact of British literature in Germany, especially the novel, has been well documented; indeed, Michael Maurer affirmed the formative connection between Anglophilia and the Enlightenment in Germany.[25] But unlike the situation in Germany, where admiration of all things British historically has been and remains a vital presence in intellectual life, there has traditionally been strong resistance by many scholars and critics of British literature to accept a model of cultural history that acknowledges the impact that the transmission of German literature and thought has had on shaping British cultural identity. This may have had something to do with the fact that women and other cultural outsiders played leading roles as literary intermediaries and that their mediating activities also constituted political acts that not only reflected sympathy with Continental ideologies and revolutions but also initiated their movement from the margins of literary culture towards the center. Also underpinning this resistance is the traditional paradigm of literary history, according to which the processes of cultural production that threaten to demote the iconic position of the author and reveal the root system of canonical works, are erased or ignored.

In order to restore this underlying institutional root system, much of the original writing generated by the Godwin Circle must be viewed in connection with the transmission activities of Fuseli, Wollstonecraft, Holcroft, and Taylor. After arriving in London in 1760, Fuseli led an aggressive campaign to introduce the cultural riches of the German language to Britain. Not merely was Fuseli *au courant* in German thought and literature, having produced the first English translation of Johann Joachim Winckelmann's *Geschichte der Kunst des Alterthums* [*The History of the Art of Antiquity*] in 1764. He had been educated in Zurich, a leading center of proto-romantic German culture in the late eighteenth century. He was also a confidant of Johann Jakob Bodmer (1698–1783) and Lavater. Encouraged to write in English by his intimate friend the publisher Joseph Johnson (1738–1809), Fuseli's influence can be felt in the pages of the *Analytical Review* where the writings of Kotzebue, Wieland, Schiller, and Goethe were reviewed on a regular basis.[26] He also composed the first authoritative history of German literature in English, which was unfortunately lost in a fire in 1770. Thus Fuseli was better positioned than anyone else in Britain at the time, and certainly more advantageously placed than anyone, before Crabb Robinson, including Coleridge, to interpret German culture for Anglophone readers. Also contributing to Fuseli's influence in the Godwin Circle was the background he shared with the Dissenters and their fellow travelers Wollstonecraft and Holcroft. Like Godwin, Fuseli was initially trained as a minister (in the liberal Protestant Zwinglian sect), but early on he abandoned that vocation in favor of a career in literature and the arts. Like Wollstonecraft, he passed through phases of enthusiasm for and subsequent disillusionment with Rousseau, whom he had met in 1767. The charismatic Fuseli also attracted disciples and none was more important as an intermediary in her own right than Wollstonecraft. Her engagement with German culture suggests the need to reassess the traditional attribution to Fuseli of some eighty reviews published in the *Analytical*, including the famous review of Goethe's dramas *Stella* (1806) and *Clavigo* (1774), and possibly to transfer several of them to his protégée.[27] Indeed, the seven reviews of German works (such as John Armstrong's 1790 translation of *Werther—The Confidential Letters of Albert; from his first attachment to Charlotte to her death*) in the *Analytical* attributed to Wollstonecraft by Marilyn Butler seems an insufficient number considering Wollstonecraft's unusually strong competence in German and the remarkable frequency with which German works were reviewed there.

Wollstonecraft's major achievement as a translator appeared in 1790. *Elements of Morality for the use of children* was freely adapted from the German text by Christian Gotthilf Salzmann (1744–1811), who was a broadly influential contemporary educational writer. Salzmann's importance was noted by Lavater, Herder, and Goethe, among others, and his *Moralisches Elementarbuch* was reprinted throughout the nineteenth century and the 1785 edition was reprinted as recently as 1980. Wollstonecraft's *Elements of Morality* is not a mechanical translation or mere hackwork; on the contrary, it represents a path-breaking exercise in the transposition of a foreign text into a domesticated form intended to make it more acceptable to a British audience. There are strong ideological and stylistic ligatures connecting *Elements of Morality* to Wollstonecraft's other works of a pedagogical and didactic character, including *Thoughts on the Education of Daughters* (1787), *The Female Reader* (1789)—a compilation of pieces by many hands, which is precisely Salzmann's organizational method in *Moralisches Elementarbuch—Original Stories from Real Life: With Conversations Calculated to Regulate the Affections and Form the*

Mind to Truth and Goodness (1788), *Mary: A Fiction* (1788), *The Wrongs of Woman, or Maria* (1798), and *A Vindication of the Rights of Woman* (1790). Wollstonecraft's novel *Young Grandison* (1790) is also, like *Elements of Morality*, essentially a reworking of a foreign work. In this case the appropriated text is *De kleine Grandison* a novel by the Dutch writer Maria Geertruida de Cambon-van der Werken, which was itself an adaptation of Samuel Richardson's original.[28] Such interconnections between Wollstonecraft's writings published as original work and her translations anticipate the instrumental function that the transmission of German culture served in the careers of women writers in the early to mid-nineteenth century in Britain and America, including Sarah Austin (1793–1867), Margaret Fuller (1810–1850), and George Eliot (1819–1880).[29]

No doubt with Fuseli's encouragement, Wollstonecraft began working on an abridged translation of Lavater's *Physiognomische Fragmente* in the late 1780s, but when Holcroft's translation appeared in 1789 Wollstonecraft's project was abandoned. Holcroft's slightly abridged translation from the German, *Essays on the Physiognomy designed to promote the knowledge and love of mankind*, appeared in the same year as Henry Hunter's complete edition which was based on Marie-Elisabeth de LaFite's complete French translation, *Essai sur la Physiognomie* (Paris: La Haye, 1781–1803). That Hunter's was the "official" translation is clear; after traveling to Switzerland and obtaining the author's imprimatur, he even engaged Fuseli as a supervisory editor with authority over both the translation of the text and the selection and production of plates. Fuseli also penned the "Advertisement" for the book which contains a vivid biographical sketch of Lavater, a friend in his youth. In contrast to Holcroft's edition, which was published cheaply for the mass market, the edition by Hunter was published by subscription and it appeared in three expensive volumes (1789, 1792, 1798) priced at £30 each.[30] The list of subscribers included other leading intermediaries of German culture—William Taylor, the translator of Goethe's *Iphigenie* (1793), and "Monk" Lewis, the Gothic novelist, who played a key role in the domestication of the German *Schauerroman* in Britain.[31] On the strength of its splendid engravings and fine binding, one reviewer considered the lavish Hunter edition "the finest printed book which has ever appeared in this or any other country."[32] Intensifying the rivalry between the two Lavater editions, Holcroft's translation was based on an authorized German abridgement (published by Winterthur, 1783–1787) made by another intimate of Lavater's circle, the academic Johann Michael Armbruster (1761–1814). The latter's alterations to the original were approved by Lavater himself in a letter dated 7 April 1783.[33] Complicating matters even further, Holcroft's edition received more favorable attention from the critics than Hunter's. Especially praiseworthy were the notices in *The European Magazine* (XVII and XVIII) and *The Critical Review* (LXVIII and LXIX). The reviewer for the latter incorrectly identified Holcroft's as the first complete version of Lavater's work to appear in English. Such an imperfect reception to Hunter's edition could only have provided an additional irritant to Fuseli. This attitude is reflected in his two-part review of Holcroft's translation in the December 1789 and April 1790 issues of the *Analytical*. Fuseli quite correctly indicates that the Holcroft translation was a full volume shorter than Hunter's and he offers a list of Holcroft's translation errors and maladroit passages.

Certainly Fuseli's hostile critique was motivated in part by his support first for Hunter's and then Wollstonecraft's rival translations; but another likely cause of his disapproval was his proprietary interest in the original *Physiognomische Fragmente*. Along with Goethe and others, Fuseli had contributed a number of aphorisms and sketches of heads that were included in the first German language edition (1775). The success of Holcroft's translation also inspired avaricious copycats, including one Samuel Shaw, whose pirated single volume edition of Holcroft's work appeared in 1792, and an anonymous publisher of the first American edition which appeared a year later. Despite any lingering bad blood between Fuseli and Holcroft, the reviewer for the *Analytical*—presumably Fuseli—excoriated the thieving Shaw as "one of those contemptible catchpennies, which cannot be too severely reprehended."[34] In 1792 G. G. J. and J. Robinson, Holcroft's publisher, responded to the threat of further piracy by issuing a one-volume abridgement that featured none of the inaccuracies that marred Shaw's hastily executed literary theft. Hunter's expensively printed translation from the French was in turn pirated by another clergyman, the Rev. C. Moore, whose edition was published in 1797. Despite its limitations, in both legal and pirated editions, Holcroft's translation remained the standard English version of Lavater's *Fragmente* throughout the nineteenth and early twentieth centuries.

Not all of Holcroft's translations created internecine rivalry within the Godwin Circle as his Lavater edition did. As a rule, his work as a translator reflected a knack for choosing texts with undeniable commercial appeal. Not untypical was the success enjoyed by his adaptation of *The Marriage of Figaro*, entitled *Follies of the Day*, which was performed on 4 December 1784 at Covent Garden with Holcroft in the lead role. Other French authors he translated included Stéphanie Félicité du Crest de Saint-Aubin (1746–1830), Claude-Étienne Savary (1750–1788), and Marie Jules César Sauvigny (1777–1851). Another successful play, Holcroft's 1790 translation of J. C. Brandes's *The German Hotel*, was frequently performed and reprinted throughout the decade. Holcroft also enjoyed success with the first English translations of Stolberg's *Travels through Germany, Switzerland, Italy, and Sicily* (1796)[35] — Fuseli's review appeared in the December 1797 *Analytical Review* (XXVI) — and the *Life of Baron Frederic Trenck* (London, 1788; Boston, 1792),[36] which has been continuously in print ever since. At this time the demand for works of real adventures was such that two other translations of Trenck's novelistic, exotic memoirs were published — anonymously — in the same year. Holcroft's selection of these texts to translate exemplifies the special nature of his relationship with German literature. Both texts afforded opportunities for submerged self-expression in the colorful careers of two liberal members of the German aristocracy which he donned in place of his own identity as an exiled, impoverished Jacobin author, subject to censorship, who was *persona non grata* in Britain following the treason trial. Stolberg's and Trenck's memoirs — as encounters with foreign otherness—reflect the substitution of Holcroft's voice in place of other "voices"; they also served as paradigms for his original *Travels from Hamburg, through Westphalia, Holland, and the Netherlands, to Paris* (1804). Holcroft's own encounter with Northern Europe must therefore be mediated by his translations of others' travel writing—and possibly also by his reading of Wollstonecraft's *A Short Residence in Sweden, Norway, and Denmark* (1796). Holcroft's editions of Stolberg and Trenck indicate that for him translation functioned as a displacement of original writing—an extreme sign of self-censorship—and represented an appropriation of an "alternative" culture in place of the official state-sponsored literary culture in Britain from which Jacobins, Dissenters, women and others were excluded and marginalized. Referring to "the occasional dilemmas of the Translator," Holcroft's Preface to Stolberg's *Travels* gives some indication of his authorial insecurity. The following passage is highly self-referential in disclosing the difficulties faced in mediating the *terra incognita* of Stolberg's experiences: in "following his erratic and devious path . . . the Translator has not infrequently found himself in a labyrinth, from which to extricate himself, and never lose sight of his author, was a task of difficulty and address." As for his confrontation with the original German he speaks of its "complex construction, indefinite grammar, licentious orthography, and perplexed idiom."[37]

The most important of Holcroft's translations in literary-historical terms—and his greatest challenge of this kind—is of Goethe's narrative poem, *Hermann und Dorothea* (1801), which was the first to appear in Britain. With this translation Holcroft joined a select company of Goethe's British intermediaries, including Taylor, Scott, Crabb Robinson, and Carlyle. As an alternative to disclosing the otherness of the existing order in Britain and the alienation that Holcroft and his fellow Jacobins and Dissenters experienced on the margins of their native culture—the positing of such otherness which had characterized his activity as a novelist, playwright, and journalist before his arrest—the translation of Goethe's text served as an exercise in centering himself in a foreign otherness. This otherness is nonetheless not entirely unfamiliar to him, since the conflict facing Hermann's family in the poem is similar to the cultural dilemma confronting Holcroft and other members of the Godwin Circle in the wake of war hysteria and government reaction: how does one adjust to the chaos and alienation of war thrust upon their settled existence by French invaders? And yet the means appear for restoring the shattered idyll and reconciling Hermann and his parents to life, and this means comes to them in the form of Dorothea the refugee. She offers a critique of the way things are while yet offering a good deal of idealistic rhetoric about the possibility of repairing the damaged fabric of society which will lead to the reconciliation of the alienated individual with society and the State. In fact, Goethe's poem extols many of the values associated with religious and political Dissent. But because of his status as an outsider in British culture even before his arrest, Holcroft was never in his own novels or plays able to attain the state of unified perception between subject and object—the self and the social world—visible in his translation. This condition, which is analogous to Bakhtinian "transgredience," is produced when "the whole existence of others is seen from outside not only their own knowledge that they are being perceived by somebody else, but from beyond their awareness that such an other even exists."[38] Holcroft thus approached the task of translating *Hermann und Dorothea* as an attempt to attain "transgredience" between the author of the original work and himself as the mediator of its otherness.

Goethe himself noticed this characteristic in Holcroft's translation. In a letter to Holcroft dated 29 May 1801 Goethe distinguishes between two approaches to translation: the first, in which the translator tries "seiner Nation den reinen Begriff eines fremden Autors überliefern, fremde Zustände derselben anschaulich machen will, wobei man sich denn genau an das Original bindet" [to convey the pure concept of a foreign author, to make the foreign context vividly realizable to the reader, by binding himself precisely to the original meaning].[39] Alternatively, the translator may choose to treat the original text as "eine Art Stoff," that is, a pliable medium which may be modified in such a way "that it becomes more familiar" to the translator's readers, even to the point where "his readers will be able to read it as an original," as though the text's otherness had been neutralized. The latter, Goethe insists, is Holcroft's method, which is in keeping with the description Holcroft provides concerning his methodology in the Preface and Notes to the translation:

> In moral sentiments, poetical feeling, and idioms of speech, Each people have their peculiarities. To these I have not infrequently dared to render my author subject; and indulge in such variations as I imagined he would have been likely to have adopted, had he written to the English Nation.... [The translator] will not honour his author by being too much his slave; though continual attempts to be his equal are but continual disappointments: at least, such honours are rarely attained, and short of duration; and even while he seeks them, he exposes himself to the dangers either of just censure or pedantic cavil.[40]

Holcroft's commentary on Goethe's poem also contains an implicit theory of translation which suggests parallels with essayist William Hazlitt's concept of "gusto" or Keatsean "intensity." Clearly, for Holcroft, the focus of the translator is on replicating emotional authenticity rather than word-for-word accuracy:

> A poet can never be translated with any due degree of the enthusiasm with which he wrote, unless the translator excites in himself the same kind of ardor. He will then, while he breathes spirit and feeling of his author, generally forget his author's words. The excellence of all translations will indeed rather consist in the feeling and the spirit than in the words.[41]

The process of selection and arrangement of suitable voices and garb for the transformation of the foreign text into something new and yet non-alienating is itself perhaps a more adequate definition for the search for a specific framework from a multitude of possible responses. And here, in Goethe's translated text, at a significant site of cultural interaction in the Romantic age, Holcroft appears to have attained reciprocal unity between subject and object to a degree that eluded him in his career as novelist, playwright, and journalist.

Writing for the comparatively liberal and cosmopolitan *Monthly Review*, William Taylor emerged as a key figure in the cultural politics of the 1790s. Less familiar to us, perhaps, than the translators Robert Pearse Gillies (1788–1858) and John Gibson Lockhart

(1794–1854), the son-in-law of Sir Walter Scott, Taylor is nonetheless the most important critic of German literature before Carlyle who stimulated the German studies of Crabb Robinson, Scott, Lewis, George Barrow, Sarah Austin, and poet laureate Robert Southey. His career as a translator and critic encapsulates the problems confronting would-be British mediators of foreign culture at the close of the eighteenth century. There is, as in Coleridge, a certain logical consistency running through Taylor's opinions, but also insensitivity to the special development in literary history represented by Goethe. Wilhelm Dilthey, for one, argues that the difficulties Goethe's contemporaries experienced in classifying him result from the confusing array of talents and interests that he embodied. The likelihood of misinterpretation is also increased by Goethe's ambivalent relationship to the *Aufklärung* [Enlightenment]. Although Goethe shares a common cultural legacy with Klopstock, for example, whom Coleridge and Wordsworth paid a visit in 1798, his characteristic form of literary expression is lyrical, generically unstable, and highly subjective. Many British critics of the time, including Taylor, Coleridge, Hazlitt, and De Quincey, did not recognize that Goethe's manner of expressing himself represented a radical new departure in modern thought and literature. In addition to his literary work, Goethe's scientific research, philosophical reflections, and even his administrative duties for the Grand Duchy of Saxe-Weimar, form a seamless unity with and do not simply fill in the pauses separating his creative periods. As Dilthey explains, these activities were indispensable aids to Goethe in his confrontation with and conquest of life and the world: "er zu Erfüllung seiner dichterischen Mission bedürfte, und nur die wissenschaftliche Überwindung der Aufklärung konnte ihm für seine poetische Welt freie Bahn schaffen" [in order to fulfill his mission as a poet Goethe first needed to create free space for his poetic world by overcoming the scientific achievement of the Enlightenment]. In later life Goethe feared that his engagement with the fine arts, the "active" life of a minister with multiple portfolios at court, as well as science and scholarship, were "falsche Tendenzen" [false tendencies]. Conversely, these interests were, in Dilthey's view, served as

> das breite Fundament für ein dichterisches Lebenswerk von ganz neuer Art, daß mit der Gestaltung der Persönlichkeit unzertrennlich verbunden war. So ist der Platz Goethes nicht unter den großen Naturforschern, Philosophen oder Staatsmännern, er ist neben Äschylos, Dante und Shakespeare.[42]

If the important new functions of the poet fused in Goethe went unnoticed by many influential contemporaries—consider Adolf Menzel in Germany and Taylor, Coleridge, Hazlitt, and De Quincey in Britain—more conventional writers posed no such problems. For example, the works of Kotzebue, Taylor's literary idol, enjoyed enormous popularity on the London stage. "According to my judgment," Taylor writes in tones of praise so immoderate that he elicited Carlyle's "good-humored" and "judicial censure"[43] in the *Edinburgh Review*: "Kotzebue is the greatest dramatic genius that Europe has evolved since Shakespeare." Taylor was determined "to give some idea of the various powers of this great writer," whose range includes "plays of every form: farces, melodramas, mixt or sentimental dramas, household tragedies, classical tragedies, and . . . that vaster and more difficult form of art . . . the gothic tragedy."[44] Kotzebue apparent defects, including his notorious prolificity and nonchalance, are, in Taylor's estimation, signs of genius. He applauds Kotzebue's penchant for grandiose special effects even at the expense of nuances of character, plot development, and dialogue. These "extraordinary" effects "concentrate the attention of an audience on the passing scene."[45] Even though Taylor concedes that "Goethe had the merit of showing" others "the way" and of having surpassed both Kotzebue and Schiller in classical tragedy with *Iphigenia in Tauris*, he nonetheless praises Kotzebue for his "superior invention," in which he excels Schiller and Goethe. Moreover, his "comic approaches his tragic force . . . and his sudden power over all the emotions has in it something magical."[46] Accustomed to Kotzebue's energy, pathos, and sentimentality, Taylor was not aesthetically inclined to admire the realism of Goethe's diction, his naturalistic portrayal of human passions, and his indifference to neoclassical conventions of pacing or time.

Taylor was baffled by the changes in Goethe's artistic development that took place in the fifty years dividing *Werther* from *Wilhelm Meister*. The abstractions of Goethe's later style and the focus on the protagonist's inner development as he experiences a broad panorama of human experience created puzzles for a critic with a predilection for sentiment, decorum, and sensationalistic stage effects. Although he approves of the "picturesque descriptions, sage reflections, and poignant situations" that are found in the novel, Taylor notes that "a senile garrulity creeps on him, his style is become more trailing, and those gushes of learning, which refresh the soul, sparkle seldomer along the smoother but expanded currents of his narrative."[47]

Taylor's survey of Goethe's major works in prose continues in the same vein of moral reproach and aesthetic disapproval. *Die Wahlverwandschaften* [*Elective Affinities*] (1809) is dismissed as "hardly worthy" of Goethe's pen. Although he is prepared to acknowledge Goethe's superior "knowledge of human nature," ingeniously represented as paralleling certain kinds of chemical reaction, he sees in this performance "some declension of his plastic power."[48] Taylor's remarks on *Dichtung und Wahrheit* suggests that he fails to recognize the organization and method of the work and its relation to Goethe's Terentian openness to human experience:

> This is not an autobiography, but rather a biographical novel, in which many things are related of the hero, which never happened to him. It is a household epopeia, which, like the Waverly novels [of Walter Scott], mingles history and invention, in a manner interesting to the reader, but dangerous to his distinctness of memory, particularly as, in this instance, he cannot turn to the pure chronicle of the historian.[49]

By translating *Dichtung und Wahrheit* with the terms reversed, as "Fact and Fiction," Taylor has misconstrued the significance of the juxtaposition of "Dichtung" and "Wahrheit." In Goethe's title the emphasis is on "Dichtung." Subordinate to "Dichtung" in Goethe's title is "Wahrheit," which is not adequately translated as "fact," but should actually be characterized as "truth." Taylor's description of *Dichtung und Wahrheit* as a kind of domestic epic is in fact an astute observation. As a "biographical novel" *Dichtung und Wahrheit* reveals what Arthur Schopenhauer (1788–1860) calls the "innere Bedeutsamkeit" [inner significance] of everyday life in contrast to the "äußere Bedeutsamkeit" [outer significance] of historical narrative.[50] And yet, because Taylor blames Goethe for failing "to separate the fiction from the fact" in this work, it is clear that he has profoundly misunderstood Goethe's technique of interpreting his age through the medium of his own personality and the formative events in his development.[51] His perplexity anticipates Saintsbury's denunciation of techniques of criticism in which the main emphasis is on the personality of the author. Goethe gives the scenes "from my life" a "typical" quality that corresponds to Aristotle's concept of "universality," Sir Philip Sidney's Horatian "speaking picture of Poesy," Hegel's "concrete universal," and T.S. Eliot's "objective correlative." As the leading poet of his age and *Sprachraum*,[52] Goethe creates out of the raw materials of his life an artistic mythos, in which the constituent elements—poetry and truth, the universal idea and the particular event—are kept in balance. Taylor denigrates the book's mythical dimension as merely "a spirit of omen-hunting, hardly consistent with the complete infidelity, to which Goethe lays claim."[53]

Taylor's judgment of Goethe did not evolve. Even Crabb Robinson's friendly disagreement and Carlyle's negative review left him unrepentant, but it is important to note that even the favorable views of Crabb Robinson and Carlyle signified rare outbursts of dissent in an age dominated by nearly universal antipathy toward Goethe. The congruence between Taylor's views and the editorial position of *The Anti-Jacobin Review* is apparent in a letter to Crabb Robinson on the taste of the British reading public and the reception of Goethe's immorality:

> The entire works of Goethe would not suit here: he has attained that divine morality which looks down on all forms of human conduct, which equal eye, and sees in the lewdness of Faustus, or the purity of Iphigenie, but that exact

adaptation of effect and cause, of conduct and motive, which he characterizes the constitution of things.[54]

Shortly afterwards, Crabb Robinson records a conversation with Taylor that took place on 19 August 1813: "In the evening a call on W. Taylor late. We talked on German literature in which Taylor is a heretic, for he does not acknowledge the supremacy of Goethe."[55]

From October 1790 to August 1799 Taylor published dozens of reviews and articles on the works of Schiller, Goethe, Klopstock, Wieland, and Kotzebue. During the same decade he produced the first English translation of Goethe's classical drama *Iphigenie auf Tauris* (1779), which published in 1796, as well as one of the best contemporary adaptations of the poem "Leonore" (1794) by Gottfried August Bürger (1747–1794). Others who paid tribute to the popularity of Bürger's signature poem, which made ballad writing fashionable across Romantic Europe, include Walter Scott and Henry James Pye (1744–1813), the future poet laureate and butt of countless puns. The decade of the 1790s was, of course, characterized by a vogue for German drama—in Britain and on the Continent—especially the pathos-drenched plays of Kotzebue. At this time no British critic emerged with enough cultural authority to take the lead in canon formation. Nearly every German writer translated into English found at least one disciple who was prepared to name him the dominant figure in German literature. To the dismay of the young Carlyle, who published a watershed series of articles on German culture in the *Edinburgh Review* and *Fraser's Magazine* in the 1820s and 1830s, Taylor sided with Kotzebue as the leading German writer of his generation. While not alone in giving voice to the public taste for Kotzebue's brand of kitsch—the Irish playwright Richard Brinsley Sheridan's successful plays, *The Stranger* (1798) and *Pizarro* (1799), were adapted, respectively, from Kotzebue's *Menschenhaß und Reue* [*Misanthropy and Repentance*] (1789) and *Die Spanier in Peru, oder Rollas Tod* [*The Spanish in Peru or the Death of Rolla*] (1795)—Taylor was perhaps more joyously uninhibited and less ambivalent than others in his praise. Kotzebue seemed without question "the greatest dramatic genius that Europe has evolved since Shakespeare," whose genius commanded "plays of every form: farces, melodramas, mixt or sentimental dramas, household tragedies, classical tragedies, and . . . that vaster and more difficult form of art . . . the gothic tragedy."⁵⁶ Kotzebue's obvious artistic defects—prolificity and nonchalance, the occupational hazards of a wildly popular author—did not earn a sideways glance; Taylor even applauded Kotzebue's tendency to exploit cheap theatrical effects and to ignore almost completely the nuances of character and plot development. Not unlike present-day directors of action films, it was Kotzebue's special talent to "concentrate the attention of an audience on the passing scene" by making "free use of the extraordinary."⁵⁷ As proof that there is truly no accounting for taste, during this period none of Goethe's and Schiller's plays were produced in Britain and Lessing's *Emilia Galotti* (1772) was performed exactly four times at Drury Lane in 1794. By contrast, performances of Kotzebue's *Pizarro* and *Menschenhaß und Reue*—in Sheridan's adaptations—were repeated over forty times in 1798 and 1799.

The popular demand on the British stage for Kotzebue's works reached such prominence that it began to outstrip the capacity of translators to produce accurate versions of his plays. Though the first complaints directed against Kotzebue in the reviews focused almost exclusively on the execrable literary quality of the bowdlerized texts, conservative critics noticed that the German playwright's "superior invention" and emotional energy masked a potentially subversive ideology of sensibility that some were quick to associate with what recently caused so much mischief in Paris. A critic writing in *The Ladies Monthly Museum* complained of *Lover's Vows* (1798) by Elizabeth Inchbald (1753–1821), an adaptation of Kotzebue's *Das Kind der Liebe* [*Love Child or Natural Son*] (1780): "We cannot but declare that the dramas of Kotzebue have, in our opinion, a tendency to encourage a laxity of principle that ought to make the English people rather cautious of giving too implicit credit to the sentiment he inculcates."⁵⁸ Such qualms are mild, almost praiseworthy compared to the vitriolic attack on Kotzebue that appeared in *The Anti-Jacobin Review* in 1799:

> Let us, for God's sake, look with a little more circumspection at the claims of these German philosophers before we so readily admit the value of them; nor suffer the public taste to be vitiated thus, without making one single attempt to expose the absurdity of its seducer. My blood boils with indignation when I see my beloved Shakespeare, Otway, Rowe, and all those ornaments of my native country thrust aside to make room for the filthy effusions of this German dunce.[59]

A bellwether for cultural and political reaction in the decade following the French Revolution, *The Anti-Jacobin Review and Magazine, or Monthly Political and Literary Censor* took up where its predecessor, the *Anti-Jacobin or Weekly Examiner*, left off. In addition to the charge of bad morals, the alarm was raised in succeeding issues about the threats posed to traditional religious values and political orthodoxy by Kotzebue and the "German School." A general fear of heterodoxy, foreign culture, and liberalism colored such comments as the following: *Pizarro* was seen to exalt "Deism, or natural religion." "By flattering the passions [Kotzebue] attempts powerfully to interest the heart, and when that is gained, insidiously instills his venomous principles."[60] Guilty as well of inverting the social hierarchy in his plays, Kotzebue frequently depicts "the great . . . as vicious" and "the low . . . as virtuous." Moreover, Elvira, the female protagonist in *Pizarro*, was condemned as a "complete Godwinite heroine."[61] Extreme even by the standards of xenophobic rhetoric of *The Anti-Jacobin Review* is the Preface to the fourth volume, published in 1799, in which cultural paranoia and anti-German xenophobia is carried to new heights:

> It is with an equal portion of surprise and alarm that we witness in this country a glaring depravity of taste, as displayed in the extreme eagerness for foreign productions, and a systematic design to extend such depravity by a regular importation of exotic poison from the envenomed crucibles of the literary and political alchemists of the new German school. The state of the foreign presses . . . is still such as to justify the most serious apprehensions in the mind of all who feel any interest in the preservation of religion and morality, and the importation of their products into this country should, if possible, be guarded against with the same provident spirit of caution which enforces a strict observance of quarantine by vessels which arrive from countries infected with the plague . . . . Even an act of despotism when exercised for the purpose of rescuing mankind

from the worse species of oppression—the subjugation of the mind to the degrading tyranny of Philosophism—would be entitled to applause.[62]

The impact of this type of conservative invective was immediate, widespread, and of fairly long duration. It is even felt in a text by the playwright Hannah More, *Strictures on the Modern System of Female Education* (1799), in which the ill effects of German literature are inscribed on the body politic:

> Those ladies who take the lead in society are loudly called upon to act as the guardians of the public taste, as well as of the public virtue, in an important instance. They are called upon, therefore, to oppose with the whole weight of their influence, the irruptions of those swarms of publications now daily issuing from the banks of the Danube, which, like their ravaging predecessors of the darker ages, though with far other and more fatal arms, are overrunning civil society.[63]

Attacks like this in the press were a product of the general atmosphere of cultural chauvinism and government repression and censorship that diverted Godwin into writing children's books and forced Holcroft to seek his literary fortunes in translation. Once noted for their interest in German and Continental literature generally, in the late 1790s journals like *The Monthly Mirror, The Critical Review*, and *The Monthly Review* abruptly stopped the practice of reviewing German books. In the face of officially-sanctioned harassment of Dissenters and radicals, Taylor dropped out of the reviewing business altogether for nearly a decade and it was not until 1808 that we find him once again reviewing German literature for *The Monthly Review*. Despite being twice marginalized as it were, initially by his preference for Kotzebue over Goethe,[64] and then by government-sponsored literary terrorism, as one of the first intermediaries between British and German culture Taylor must be credited for performing a valuable service. Since unmediated experience of foreign literature is not possible for the monoglot English reader, the foreign text first must be appropriated, annexed, and domesticated by the translator. Far from simply introducing the readers of *The Monthly Review* to a new taste in literature, Taylor was among the most important cultural intermediaries in dissenting, radical circles.

Taylor's limitations as a critic and cultural mediator are perhaps nowhere more apparent than in his misjudgment of Goethe. For example, while Goethe shares a common cultural legacy with Lessing, his poetic gift and his sensibility, which encode highly personal feelings and experiences, are at odds with Enlightenment ideals of detachment and objectivity. Taylor was not alone in failing to recognize that Goethe's subjectivity represented a radical new departure; one recalls that while traveling in Germany Coleridge and Wordsworth anachronistically beat a path to Klopstock's door. Coleridge also planned to write a full-scale study of Lessing's life and works. In step with Coleridge, whose response to Schiller's Karl Moor is well known ("Southey, who is this convulser of the heart?"), Taylor esteems Kotzebue's energy and Schiller's sublimity as chief literary values and he could not help missing the greater subtlety in Goethe's naturalism.

Despite his flaws as a mediator and translator of German culture in Britain—flaws that he shared with much more eminent contemporaries, Taylor may be singled out as arguably the most important early initiator of intercultural and interlinguistic exchange between Britain and Germany. The difficulties he faced—from a proliferation of faulty translations to censorship—simply indicate, as the translation theorist Antoine Berman has argued, that "every culture resists translation"—and the fact that the current crisis over European unity issues from Britain is additional evidence of such resistance. Even Taylor's modest accomplishments as a reviewer and translator reinforce Berman's view that "the very aim of translation [is] to open up in writing a certain relation with the Other, to fertilize what is one's Own through the mediation of what is Foreign." Translation is thus "diametrically opposed to the ethnocentric structure of every culture, that species of narcissism by which every society wants to be a pure and unadulterated Whole . . . . The essence of translation may be likened to an opening, a dialogue, a cross-breeding, a de-centering" of one's culture that inevitably provides resistance of the sort represented by the *Anti-Jacobin* and *The Anti-Jacobin Review*.[65] Politically motivated resistance to the importation of foreign texts in Britain is to blame for the deformations in Taylor's response to German literature, such as his anachronistic preference for Kotzebue over Goethe (as it does for Coleridge and Wordsworth's initial preference for Klopstock). Nonetheless, far from simply introducing the readers of *The Monthly Review* to a new taste in literature, Taylor was participating in the unheralded but important mission of the translator from the German language as praised by Goethe:

> Wer die deutsche Sprache versteht und studirt befindet sich auf dem Markte wo alle Nationen ihre Waaren anbieten, er spielt den Dolmetscher indem er sich selbst bereichert. Und so ist jeder Übersetzer anzusehen, daß er sich als Vermittler dieses allgemein geistigen Handels bemüht, und dem Wechseltausch zu befördern sich zum Geschäft macht. Denn, was man auch von der Unzulänglichkeit des Übersetzens sagen mag, so ist und bleibt es doch eins der wichtigsten und würdigsten Geschäffte in dem allgemeinen Weltwesen.[66]

The truth of this last observation was seen in the extraordinary popularity that even poor, inaccurate translations of German texts enjoyed in Britain in the 1790s. For Goethe, translation was the main factor in the emergence of a truly globalized culture, which he christened *Weltliteratur* [world literature]. A passage from Goethe's correspondence with Carlyle contains the clearest statement of the significance of translation for the development of genuine cultural "universality":

> Offenbar ist das Bestreben der besten Dichter und ästhetischen Schrift-steller aller Nationen schon seit geraumer Zeit auf das allgemein Menschliche gerichtet. In jedem Besondern, es sei nun historisch, mythologisch, fabelhaft, mehr oder weniger willkürlich ersonnen, wird man durch Nationalität und Persönlichkeit hindurch jenes Allgemeine immer mehr durchleuchten und durchschimmern sehn .... Was nun in den Dichtungen aller Nationen hierauf hindeutet und hinwirkt, dies ist es was die Übrigen sich anzueignen haben. Die Besonderheiten einer jeden muß man kennen lernen, um sie ihr zu laßen, um gerade dadurch mit ihr zu verkehren; denn die Eigenheiten einer Nation sind wie ihre Sprache und ihre Münzsorten, sie erleichtern den Verkehr, ja sie machen ihn erst vollkommen möglich .... Ein wahrhaft allgemeine Duldung wird am sichersten erreicht, wenn man das Besondere der einzelnen Menschen und Völkerschaften auf sich beruhen läßt, bei der Überzeugung jedoch festhält, daß das wahrhaft Verdienstliche sich dadurch auszeichnet, daß er der ganzen Menschheit angehört.[67]

Goethe's translations—and his translations from Cellini, Diderot, Voltaire, Euripides, Racine, Corneille, as well as his translations of Italian, English, Spanish, and Greek poems, fill a good-sized volume in the *Weimarer Ausgabe*—and the translations Taylor, Wollstonecraft, Holcroft, and Coleridge—to name just some prominent translators from the German in the 1790s—fulfill the essential function of incarnating cross-border cultural exchanges. Regardless of the quality of these efforts—and here Taylor's reviews and translations succeed to the same degree as Goethe's—translation as the expression of *Bildung* consists in a multiplicity of intercultural and interlinguistic acts—engaged in by individuals and nations. As Berman has suggested, these are "interactions in which they construct their own identity and their relations to the foreign." Thus translation is the essence of the *Bildung* of Romanticism, since the formation of the self—and by extension, an entire people—also demands the appropriation of the Other in a form that makes contact possible and fulfilling. The movement of translation like that of *Bildung* is circular and "starts from what is one's own, the same, in order to go towards the foreign, the other. . . and, starting from this experience, to return to its point of departure."[68] Since unmediated experience of the Other is not possible, appropriation of the foreign takes the form of an annexation, a use of the Other, the foreign, the past, for the needs of the Self, the familiar, and the present.

Chapter Two
Goethe, the Reception of Kant, and the Romantic Culture War in Britain

> "Ich fragte Goethe, welchen der neueren Philosophen er für den vorzüglichsten hallte. 'Kant,' sagte er, 'ist der vorzüglichste, ohne allen Zweifel. Er ist auch derjenige, dessen Lehre sich fortwirkend erwiesen hat und die in unsere deutsche Kultur am tiefsten eingedrungen ist. Er hat auf Sie gewirkt, ohne daß Sie ihn gelesen haben. Jetzt brauchen Sie ihn nicht mehr, denn was er Ihnen geben konnte, besitzen Sie schon.'"
>
> J.P. Eckermann, *Gespräche mit Goethe*[1]

As we have seen, the mediation of German literature and thought is one of the defining features of British culture from the late eighteenth century to the decades following World War II.[2] During the Romantic Age this process occupied writers from all strata of the literary world, from leading poets and critics to professional reviewers and hack translators, and engaged all factions, including Tories, Whigs, and Jacobins. Moreover, if one examines the largely unknown review criticism of William Taylor, William Hazlitt, Thomas De Quincey, and Henry Crabb Robinson, clear parallels emerge between the increasingly sophisticated treatment of Immanuel Kant (1724–1804) and the development of review criticism as a more sophisticated enterprise. Having evolved from mere appendages of the book trade to assume a condition of greater freedom, reviewers often chose to exercise their new found independence in meditations on Kant, who, along with Goethe, was identified as one of the key figures in the German challenge to the epistemological and aesthetic status quo in Britain and on the Continent.[3]

Most significantly, the reception of Kant reflects in microcosm the cultural politics of the post-revolutionary era, including the debate that arose over British cultural identity. The xenophobic, nativist position that may be inferred from the Kant criticism of Taylor, Hazlitt, and De Quincey and that is echoed in the hostile reaction to continental influence printed in the pages of *The Anti-Jacobin Review* and the *Edinburgh Review*, stands opposed to the truly cosmopolitan vision, based on direct personal contact with German intellectuals and genuine scholarly engagement, fashioned by Crabb Robinson. From the culture war waged in the reviews and canvassed in this chapter to the longstanding rivalry between English and comparative literature departments in American universities, extreme ambivalence, if not open hostility to continental influence, appears to be a characteristic expression of British culture and of Anglophiles based in former British colonies. This is only partly to be explained by the existence of real or perceived threats from across the English Channel.

The present discussion, which was suggested by *Immanuel Kant in England* (1931), René Wellek's influential study, is more concerned than Wellek with the cultural politics that shaped the period's reception of Goethe and other German cultural figures by early Romantic reviewers. After first examining the Kant criticism of Taylor, Hazlitt, and De Quincey the merits of the little-known "Letters on the Philosophy of Kant" by Crabb Robinson will be analyzed. These epistolary essays, which were published more than a decade prior to Coleridge's *Biographia Literaria* (1817) and two decades before Carlyle's essays and translations, offer an interpretation of Kant's thought of unparalleled discernment, coherence, and originality.

Scholars of the Romantic period know William Taylor (1765–1836) as a close friend of poet laureate Robert Southey (1774–1843) and the author of a reference work, *English Synonyms Discriminated* (1813), which is cited by Coleridge in chapter 4 of the *Biographia Literaria*. Contemporaries also admired Taylor as one of the most capable and prolific reviewers working for *The Monthly Review*, *The Monthly Magazine*, and *The Critical Review*. Covering a broad range of topics, including ancient and modern history, linguistics and philology, theology and politics, travel and ethnography, philosophy and literature, his contributions to these periodicals run literally into hundreds of pieces.[4]

More than any other critic active before Coleridge and Carlyle, Taylor is responsible for creating an audience for German literature

Chapter Two: Goethe and the Romantic Culture War in Britain 59

in Romantic Britain and for encouraging the German studies of canonical figures such as Scott, Coleridge, Southey, and Walter Savage Landor.[5] Besides publishing reviews of leading German authors across a broad range of fields—Kant, Wieland, Herder, Klopstock, Goethe, Schiller, Kotzebue, A.W. Schlegel, J.G. Eichhorn, H.E.G. Paulus, and J.D. Michaelis—Taylor also translated Bürger's influential and widely-admired poem "Lenore" (which is said to have inspired Scott's translation of Goethe's *Götz von Berlichingen*, published in 1799, and his first experiments in the ballad form), Goethe's *Iphigenie auf Tauris* (also translated in 1790 and published in 1795), and G.E. Lessing's *Nathan der Weise* [*Nathan the Wise*] (translated in 1790 and published in 1805). Taylor, who elevated reviewing to new respectability, was admired by his peers for the depth as well as the breadth of his learning, as the following comment by Hazlitt makes clear: "The style of philosophical criticism, which has been the boast of the *Edinburgh Review*, was first introduced into *The Monthly Review* about the year 1796, in a series of articles by Mr. William Taylor, of Norwich."[6] In addition to his innovations in reviewing, which anticipated the publication of long reviews in the *Edinburgh Review*, Taylor was also a forerunner of that class of professional reviewers who were able to support themselves solely by their writing.[7]

Yet, for all his importance as a literary innovator and early cultural intermediary, the opinions that fill Taylor's reviews have not stood the test of time. Quixotically, he remained all his life convinced that Wieland and Kotzebue, rather than Goethe and the German Romantics, represented the dominant tendency in German literature. Deemed utterly "preposterous" by Saintsbury, the great Edwardian arbiter of taste, because they were already outdated when they appeared in a collected edition (1828–1830), Taylor's articles on German thought and literature elicited "good-humoured, judicious censure" in the review that launched Carlyle's career as a critic.[8]

Taylor's reaction to Kant consistently reflects the anachronistic tendency that detracts from his literary criticism in general. In a review of the German émigré scholar A.F.M. Willich's *Elements of the Critical Philosophy* (1798), one of the earliest systematic efforts to transmit Kant to Britain, Taylor expresses profound skepticism toward ideas that seem superficially so foreign to the British philosophical tradition. Typically shallow is the observation that Kant "is nearly seventy-five years old; a singular period of life for the construction of a new system of philosophy!"[9] Taylor finds justification for his qualms in the hero-worship of Kant's German admirers, which he finds unseemly:

> His scholars, like the disciples of Plotinus, seem only in doubt whether to revere him as a sage or to worship him as a divinity; from the angelic and seraphic doctors of their forefathers, they turn with awe to this incarnate logos; and they want only the trumpet of Eloa to sound his name from sun to sun.[10]

With characteristic British skepticism Taylor condemns the specialized vocabulary that accompanies Kant's "syllogizing" method because it permits "dialectic obscurity to pass for intellectual subtlety." Even the assistance provided by Willich's glossary of the critical philosophy is rejected because "these explanations have not rendered it much more intelligible."[11]

As a cultural nationalist, Taylor demonizes Kant as a subversive outsider, whose teachings threaten to "overshadow the modern world" with "the same obfuscation of the public mind, which, by a similar process, the Platonists of Alexandria [the Sophists] superinduced on the antient [sic]."[12] Consonant with the editorial position of *The Anti-Jacobin Review* toward continental, especially German, thought Taylor blames the post-1789 "general dissolution of morals" in France on the acceptance of Kant's "cloudy phraseology which may intercept from below the war-whoop of impiety, and from above the evulgation of infidelity." Motivated by anti-Catholic prejudice as well as anti-Jacobin paranoia, Taylor accuses Kant's disciples of adopting this system as a "cypher of illuminism," code for Jesuitical conspiracy, that permitted "public discussions of the most critical nature . . . without alarming the prejudices of the people or exciting the precautions of the magistrate." The last straw, according to Taylor's xenophobic fantasy, is that both Kant and "the philosophers of the Lyceum" seek "to entomb with reasonings the reason of the modern world."[13]

The vehemence of Taylor's critique of Kant was not out of the ordinary for its time. Indeed, it is typical of older professional critics, whose taste as well as their political, religious, and other cultural commitments were formed during the Enlightenment, to espouse a nationalistic and conservative aesthetic ideology that underpins their views. But even in younger critics associated with Romanticism, such as Coleridge, Hazlitt, and De Quincey, hostility to German culture, whether embodied in animus toward Goethe or Kant, is not uncommon and yet, it is nonetheless surprising, given that the literary apprenticeship of many leading Romantic writers consisted of emulating, appropriating, and translating German writers. A short list of these translators includes Coleridge, Sarah Austin, Lord Byron, Percy Bysshe Shelley, Sir Walter Scott, and Carlyle. According to Leslie Stephen's entry on Scott in the *Dictionary of National Biography*, the latter's translation of Goethe's drama, *Götz von Berlichingen*, was published with the help of M.G. "Monk" Lewis, another British "Germanico," who took an active part in translating and adapting German plays for the London stage.[14] Without taking sides in the debate over Coleridge's alleged plagiarisms of Kant, Fichte, Schiller, and Schelling, it is nonetheless clear that, without the corroboration he found in German sources for his own aesthetic, religious, and metaphysical ideas, British Romanticism would, as Wellek put it, have "remained dumb in matters of the intellect."[15]

Hazlitt and De Quincey were also among those young writers who "Germanized" themselves, much as young American scholars oriented themselves toward Paris in the 1980s, and set up shop as critics of German thought. Hazlitt published a long two-part review of Germaine de Staël's *De l'Allemagne*, her monitory appeal to a French audience that, to avoid censorship, was first published by John Murray in 1813. Consistent with Coleridge's recommendation of Kant as an antidote to eighteenth-century empiricism, Hazlitt describes the critical philosophy as a "formal and elaborate antithesis" to John Locke. Convinced that his grasp of Kant is superior to Staël's, Hazlitt notes that "the harmony of his style and the graces of her exposition" conceal "the abruptness of the reasoning."[16] In a subsequent review of Coleridge's *Biographia Literaria*, Hazlitt employs crudely dismissive rhetoric, an arrow drawn from the quiver of reviewers for the *Anti-Jacobin* (or Taylor), to dismiss Kant's system as "the most willful and monstrous absurdity that was ever invented."[17]

How is one to account for such a rash opinion that hardly seems worthy of Hazlitt's pen? Wellek is persuaded that Hazlitt's piece embodies "much more than a declaration of antipathy against technicalities the importance of which he did not grasp, but rather a grotesque example of misunderstanding which scarcely can be paralleled from the literature of the time."[18] A survey of contemporary critiques of Kant in Britain reveals that Wellek's confidence that this is an exception is misplaced. Whether the product of conservative cultural politics or simply a deficient education (i.e., lack of German language skills), few, if any, of Hazlitt's contemporaries would be spared the same embarrassment. It would be a mistake, for instance, to expect a lack of distortion in De Quincey's writings on Kant; his track record for deliberate or unintentional misunderstanding in his reviews of German authors surpasses that of all other critics in his generation. Quick to exploit the public's growing fascination with German literature, which De Quincey considered "beyond all question . . . the wealthiest in the world," his contributions to a critique are nonetheless tinged with a perplexing hostility.[19] In addition to an utterly wrongheaded review of Carlyle's translation of Goethe's *Wilhelm Meister's Apprenticeship*, he published some dreadfully inaccurate translations from the writings of Jean Paul Richter,[20] a mean-spirited attack on Goethe's character, in which he adopts the moralizing tone of *The Anti-Jacobin Review*, a few fragmentary translations of Kant, and related critical-philosophical essays, including the first history of Kant's reception in Britain.[21]

In this piece, "Letter V: On the English Notices of Kant," the last installment in a series of "Letters to a Young Man whose Education has been Neglected," De Quincey expresses concern that the "gross misrepresentations" of other critics and intermediaries, including Willich, Coleridge, Dugald Stewart (1753–1828), and Staël, may have

Chapter Two: Goethe and the Romantic Culture War in Britain 63

misled his addressee and undermined his advice "to take special notice of German literature, as a literature of knowledge, not of power." De Quincey considers it his "business to point out any facts which may tend to disarm the authority of these writers, just so far as to replace you in the situation of a neutral and unprejudiced student."[22] What follows, however, is not anything like an authoritative interpretation of Kant's thought, but merely a litany of errors, distortions, and complaints. Stewart, who represented the British academic establishment from which De Quincey, the ink-stained wretch, felt alienated, is reprimanded for his total neglect of Kant's importance to modern philosophy. As for the synopsis of Kant's ideas in *De l'Allemagne*,[23] De Quincey reiterates the standard indictment against Staël that her penchant for simplification "has contrived to translate his philosophy into a sense which leaves it tolerably easy to apprehend; but unfortunately at the expense of all definite purpose, application, or philosophic meaning."[24] By contrast, Coleridge is, to no one's surprise, criticized for insufficient clarity in chapter 9 of the *Biographia Literaria*: "by expounding the oracle in words of more Delphic obscurity than the German original could have presented to the immaturest student." Because of a tendency to intertwine the thoughts of others in the fiber of his own intellect such a result is, as De Quincey, his close contemporary, expected from him: "Mr. Coleridge's mind . . . never gives back anything as it receives it." It is this remorseless tendency to appropriate and to conflate—"this indocility of mind"— that "unfits a man to be the faithful expounder of a philosophical system." Therefore De Quincey concludes that Coleridge has "unfortunately too little talent for teaching or communicating any sort of knowledge."[25]

There is no denying the accuracy of these observations. The vehemence of De Quincey's assault on Coleridge was motivated in part by disillusionment. Despite claiming a more profound understanding of German culture than any of his contemporaries, Coleridge proved a less than reliable intermediary for younger writers, who were besotted with his poetic gifts and brilliant table talk. Yet, conceding De Quincey's insight into Coleridge's shortcomings, it is only fair to examine his most extensive commentary on Kant, "German Studies and Kant in particular."[26] Pulling no punches, Wellek puts it best, insisting that it reflects "a gross misunderstanding of the purpose of the Kantian philosophy" and a "certain fundamental insincerity in his relation to Kant." Despite evidence that De Quincey studied Kant in the original and could therefore claim an intimacy unsurpassed by his contemporaries, "this experience," Wellek suggests, "however actual and indisputable, remained only skin-deep, the expression of a mood, of a moment's despair and tedium." Unlike Coleridge and Carlyle, whose writings reflect genuine affinity with the program of German idealist philosophy, De Quincey demonstrated "no deeper relation to philosophical thought."[27]

For an accurate as well as sympathetic contemporary analysis of Kant, one must turn to a figure whose writings on German culture predate those of Coleridge, Hazlitt, and De Quincey. Crabb Robinson was celebrated in the literary salons of nineteenth-century Europe as the friend of Goethe, Coleridge, and William Blake. He is remembered, if at all, along with the painter Benjamin Robert Haydon (1786–1846), as one of the most important diarists of the Romantic Age. Self-effacing in a way that focuses attention on his subjects, Crabb Robinson inverts the usual function of literary memoirs (from which, according to Goethe, one always learns more about the writer himself than any of his experiences), and provides greater scope for the reader to identify with the remarkable men and women he encountered over a long life devoted to literature.

Crabb Robinson was, however, not satisfied with his myriad activities as diarist, lawyer, traveler, patron of poets and artists, and ardent admirer of German culture. In addition to these credentials, he also sought to make his mark, in his early years, as a critic. Among the first in Britain to recognize the importance of Goethe's lyric and epigrammatic poems, he also published a series of three "Letters on the Philosophy of Kant."[28] These were published from August 1802 to May 1803 in *The Monthly Register and Encyclopedian Magazine*, an upstart London journal designed to satisfy the increasing popular

Chapter Two: Goethe and the Romantic Culture War in Britain 65

demand for news of cultural developments on the Continent. Familiar in tone, these epistolary essays were written during a lengthy residence in Jena and Weimar, where, thanks to a letter of introduction from Taylor and his own gregarious open nature, Crabb Robinson got on well with the luminaries attached to the court of Grand Duke Karl August.

While it is true that many British pilgrims flocked to Weimar, including Taylor, Lewis, R.P. Gillies, and William Makepeace Thackeray (1811–1863), there were also a number of young Harvard College students such as Edward Everett, George Bancroft, George Ticknor, and Henry Wadsworth Longfellow. Few visitors were treated with the high regard that Crabb Robinson was held in the Goethe household.[29] But this is just one of the advantages that he enjoyed over another Englishman who had taken up residence in nearby Goslar and attended lectures in Göttingen not long before this time. Exaggerating what was accomplished during Coleridge's residence in Germany (1798–1799) is a standard feature of Coleridge scholarship. And while it is true that Coleridge acquired some German, and worked in the renowned Göttingen University Library, his sojourn cannot compare to Crabb Robinson's in terms of access gained to leading cultural figures and absorption of the language and culture. In contrast to Coleridge's marginal existence in Göttingen, Crabb Robinson enrolled as a fully matriculated student at the University of Jena, learned to speak German with near-native fluency, and counted among his friends many leading writers, including Goethe, Schiller, Schelling, A.W. Schlegel, Wieland, and the Brentanos— Christian, Bettina, and Clemens. Indeed, Crabb Robinson's friendships with Schelling, who vied with Fichte and Schopenhauer as claimant to Kant's legacy, endowed him with truly unrivalled credentials as an elucidator of the Kantian system and helped him avoid the mistakes of Taylor, Hazlitt, De Quincey, and Coleridge.

Due, however, to the vagaries of the publishing world, Crabb Robinson was prevented from exploiting his advantages as an intermediary between Britain and Germany. In the summer of 1803 *The Monthly Register* was taken over by a new editor-publisher, who scrapped plans for more letters on Kant, and a new series of essays on Goethe. This turn of events dealt a blow to the aspiring critic. In later years, when asked about his essays on German culture, he replied with characteristic modesty that they "attracted no notice and did not deserve any."[30] The frustration of his early literary ambitions could only have intensified through his association with so many successful writers at home in Britain and on the Continent. But posterity has been kinder to this literary stepchild than its parent.

Wellek was the first modern critic to treat Crabb Robinson's "Letters on the Philosophy of Kant" as more than mere dilletantish oddities: "They are extraordinarily accurate and vivid. They grasp the central problem of Kant's epistemology and try to give an interpretation of Kant's teaching which is by no means altogether usual and hackneyed today."[31] Crabb Robinson's use of the epistolary mode suggests more than superficial parallels with Paul's evangelizing letters to the still-to-be converted Hellenes. It is, in fact, this proselytizing tone that distinguishes Crabb Robinson's epistles on Kant from the minor eighteenth-century genre exemplified by Charles-Louis Montesquieu's *Les Lettres Persanes* (1721) and Oliver Goldsmith's *Citizen of the World* (1762). Not interested in making satirical or moral comparisons between cultures or in recording impressions while living abroad—Coleridge's observations in *Satyrane's Letters* (1798–1799) are entirely of the latter type—Crabb Robinson seeks instead to make converts to the foreign "creed" of the idealistic philosophy. His purpose is similar to Staël's in *De l'Allemagne*: both authors present the German ideology, headed by Kant's teachings, with its organic conception of mind and universe, and its privileging of *Vernunft* [intuitive reason] over logic and *Verstand* [the practical understanding], as necessary therapy for their respective ailing national psyches.

This part of Crabb Robinson's discussion anticipates Carlyle's commendation of German thought and literature as a modern spiritual anodyne. According to Carlyle, who was writing over twenty years later, "the higher literature of Germany . . . that wide-spreading, deep-whirling vortex of Kantism, so soon metamorphosed into

Fichteism, and then as Hegelism, and Cousinism," contained a "new revelation of the Godlike." Carlyle sees in the growing interest in German thought a way of countering the leading tendencies of the age, what he denounced as "Pyrrhonism and Materialism," and making "Faith in Religion" (Carlyle's capitalization here) once again "possible and inevitable for the scientific mind."[32] In a Carlylean observation, Crabb Robinson deems it significant that German culture should have produced both "a great poet and a great philosopher" at the same time.[33] The appearance of Goethe and Kant together at the end of the eighteenth century suggests the reconciliation of poetry and philosophy. This ascertainment was corroborated sixty-five years later as Crabb Robinson recorded his impressions of Matthew Arnold's essay, "On the Function of Criticism at the Present Time." Echoing Crabb Robinson's first letter in the series, Arnold writes, in one of the most famous lines in English criticism, that "the creation of a modern poet, to be worth much, implies a great critical effort behind it; else it would be a comparatively poor, barren affair."[34] Reminiscent of Carlyle some thirty-five years before when he admonished readers of *Sartor Resartus* to "Close thy Byron, open thy Goethe," Arnold argues that Goethe's achievement as a poet will endure longer than Byron's because "Goethe's was nourished by a great critical effort providing the true materials for it, and Byron's was not."[35] Crabb Robinson notes his agreement with Arnold that the basis for Germany's modern cultural rebirth is precisely this reciprocal, mutually reinforcing relationship between the imaginative and the critical faculties.[36]

Crabb Robinson's first letter (August 1802) opens with an account of the vertiginous effects of Kant's teaching on the mind of the author. His outlook, formed by the writings of John Locke (1632–1704), David Hartley (1705–1757), and the British empirical tradition—not to mention his upbringing in a dissenting household—functions as representative of the Romantic generation. The discovery of Kant shattered these Enlightenment idols, leaving Crabb Robinson with "no compass to guide me." In keeping with his proselytizing mission, the first letter reenacts the drama of Crabb Robinson's conversion experience and the resulting crisis of intellectual disinheritance:

> I was, in the true sense of the word CONFOUNDED. In the critical school I found the first principles of Locke's philosophy, not refuted at length, but dispatched with insolent brevity, as too grossly false to require a minute refutation; my favorite authors not unknown, but known and almost despised; my own habit of thinking represented as the utmost reproach to a rational being; a sort of Esau-like relinquishing of our birth-right, the right to reason and determine.[37]

Based on his intellectual and religious formation, which predisposed him to reject the "transcendental speculation" of Kant, Crabb Robinson admits to having undergone a complete change of heart after long and "exclusive study." Thus, the "Letters" should be read partly as an intellectual autobiography and partly as a rejoinder to the distorted and outlandish claims published in the popular press that Kant and his followers had set out to destroy Christianity. In contrast to the skepticism of Enlightenment thinkers, Crabb Robinson asserts that Kant's teachings are actually not incompatible with religion. In a phrase borrowed from Goethe—and recycled by Carlyle in *Sartor Resartus* thirty years later—Crabb Robinson derides philosophical skepticism as "the *sans-culottism* [Jacobinism] of philosophy" and credits Kant with having revealed that systems based on "materialism and necessity" are, in fact, indistinguishable from "atheism."[38] Kant's method of disarming skepticism proceeds by "showing the precise limits of knowledge and the extent and degree of belief which we are compelled to give to notions that are susceptible of certain evidence." While thus affirming the power of human intellect, Kant does not, however, undermine faith in a supreme deity. On the contrary, Crabb Robinson insists, in a pithy recitation of the credo of Romanticism, that Kant "affirms the right, and even necessity of pure reason, of the belief in God and a future state; he asserts free will, repels the dogmatic notion of materialism, and indignantly rejects the notion of self-love as the basis of moral sentiment."[39]

Chapter Two: Goethe and the Romantic Culture War in Britain 69

While the skepticism of David Hume (1711–1776) may be presumed to be genuine, Kant only "seems to be hyperskeptical"; he actually seeks to effect "a sort of peace and union" between philosophy and religion. Kant's attack on "skepticism by destroying the dogmatism which generated it"—a method that "cannot but terrify the orthodox"[40]—greatly appealed to Crabb Robinson, who, as a follower of William Godwin, sought to effect a kind of cleansing of the temple of philosophy in order to assert a more humane system. Therefore, somewhat paradoxically, Kant's "hyperskepticism" reveals that faith "is not merely a wish or a hope, but a confidence as strong and as irresistible as knowledge itself." The "certainty" of faith, then, remains unchanged, but, and here is the telling part of Kant's logic as understood by Crabb Robinson the Dissenter, "the grounds of faith are reversed." Contrary to the popular contemporary caricature of Kant as "a reviewer of useless speculation, and . . . a descendant of the old [Roman Catholic] schoolmen," he is instead "the direst foe of the metaphysicians, and possesses nothing of the schoolmen but their acuteness and profundity."[41]

As if responding to Taylor's paranoid and xenophobic ravings against Jacobins and Papist conspiracies in *The Monthly Review*, Crabb Robinson rejects any parallels between Kant and the "illuminati of the French atheists," including "that arch descendent of Loyola, the Ex-Jesuit Baruel."[42] Yet, in so hastily dismissing the charge that Kant bears some responsibility for loosening the moorings of faith in what Carlyle calls the "Atheistic Century,"[43] Crabb Robinson seems blind to the metamorphosis that Kant undergoes in his quirky, idiosyncratic interpretation. If only he had been more sensitive to the potentially devastating inferences to be drawn from Kant's teachings, he might have not so easily maintained his sangfroid in a controversy that roused philosophers Friedrich Heinrich Jacobi (1743–1819)—who popularized the term "nihilism" and blamed Goethe for celebrating individualism—and Søren Kierkegaard (1813–1855) to defend the prerogatives of faith against Romantic relativism.

Crabb Robinson's views are generally in accord with Coleridge's critique of British Associationism (while it is possible that Coleridge read the "Letters on the Philosophy of Kant" in *The Monthly Register*, his survey of British Associationism in the *Biographia Literaria* was certainly derived in part from J. G. E. Maaß's *Versuch über die Einbildungskraft* [*Essay on the Imagination*] (1792), but rather than suggesting parallels to specific features of Coleridge's argument, it is the moral vision underlying Crabb Robinson's interpretation of Kant's teachings that anticipates the critique of the "consequences of the Harleian Theory" in chapter 7 of the *Biographia Literaria*. His polarization of German idealism and French materialism is part of the stock-in-trade of British Romantic ideology and the rhetoric he employs to demonize French thought is remarkably Carlylean in its vehemence: "The German school is one great antithesis to the French school . . . . This is a coupling of life and death together: between the French and German schools there can be no peace, it is a war of extermination." Kant and German philosophy provide an "antidote" to "Locke full-grown" and the corrupting influence of materialism on ethics, religion, and art. In "this quintessence of French philosophy" only "the dregs of life are left, nothing but conscious organization and living mechanism."[44] This is also strikingly reminiscent of Staël's treatment of the opposition between French and German culture in *De l'Allemagne*. She insists that the two nations occupy

> deux extrémités de la chaîne morale, puisque les uns considèrent les objets extérieurs comme le mobile de toutes les idées, et les autres, les idées comme le mobile de toutes les impressions. Ces deux nations cependant s'accordent assez bien sous les rapports sociaux; mais il n'en est point de plus opposées dans leur system littéraire et philosophique.[45]

Of course, any parallels with Staël are not entirely coincidental. The German Romantic writer A.W. Schlegel (1767–1845), who traveled for a time as a member of Staël's entourage, was primarily responsible for schooling her in German thought and literature. It is also true that Crabb Robinson, a student of Schelling and a foreigner who had successfully come to grips with the most difficult aspects of contemporary German philosophy, was brought in by Karl August

Böttiger (1760–1830), a mutual acquaintance and member of the Weimar circle of intellectuals clustered around Goethe, to serve as her special tutor.⁴⁶ In subsequent years, Crabb Robinson was convinced that proof of their collaboration is visible in the pages of *De l'Allemagne*. It is, indeed, ironic that Crabb Robinson, a British commoner and a Dissenter at that, should have been chosen to tutor Staël, a wellborn Swiss Protestant, whose work as a cultural intermediary exerted enormous influence in Britain and the United States, not to mention France and Germany, whose culture she mediated for all the others. The mediation of a mediation (Crabb Robinson's) that in turn stimulated the efforts of other intermediaries, *De l'Allemagne* supports the notion that Romantic culture is the result of cultural interaction and the interplay of literary intermediaries in a cosmopolitan context.

Disguised as a letter from a British student in Jena to a friend back home, the second letter (November 1802) in the series seems derived from Crabb Robinson's surviving correspondence with his brother Thomas, to whom most of his private correspondence from Germany was addressed. The focus of this letter is a discussion of the respective merits of Kant and Locke. Responding to accusations that he favors a system of "lyrical metaphysics," the student responds by offering a Romantic critique of materialism:

> And I pity you for having no metaphysics, only a mere physics. It is the essence of the sensible philosophy to degrade the mind into a necessarily passive machine. Locke, indeed, avoided this reproach by incurring a greater inconsistency: but the more celebrated of his followers have raised on his principles a system, according to which there can be neither poetry, religion, nor love.⁴⁷

This invocation of the holy trinity of German Romanticism—poetry, religion, and love—is a reminder to us that Crabb Robinson attended Schelling's lectures in Jena. Schelling, as Wellek explains, "extolled poetry to be the truest revelation of the Absolute, it justified religion by philosophy and it found a new meaning for the mystery of love."⁴⁸ Although at times it seems that Crabb Robinson is less interested in the actual basis for Kant's notoriety—his revolutionary epistemology—he is so determined to remove the stigma of mysticism from contemporary German thought that he defends Kant's virtually impenetrable technical vocabulary. Crabb Robinson's tolerance of jargon contrasts sharply with Taylor's impatient dismissal of the lexicon of German Idealism: "[Kant] had thoughts which had never been thought before; and his new coin required a new stamp."[49]

From a defense of Kantian terminology Crabb Robinson moves on to the question of whether a priori knowledge (metaphysics) is superior to a posteriori evidence (physics). He offers a commonplace paradox that illustrates how even the skeptical British mind has accommodated itself to the a priori: mathematics, the cornerstone of the experimental sciences, is actually "grounded on positions experimentally impossible." This paradox confirms that ideas are anterior to sense, since "the intellect or reason can think what the sense cannot behold."[50] In an actual rather than fictional letter to his brother, Crabb Robinson reinforces this point by comparing the subjective basis of knowledge to a magic lantern:

> In order to show the figures [projected by the lantern] there must be a bright spot on the wall, upon which the coloured figures are to be exhibited. Without figures, the luminous spot is an empty nothing, like the human mind till it has objects of sense. But without the spot the figures would be invisible, as without an a priori capacity to receive impressions we could have none.[51]

That the origin of knowledge as representation in the perceiving subject establishes the possibility of synthetic judgments, it also requires that the model of the mind derived from empiricism must be replaced with the Kantian paradigm advocated by Crabb Robinson. Here his position coincides with one of the fundamental ideas associated with both British and German Romanticism, namely, that "the mind of man is essentially active, not the mere recipient of impressions"[52]—it is a lamp rather than a mirror. The ultimate "basis of truth" is thus not confined to experimental science, but is found in metaphysics and a priori conceptions, which are seen as "the essential laws of mind." By appealing to another position derived from mathematics, Crabb Robinson seeks to clarify the distinction between analytical and synthetic judgments and to prove that achieving any kind of result requires resorting to synthetic judgments, for which there are, however, no proofs available in the world of experience:

> Beyond all doubt—analyze 2 + 2 as long as you please; the result can never be otherwise than 2 + 2 = 2 + 2; that the result is 4 is a synthesis of reason, for 4 does not lie in 2 + 2, though we necessarily think so, for we confound our acquired synthetical knowledge with what lies in the simplest subjects.[53]

Consistent with the position outlined in this letter to his brother, Crabb Robinson seeks to convert the reader to his view that Kant's "Criticism of Pure Reason" provides one with a means of determining how "knowledge, *a priori*" arises out of the faculty of reason, what the extent of this knowledge is, and how to distinguish between "mere objects of experience" and "supersensible" objects. In case readers back in Britain object that all of this is foreign mumbo jumbo, Crabb Robinson's fictional proselytizer notes that just as soon as one seeks to ground the possibility of knowing upon "a system of a priori conceptions," one becomes engaged in solving the "sublime" problems of "the transcendental philosophy."[54]

Crabb Robinson is convinced that Kant's epistemology has opened a new world of certainty to the notice of humankind. Unlike the contingent forms of knowledge afforded by empiricism, Kant's teaching offers a measure of certainty unavailable to "the school of Locke," which mistakenly "degrades rational truths to matters of fact: and Hume affirmed the truth, that facts afford no certainty, only probability."[55] Citing Hume, Crabb Robinson invokes the all-important affinity between Kant and British philosophy. (Indeed, among Kant's followers, Schopenhauer regarded Hume so highly that he was inspired to learn English in order to translate *An Enquiry Concerning Human Understanding*.) In this light, the transcendental philosophy, treated with such disdain by Taylor, Hazlitt, and De Quincey, can be seen as the consummation of native British skepticism, only deepened and systematized by Kant.

Of the three letters published in the series, the third (April 1803) contains the most numerous examples and the most polished argument. Crabb Robinson begins by recapitulating the main concerns of the previous letter: the proposition that there is "something in our knowledge which is not experimental." He insists that even in cases where the mind is the object of its own knowledge and thus becomes simultaneously subject and object, "it does not lose the priority of its nature." To lend support to this argument Crabb Robinson appeals to Spinoza (1632–1677), whose work he might easily have discussed with Goethe over dinner in Weimar: "*Substantia prior est suis affectionibus*: the substance is prior to the affections; the organ, to the sense; the basis, to the structure."[56] This is also the position of Fichte and Schelling. The issues that dominate an unpublished fourth letter—the status of time and space according to Kant and the ontological status of objects of subjective knowledge—are discussed next. Crabb Robinson defends Kant's assertion that the priority of the mind is demonstrated by "the nature of things" and of time. Citing Fichte's refutation of Leibniz, he insists that there are concepts, such as "the one, the same, cause," that do indeed enjoy independence from consciousness. As Crabb Robinson interprets Kant,

> the mind itself could not exist without external objects, which furnish us with the matter of experience, and are collectively the world. And when we consider the same representations in reference to the necessity of external objects they are *a posteriori*: but this distinction itself is purely logical or ideal.[57]

In closing his argument, Crabb Robinson appeals directly to Kant, who describes this antithesis as the opposition of "matter (the a posteriori) and form (the a priori) in our representations."[58] Crabb Robinson's interpretation is at odds, however, with Schopenhauer's insistence that it was Kant's "erster Fehler [first mistake]" that he failed to acknowledge the irrefragable priority of the subjective knower. "Die Welt," Schopenhauer claims,

> ist meine Vorstellung . . . . Keine Wahrheit ist also gewißer, von allen andern unabhängiger und eines Beweises weniger bedürftig, daß alles, was für die Erkenntnis da ist, also diese ganze Welt, nur Objekt in Beziehung auf das Subjekt ist, Anschauung des Anschauenden, mit *einem Wort*, Vorstellung.[59]

Chapter Two: Goethe and the Romantic Culture War in Britain

There are no references to Schopenhauer in Crabb Robinson's voluminous diaries or correspondence, even though Schopenhauer, along with Schelling, Crabb Robinson's teacher, was Kant's leading follower, and no thinker of the time more legitimately claimed Kant's mantle.[60] Even if his "Letters on the Philosophy of Kant" lack Schopenhauer's brilliance and stylistic verve, they are far superior to the philosophical criticism of Taylor, Hazlitt, and De Quincey. Indeed, they embody the most important attempt in the early Romantic Age to offer an accurate interpretation of Kant's "peculiar logical method." Published more than a decade before Coleridge's *Biographia Literaria* and more than two decades before Carlyle's German criticism, Crabb Robinson's epistolary essays lay the foundation for Kant's reception in Britain. Over two centuries after their publication in *The Monthly Register*, the sense of intellectual discovery that they convey remains fresh, as does the enthusiasm and missionary zeal with which a young British Dissenter announced the "Copernican revolution" in modern European philosophy that was set in motion by the writings of Kant, and plunged headlong into the war of ideas that was being waged in Britain in the early years of the nineteenth century.

Chapter Three
The Accidental Intermediary: Henry Crabb Robinson and the Translation of Goethe's Poetry

> "Die Vaterbindung, Vaternachahmung, das Vaterspiel und seine Übertragungen auf Vaterersatzbilder höherer und geistiger Art – wie bestimmend, wie prägrend und bildend wirken diese Infantilismen auf das individuelle Leben ein! .... So kann die imitatio Goethe mit ihren Erinnerungen an die Werther, die Meister Stufe und an die Altersphase von Faust und Diwan noch heute aus dem Unbewußten ein Schriftstellerleben führen und mythisch bestimmen,– ich sage: aus dem Unbewußten, obgleich im Künstler das Unbewußte jeden Augenblick ins lächelnd Bewußte und kindlich tief Aufmerksame hinüberspielt."
>
> Thomas Mann[1]

If Henry Crabb Robinson had only published his papers on Kant—the central figure in modern philosophy—he would still deserve to be remembered as one of the foremost interpreters of German thought in early nineteenth-century Britain. With the publication of five additional "Letters on German Literature," which appeared concurrently with the "Letters on Kant" from August 1802 to April 1803 in *The Monthly Register and Encyclopedian Magazine*, he joined Taylor, Scott, and Coleridge as one of the most important early translators and critics of German literature in Britain. These "Letters," moreover, reflect surprising critical independence and signal an important departure from the work of his better-known contemporaries. While Taylor, Scott, and Coleridge focused on German dramatists and translated, respectively, Goethe's *Iphigenie auf Tauris*, *Götz von Berlichingen*, and Schiller's *Wallenstein*, Crabb Robinson sought to publicize what was at that time a lesser-known side to Goethe's multi-faceted corpus—his achievement as a lyric poet. Crabb Robinson's view of Goethe as the leading poet in Germany *and* Europe anticipates the position that would, in the writings of Thomas Carlyle, Ralph Waldo Emerson, Matthew Arnold, and G.H. Lewes, come to dominate Anglophone literary criticism in the nineteenth century. The value of his translations and critical commentary has been assessed until now. In an early article, A. G. Alford surveys the major critical statements and translations of Goethe's works published in the last two decades of the eighteenth century. Upon examination of Crabb Robinson's essays, he describes the first decade of the nineteenth century as "a period of apathy" in which "no new translations appeared and no criticisms."[2] Diana Behler thoroughly canvassed the impact of Crabb Robinson's mediation of German culture in a series of four articles published over a decade, but she does not discuss his Goethe translations. More recently, the Henry Crabb Robinson Project at the Queen Mary University of London began to generate work that will elevate Crabb Robinson's critical and intellectual interest a fully deserved niche beside his canonical Romantic contemporaries.[3]

Crabb Robinson's assertion of Goethe's preeminence among German poets was, for its time, highly audacious and he stood virtually alone in defending Goethe against charges of immorality raised by the chauvinistic reviewers of the *Anti-Jacobin, or, Weekly Examiner*—George Canning (1770–1827), George Ellis, and John Hookham Frere. He also had the temerity to challenge the views of those few influential critics, such as Taylor, Holcroft, and Gillies, who were sympathetic to German literature, but who ranked Kotzebue, the sensationalistic playwright, higher than Goethe. By contrast, the virtually unknown Crabb Robinson, who spent nearly five years (1800–1805) traveling and studying in Germany, felt that a distorted view of the relative merit of German writers was possibly even more hazardous to the proper development of British taste than the outright rejection of German literature. Hence, the polemic in his "Letters on German Literature" is not directed against the reliably partisan editorial policy of *The Anti-Jacobin Review*, but is meant rather to correct the well-meaning but misguided efforts of his slightly older contemporaries who were seemingly oblivious to Goethe's merits. What Crabb Robinson has in common with "minor" critics, such as William Taylor and Thomas Holcroft, and the authors of numerous counter-"Wertheriads," is that his and their breakthrough into print is associated with mediating or even imitating Goethe.

Whether a writer is a minor (Taylor or Crabb Robinson) or a major figure (Coleridge, Wordsworth, Shelley, Byron), he or she must either accept or reject the influence of Goethe as the "strong poet" dominating the Romantic generation.

The first and third of the "Letters" serve as the theoretical focus of the series, while the second, fourth, and fifth present Crabb Robinson's translations and commentary on Goethe's poetry. The first letter (August 1802) begins with a series of arguments aimed at persuading the skeptical British reading public of the merits of German literature. As a first step, he offers to explain methods of versification employed by German writers and he provides, as examples, the first published translations of several poems by Goethe and Schiller in English, including selections from the *Venetianische Epigramme* and the *Zahme Xenien [Gentle Distichs]*. Describing contemporary German poets as the "true modern classics" and "the restorers of Greek art and Greek taste," Crabb Robinson claims that notwithstanding the efforts of previous translators, readers in the British Isles really know "nothing about German literature."[4] Despite what Taylor and others asserted in reviews and offered as translations in *The Monthly Review*, *The Monthly Magazine*, and *The Critical Review*, the authors of the wildly popular *Schicksalsdramen*—the first works to be translated into English—are not, in Crabb Robinson's view, the best or even representative products of the German muse. Invoking the distinction between low- and highbrow culture, he assures the reader that

> Kotzebue's and Iffland's plays and Lafontaine's novels are not German literature; though popular German works, they are not considered as classical here [in Germany where Crabb Robinson wrote his "Letters"]. Are you willing that English dramatic poetry should be judged of here by the works of Reynolds and O'Keefe; or the English novel by Mrs. Richardson or Mrs. Gunning?[5]

Goethe, Crabb Robinson emphasizes, and not Kotzebue, August Wilhelm Iffland (1759–1814), or August LaFontaine (1758–1831), is *"Germany's great poet."*[6] With this claim, by which he anticipates, twelve years prior to the publication of *De l'Allemagne*, Staël's identification of the signal forces shaping German literature, he seeks to reverse the tendency of late eighteenth-century British criticism of

German literature. In this way Crabb Robinson foreshadows Carlyle's critique of Taylor's *An Historic Survey of German Poetry* that would appear twenty-five years later in the *Edinburgh Review* (No. 105) and, beyond that, the interest taken in Goethe by such leading Anglo-American critics as Arnold, Emerson, and George Santayana.[7]

The issue at hand here is the age-old problem of reconciling differences in national taste between peoples divided from one another by language, history, religion, and custom. How, for example, do British monoglot readers acquire a clear sense of what is of genuine value in a foreign literature? How much does this depend on the vagaries of the publishing industry and how much on choices made by translators? "Nothing is harder," Carlyle vented as he suffered in the throes of translating *Wilhelm Meister*, "than to form a true judgment of foreign minds and forms of character." But, he admitted, there is still no "work nobler than transplanting foreign thought into the barren domestic soil."[8] The sensational, if senseless, popularity of Kotzebue and his imitators in Britain is, if mysterious to Crabb Robinson and others, who, like Carlyle, earned their stripes as toilers in the vineyard of translation, it is no less surprising than the judgment of French critics and Symbolist poets who raised Edgar Allan Poe to the status of the representative nineteenth-century American poet.[9]

As for the "few valuable works" that had been translated by contemporaries, such as some of the writings of the poet Wieland, Crabb Robinson is adamant that even these, when compared to the works of Goethe, "are not characteristic of the peculiar spirit of German literature." And those that are, he finds, "in being imported . . . are polluted by coming through impure channels." It is certainly a law of the literary marketplace that "each walk of literature is first trodden by the few, ere the doors are open to the vulgar," but in the case of German literature in Britain it is lamentable that "the manufacturers of translations have rushed at once into the garden."[10] There is, however, more than mere caprice or hack writing at work in sabotaging the development of British sophistication with regard to foreign, especially German, literature. In Crabb Robinson's view two factors are responsible: first, the lack of a consistent, institutional process governing the selection of texts to be translated and offered to the reading public and, secondly, the more intractable and perhaps ever-present problem of overcoming the disparity between the limited abilities of English translators and the increasing public demand for German texts. The impact of both factors acting in combination has had, as Crabb Robinson observes, an insidious effect on the periodical criticism that formed the taste of many readers. He cites a particularly egregious case "one of our reviews spoke of Schiller and Kotzebue as the German Shakespeares"—which, in the absence of translations of Goethe's plays, reflects the writer's ignorance of the full range of German literature rather than flawed judgment.[11]

Crabb Robinson's attempt to educate British readers begins with a discussion of German prosody, specifically with a comparison between the efforts of John Milton (1608–1674) and Klopstock to "nationalise the Greek and Roman metres" in English and German, respectively. Coming more than a century after Milton, Klopstock's achievement in *Der Messias* [*The Messiah*] (1748) refutes the argument, maintained by champions of Latinate (read French) culture, that a modern Germanic language "is not capable of the ancient metres . . . that the ancients had other organs, and their language other elements than ours." Although "the language of Klopstock was . . . unquestionably less advanced in cultivation than the English language in the middle of the seventeenth century," he "brought to his task a mind not less deeply impressed with the national importance of his work." The result was "a revolution in the language and literature of his country." In substituting iambic pentameter for the "Gothic barbarism of rhyme," Klopstock anticipates the standard measure of the irregular Romantic ode, as exemplified by Hölderlin, Schiller, and Novalis in German, and Wordsworth, Coleridge, and Keats in English.[12]

Next, inspired by the German philosopher and cultural anthropologist Johann Gottfried Herder's remark that "'the English muse is a thinking muse'" and noting the predilection of certain British poets, such as Dryden, Pope and Johnson, for *"thinking verses,"* Crabb

Robinson suggests that contemporary British poets would do well to follow the example of Goethe and Schiller, who, in reviving the epigram as a living, effective verse form, have demonstrated how "the terse sententious pentameter" may be "admirably adapted to a stroke of wit, or strong moral sentiment" or to the expression of elegiac emotion.[13] As illustrations of both types of epigram Crabb Robinson offers the first English translations from Goethe's *Venetianische Epigramme*, including those to which he gives the following English titles: "The Gondola," "The Patricians," and "My Employment." If not the most highly wrought art, these translations are sensitive, accurate imitations of the originals and they also succeed in suggesting Goethe's mastery of the genre as well as domesticating the foreignness of this form. Crabb Robinson also introduces the reader to the *Zahme Xenien* the collection of satirical distiches jointly authored by Goethe and Schiller. A mosaic of hilarious portraits and irreverent observations, this work is comparable in spirit, if not in its structure, to Pope's comic masterpiece of "personal satire," *The Dunciad* (1728/1743). Like Pope's acerbic attacks on his enemies Goethe's distiches "were directed indiscriminately against the real dunces, and against those who had given no other proof of dullness than that of not being sufficiently warm admirers of the two literary heroes," their authors.[14] Of special interest to Crabb Robinson are Goethe and Schiller's distiches on philosophical themes, including two that represent efforts to clarify Kant's views on the subordination of time and space to human perception and the priority of synthetic to analytical judgments. They also offer satires on the "empirical school," Kant's epigones and the hordes of commentators encumbering the Königsberg sage like so many Lilliputians. Other translations offered from the *Xenien*, which have not lost the satiric bite of the German texts, include burlesques of various competing literary schools, ridicule for the hapless translator (by now a familiar theme) of Torquato Tasso's *Gierusalemme liberata* [*Jerusalem Delivered*] (1581), scathing abuse for German political aspirations, a comment on the apparently natural opposition between genius and conventional taste, and, finally,

Johnsonian sarcasm for the infallible omniscience of the Astronomer.[15] Crabb Robinson's first letter concludes with a more than credible translation of Schiller's "Das Genie" ["The Genius"]. The skill in evidence in this piece is a harbinger of the "Second Letter on German Literature," the briefest in the series, which contains just two short translations.

The four remaining letters are much briefer than the first and, except for the third, and consist almost entirely of translations and commentary on German prosody.[16] The third, addressed simply to "Mr. Editor," contains no translations, but does make several astute remarks that anticipate Carlyle some twenty-five years into the future. It conveys experiments in versification conducted by contemporary German writers. Crabb Robinson offers the observation that "the spirit of invention which distinguishes the modern German philosophers is equally apparent in their poets." This technical originality is reflected in the attempt by Ludwig Tieck (1773–1853) in the long ballad, "Die Zeichen im Walde" ["The Signs in the Forest"], to substitute feminine assonance for rhyme. Such an experiment seeks "to determine how much the ear can endure without losing the sense of unity: and on the other side, by the most inartificial and seemingly lawless, rhyme-less form, to ascertain with how little the ear can be satisfied and the sense of unity gratified."[17] Crabb Robinson explains that, owing to the wealth of "female rhymes" (with vowel endings) in the German language, many popular German poets have laid claim to the "Italian stanza" and experimented with reviving the sonnet and terza rima "without masculine terminations." Despite its vogue, he does not condone this practice. The arbiter of taste for him is not the general tendency emerging in the poetry of the German Romantics, but the exceptional genius, and *"Goethe,"* he observes, "has . . . not adopted this novelty; indeed it is his character in all things to be the leader; he imitates no one."[18]

Side by side with experimentation in prosody is the effort by many contemporary German poets to rescue other neglected metrical forms, such as the alexandrine, "from oblivion." This verse form, considered "obsolete" in Britain, thrives in mid-eighteenth-century Germany because, as Crabb Robinson explains, "the Germans had no stage of their own, and were the mere imitators of England and France; all their tragedies were in alexandrines."[19] He cites two examples of this antiquarian tendency, Goethe's play *Die Mitschuldigen* [*Partners in Guilt*] (1777–1787) and the Prelude to Schiller's three-part drama *Wallenstein* (1798–1799). While excluded from Coleridge's great translation of the latter because, as the translator argues in the "Preface of the Translator to the First Edition," this section "would have been unadvisable from the incongruity of those lax verses with the present taste of the English public,"[20] Crabb Robinson defends the Prelude as perhaps the most interesting part of the drama: "This little piece, Wallenstein's Camp, has probably not been translated; but perhaps it has more true dramatic merit than Piccolimini, and Wallenstein's Death."[21]

In the fourth letter Crabb Robinson presents for the first time in English four more poems, all of which date from Goethe's early burst of creative activity in Frankfurt (1771–1774). The same period is associated with the composition of Goethe's first drama, *Götz von Berlichingen* (1773), and his first novel, *The Sufferings of Young Werther* (1774). The translations offered here "as near the original as possible" are based on "Der Wanderer," "Mahometsgesang," "Prometheus," and its pendant poem, "Ganymed." Notwithstanding Goethe's achievement in these poems Crabb Robinson notes that "they belong to the less popular and earlier productions of Goethe, and are overlooked in the more elaborate beauties of Werter [sic], Iphigenie, Tasso, Faust, Withelon, Maister [sic], etc." Taking into account the diverse, at times controversial subject matter as well as the obvious power of expression in these poems, Crabb Robinson challenges the reader to name an "English poet who has wrought *such* themes with *such* talents."[22] He suggests the qualities that set these poems apart from the British tradition and also from later phases of Goethe's career. Chief among these qualities is an unprecedented union of powerful subjective feeling and reflective thought. These poems, he writes, will all strike you alike by their originality. I do not think that the whole body of English poetry contains any thing which resembles these pieces, in the point of view in which the objects are seen, nor in the feeling; and this reflection and this feeling are (except in the case of the Wanderer) expressed more immediately, and more in the declamatory style, than we find in Goethe's subsequent works.

The mature Goethe's decision to abandon "the style in which he has produced these masterpieces" is the result, according to Crabb Robinson, of a conscious decision to accept new challenges.[23]

"Der Wanderer," the first poem examined in the fourth letter, is described as "a striking and pathetic exhibition of beautiful nature and beautiful art, each heightening the other" and Crabb Robinson's interpretation leans heavily on the biography of the poet, a life previously unknown to English-speaking readers. There is, moreover, the suggestion of an analogy to the psychological and dramatic situation presented in *Werther* (unrequited love that leads to the protagonist's suicide), especially in the letters of 26 and 27 May. The unnamed protagonist of the poem belongs to the same class of world-weary empaths as Werther, Byron's Childe Harold, and Pushkin's Eugene Onegin. He wanders in order to cure his ennui and Weltschmerz. The setting of the poem, in which the protagonist encounters unreflective people at one with their surroundings, serves as a counterpoise to his alienation and is comparable to the imaginative landscape of Werther's beloved Wahlheim (derived from *Wahlheimat*, which translates as "adopted" or "chosen home," it expresses the utopian significance of this place for the protagonist). Owing to its one geographical reference point (the wanderer, we notice, takes his leave by way of the "Cuma road") and the protagonist's obvious *Sehnsucht* or longing, the poem may also function as an anticipatory dream of its author's forthcoming precipitous flight to Italy. And just as Goethe himself was less interested in Italy's monuments of Christian culture than in her pagan ruins, the attention in "Der Wanderer" is focused on a moving human encounter that takes place amid the remains of a temple. The simple life led by the young peasant woman amid such fallen splendor suggests to the traveler the theme of human transiency and the duration of art over the ages:

> A man of feeling, or rather a poet, we may even suppose Goethe himself, finds by the hut of a peasant woman who suckles her child, ruins of ancient architecture, and contemplates at once, that *beauty of art*, which, though the product of immortal genius, is itself perishable; and that *beauty in man*, which though short lived in the individual, is immortal in the species. Her sensations are portrayed in a few lines, but they are Goethe's.[24]

Crabb Robinson's commentary articulates the importance of this theme to Goethe and anticipates its expression in the later masterpiece, "Dauer im Wechsel" ["Permanence in Change"] (1801).

A comparison of selected passages from *Werther* and Crabb Robinson's translation suggests important affinities between leading themes of the novel—the celebration of nature, art and love—and "Der Wanderer." The letter of 26 May begins with Werther's justification for stopping in a country village. Goethe's sentimental description of the scenes in Wahlheim mirrors the mood of the stranger as he takes stock of the primitive Campagna homestead. In the translation that follows, a peasant woman expresses wonder that anything besides commercial interests could bring the wanderer to her doorstep:

> And what does bring thee here
> Thus through the mid-day heat and dusty road?
> What is they business? Dost thou carry goods
> Into the neighboring towns? I see thou smilest
> At my questions, stranger.

In response to her naive questions the wanderer replies simply, "Nay, I have no goods," and asks to refresh himself at the family well. Following her along a path, he discovers fragments of the sophisticated handiwork of ancient times. He realizes that the flagstone path had been built by the same "plastic spirit" of antiquity:

> Traces here
> Between these shrubs of man's arranging hand!
> Thou hast not join'd these aptly fitted stones
> Thou richly scattering nature!
> *************
> An architrave lies hidden under moss!
> Thou plastic spirit I recognize thee,
> Thy seal is stamped here!

The peasant woman's cottage, which he finds a bit further on, is, he learns, built on a "temple's ruins." Here he senses that the presence of human genius is, despite the encroachment of nature, still discernible in the fallen "masterpiece." Enacted in the little stretch of ground between the spring and the cottage is a scene from the primordial conflict between nature and the human impulse to articulate form. The wanderer is so moved that he addresses the "genius" of the ruined temple and the fragments of statues, whose beauty and nobility have been concealed but not entirely effaced by nature's irreverent and filthy vitality:

> Ivy has twined itself around
> Thy slender god-like form. And you, ye pair
> Of columns, how ye rear yourselves above
> The vileness that defiles your pedastals!
> And thou! a solitary sister there,
> Thy sacred head, crowned with gloomy moss,
> Majestically mourning, do'st look down
> Upon thy fallen sisters, who there lie
> Crush'd at thy feet! Under the brambles'
> Shade they lie obscur'd by earth and rubbish:
> And high grass nods o'er them. Nature, can'st thou
> So prize thy master-piece's master-piece?
> Remorselessly thy holy spot pollute
> And strew thy thistles there?

The wanderer pauses to consider the child feeding at its mother's breast—analogous to Werther's observations of the children playing in Wahlheim—a child who shall grow under the watchful eye of a magnificent *genius loci*. In translating the poet's apostrophe to the infant, Crabb Robinson is careful to retain the poet's emphasis on "Ruh" [rest] and "himmlicher Gesundheit" [heavenly health]:

> Sweet is thy rest! Swimming in heavenly health
> Thou breathest peace! Born 'midst the sad remains
> Of holy times of old; O, may their spirit
> Rest on thee: for he, o'er whom *that* hovers,
> Enjoys each day self-conscious like a god.

The wanderer's musings end, as Werther's do, in his letter of 27 May, with a Romantic encomium on the joys of the unexamined life. The happiness of humanity in the state of nature stems partly, at least, from its "functionalistic" attitude toward ornament. According to Goethe's larger vision, this practical impulse is good because it is essentially "natural" and shared by lower creation. It is also typical of the poet that he concludes by expressing his highly personal anti-tragic, vaguely hedonistic version of the pathetic fallacy:

> Nature! Thou, ever brooding, didst create
> Each being to enjoyment. All thy sons
> Have each his portion and his mansion here
> The swallow builds in the cornice his high nest,
> Unconscious of the ornament abides;
> The little worm spins round the golden branch,
> A winter habitation for its brood.
> And thou, O man! patches a hovel up
> For thy low wants, amid the wreck sublime
> Of ancient days; hast joy too over graves.

The traveler's parting wish that throughout his journey he may be received at day's end by "such a woman/With such a child in her arms" evokes the idyllic scene described by Werther in his letter dated 26 May.

Crabb Robinson's adaptation of the controversial "Mahometsgesang" reflects rather prescient critical judgment and his growing confidence as a translator. Rendered with lyricism combined with dense allusiveness, "The Song of Mahomet [sic]" is accompanied by insightful commentary on Goethe's formal and thematic innovations in the poem. At the outset Crabb Robinson anticipates any possible uneasiness that the English reader might feel in response to Goethe's vivid imaginative sympathy for the Islamic prophet: "it is possible, that to some few the title may be offensive; others, perhaps, without this explanation, would not even understand the poem." (Carlyle would encounter similar qualms in presenting Muhammad as the type of the prophet in his lectures *On Heroes and Hero-Worship* in 1840.) Instead of "the soft, sentimental piety of Christianity," Goethe offers "the turbulent intolerant theophilism of a boisterous and heroic mind. The allegory is as exquisitely wrought as it is boldly conceived."²⁵ Significantly, the poem also embodies Goethe's much-vaunted realism or "objectivity" in representing even unconventional character types. This tendency, which was condemned by many British critics of the period, is fully developed in the creation of such controversial figures as Werther, the Harper in *Wilhelm Meisters Lehrjahre*, and, most notably, Mephistopheles, the emissary of Satan who wills what is evil but accomplishes goodness in *Faust*. Countering the previous unchallenged influence of Goethe's detractors in Britain, Crabb Robinson reminds his readers that questions of verisimilitude, ethics, and ideology are irrelevant here; Goethe's supreme imaginative artistry, which just as readily conceives of a Gretchen as a Mephistopheles, is of supreme importance. "It is," he insists,

> by no means necessary that we should believe in the historical truth and propriety of the picture. Goethe had nothing to do with the probable hypocrisy of Mahomet [sic], and the barbarous character of his religion. Goethe had an *index*, which he would poetically exhibit. And his poem is a local habitation of it, and he found a name for it in the person of Mahomet [sic].²⁶

In other words, the "index" or symbol represented by Muhammad is what matters in the poem. His religious chauvinism and attempted conquest of Europe are of interest because, as Coleridge describes the process in chapter 15 of the *Biographia Literaria*, "a human and intellectual life is transferred to them from the poet's own spirit."²⁷

The fourth letter concludes with a discussion of two poems that depict contrasting attitudes toward the supreme power ruling the universe. In Crabb Robinson's view, "*Prometheus* and *Ganymed* may be considered as personified impiety and devotion. The lover and the hater of the gods are antithetically displayed."²⁸ Goethe's representation of Prometheus, "more noble and heroic, and more entitled to our sympathy than Milton's Satan," inspires Crabb Robinson's best translation in the series. The original poem is one of the classic statements of the *Sturm-und-Drang* assertion of human autonomy, freedom and creativity. Here Goethe gives voice to the conscience of a rising generation opposed to arbitrary aesthetic, religious, and political authority. Crabb Robinson's painstaking fidelity to the simplicity and power of the original results in an excellent English poem and the first and by no means the least important English treatment of the myth that becomes, by virtue of Byron's great lyric (1816) and Shelley's "lyrical drama," *Prometheus Unbound* (1818–1819), one of the definitive symbols of the Romantic movement.

According to Crabb Robinson's interpretation of the poem, Prometheus "proudly and triumphantly avows his contempt of the Thunderer; he bids defiance to Jupiter, and swears to perpetuate his hatred against him, in the minds of the men he had created."[29] In the first lines of the poem Jove's unlimited might, expressed in his absolute power over nature, is contrasted with his impotence to influence the lives of men and women:

> Cover thy heaven, Jove,
> With cloudy vapour,
> And, like the boy
> Who cuts down thistles,
> Shew thy strength on oaks
> And mountain tops.
> Thou canst not touch
> My earth; the cottage
> Which thou hast not built,
> Not this hearth,
> Whose glow thou enviest me.

While the emphasis in Goethe's first stanza is on the nobility and self-reliance distinguishing human beings, Byron characteristically focuses on the "silent suffering, and intense" of Prometheus and on the consequences of the pity he felt for the race of men. The contrast between heaven and earth suggested at the beginning of Goethe's poem is developed further in the second stanza where it is implied that the prodigious excess that characterizes the behavior of the gods is supported by the survival of centuries-old superstitions:

> I know nothing poorer,
> Under the sun,
> Than you, ye gods,
> You nourish sparingly,

> With smoke of sacrifice
> And breath of prayer,
> Your majesty,
> And you would starve,
> If children, beggars,
> Were not hoping fools.

By contrast, in Byron's second stanza a stronger sentiment dominates in contrast to Homer's playful treatment of the foibles of the gods, or Goethe's mild contempt for the supernatural. Byron associates Jove's regime with the principle of evil and arbitrary destruction. At this point Byron and Shelley's conceptions of the father of the gods intersect:

> Titan! to thee the strife was given
> > Between the suffering and the will,
> > Which torture where they cannot kill;
> And the inexorable Heaven,
> And the deaf tyranny of Fate,
> The ruling principle of Hate,
> Which for its pleasure doth create
> The things it may annihilate,
> Refused thee even the boon to die . . . (lines 15–23)

In Goethe's configuration of the myth Jove is merely unresponsive to the needs of mankind and the silent supplications of Prometheus. His cruelty consists in nothing more than a profound disjunction between the spiritual needs of men and his incapacity to respond to them:

> When I was a child,
> And nothing knew,
> I turn'd my puzzled eye
> To the sun, as if above
> Was an ear, that would
> Listen to my sufferings,
> And a heart like mine
> To pity the oppress'd.

In Byron's poem the sympathy expressed by Prometheus for the human condition is contrasted with the callousness and blatant cruelty of the gods. Like Goethe, Byron emphasizes the sacrifice involved in Prometheus's act of defiance, which suggests parallels between his fate and the destiny of the human race. Both Byron's more complex and Goethe's plainer style succeed in celebrating the rebellious spirit of the first creative genius. At mid-century Matthew Arnold attempts to account for the sharp differences between Goethe's style and that of the British Romantic poets. These differences become obvious when we compare the style of *Faust, Part I* (1808) and Byron's treatment of the same theme in *Manfred* (1817). The contrast would still be apparent if we were to compare *Manfred* with *Faust, Part II* (1832) because, as Arnold explains, "even Goethe at the end of his life has not the inversions, the taking tourmente style we admire in the Latins, in some of the Greeks, and in great French and English authors." Unlike Goethe, the British Romantics "still think that the object of poetry is to produce exquisite bits and images." Arnold is convinced that the contrast between Goethe and Byron reveals that "modern poetry can only subsist by its contents," and not over-reliance on rhetorical effects. With the function of poetry raised to "criticism of life" and the added responsibilities that this entails, "the language, style and general proceedings of a poetry which has such an immense task to perform, must be very plain, direct and severe . . ." Thus Arnold considers Goethe's "great plainness of speech" as much more appropriate for a "mature . . . age of the world," since "the poet's matter," being the purpose of his work, "increases with every century."[30]

Continuing faithfully to mediate Goethe's simplicity of expression, Crabb Robinson captures the sense of autonomy and isolation, the great passion and the deep humanism expressed in the last lines of the poem:

> Here I sit and form
> A man like myself;
> A race like me,
> To suffer, and to weep,
> And have enjoyment,
> And to despise,
> As I do, thee.

By contrast, Byron's concluding apology for Prometheus's rebellion corresponds to the tragic definition of life suggested in Keats's image of "the vale of Soul-making,"³¹ in which meaning is attained through suffering:

> Still in thy patient energy,
> In the endurance, and repulse
>   Of thine impenetrable spirit,
> Which Earth and Heaven could not convulse,
>   A mighty lesson we inherit:
> Thou art a symbol and a sign
>   To mortals of their fate and force.

Suffering is also an indispensable component in Goethe's treatment of the myth. However, what Crabb Robinson calls the "large vision of Goethe" characteristically excludes tragedy. "Prometheus" and its counterpart, "Ganymed," give the reader a glimpse of Goethe's attempt to reconcile the extremes of pleasure and pain as well as the transcendent possibility of love and the necessity, at times, of the cleansing effect of anger.

Key differences between Goethe's "Prometheus" and Byron's poem suggest important affinities between the German *Sturm und Drang* and British Romanticism. It is, in fact, remarkable that Crabb Robinson should have chosen the poems he did to translate. His choices disclose correspondences with the taste and critical orientation of Coleridge and Carlyle. Coleridge's interest in German literature grew with his first contact with that representative *Sturm-und-Drang* hero, Karl Moor, protagonist of *The Robbers* (1781). In one of the most memorable passages in his collected correspondence, Coleridge records his ecstatic reaction: "Who is this Schiller, this convulser of the heart? I tremble like an aspen leaf. Upon my soul, I write to you [Southey] because I am frightened . . . . Why have we ever called Milton sublime?"³² Despite the misgivings that were brought on by criticism of his translation of *Wallenstein* (1800), misgivings that would mar his admiration for Schiller, there is much tangible evidence of Coleridge's early enthusiasm for the literature of the

Sturm und Drang. And as Saintsbury comments, adding a characteristic qualification, on Coleridge's liking for Schiller, "that at one early period he apparently thought Schiller more sublime than Milton is not in the least to his discredit."[33]

Owing to the delay involved in the transmission of German literature to Britain, Thomas Caryle's taste was formed as well by the writers of the *Sturm und Drang* and German Classicism. His chief favorites are Goethe, Schiller, and Jean Paul. In the series of Johnsonian prefaces accompanying his translations in *German Romance* (2 volumes, 1827) Carlyle expresses a lack of sympathy for the Romantic generation. In the General Preface his declared discomfort with such German Romantic writers as E. T. A. Hoffmann (1776–1822) and Ludwig Tieck lead to a number of unexpected decisions, not the least of which is the addition to the collection of two pieces by Jean Paul, "Army-Chaplain Schmelze's Journey to Flätz" and the "Life of Quintus Fixlein." This reflects less an attempt to expand the canon of Romanticism to include Jean Paul than his own preference for the whimsical novelist. This seems to confirm what L. A. Willoughby has written concerning the pattern of transmission and reception between Britain and Germany: "it was the classical Goethe and Schiller, and not the contemporary German Romantic School, who acted as a spur to our Romantic Poets."[34] Perhaps the most evocative evidence of this connection is Coleridge's epigraph to the *Biographia Literaria*, which was taken from Goethe's *Propyläen* (1798):

> So wenig er auch bestimmt sein mag, andere zu belehren, so wünscht er doch sich denen mitzutheilen, die er sich gleichgesinnt weiß, (oder hofft,) deren Anzahl aber in der Breite der Welt zerstreut ist; er wünscht sein Verhältniß zu den ältesten Freunden dadurch wieder anzuknüpfen, mit neuen es fortzusetzen, und in der letzten Generation sich wieder andere fur seine übrige Lebenszeit zu gewinnen. Er wünscht der Jugend die Umwege zu ersparen, auf denen er sich selbst verirrte.[35]

In contrast to the defiance expressed in Goethe's "Prometheus," "Ganymede's Song" is, as characterized by Crabb Robinson, "one stream of love; longing, burning, love."³⁶ The first stanza is an apostrophe to the father of the gods as Zeus's immortality intensifies the bliss that his mortal lover feels in his presence:

> As in the morning sun,
> Thou dost glow round me,
> Spring, thou beloved!
> Love's joy, thousand fold,
> Presses upon my heart,
> Feeling most holy,
> Of thy eternal warmth,
> Infinite beauty.

Taken together these two poems express more than contrasting attitudes toward the gods. They also establish the more subtle limits "between the *bounds of humanity and the Divine*:"

> The one exhibits man as belonging merely to the natural or material world; and the reflection on his absolute powerlessness and nothingness, opposed to the mighty unknown powers above him, is dismal and terrific: but the picture which the counterpart exhibits, raises man, by showing him, as a member of the intellectual and moral world, in which he is a god.³⁷

In contrast to the Luciferian tendency of Prometheus, whose rebellious disposition draws him down to earth, in "Ganymede" the favorite of the gods feels the transcendent urge of love lifting him upwards to heaven.

In the fifth letter, entitled simply "More Distiches," Crabb Robinson offers an ironic defense of Goethe and Schiller's experiments in blending Latinate formal conventions with the German language. Returning to the issues touched on in the first letter, he seeks to demonstrate the advantages of a verse form that could enrich the formal possibilities of British poetry and increase its philosophical depth. If, in later life, his enthusiasm for Goethe seemed to fade, his faith in Goethe's achievement abided. Just before his death he insisted that "Goethe has done more than any man to bring back the public taste to works of imagination—a faculty which does not refuse all alliance with frightful realities, but which refines and idealizes them."[38] This suggests that by investing modern life with imaginative legitimacy Goethe anticipated the achievements of realism in verse and prose fiction.

Crabb Robinson was alert to Goethe's revolutionary impact on European culture and for this vigilance and for his intelligent response to Goethe's occasional poems he has earned posterity's regard. In his pieces in *The Monthly Register* the reader encounters the first significant effort by a member of the Romantic generation to translate and to offer an analysis of Goethe's poetry. At the same time, Crabb Robinson makes the first strides toward a symbolic interpretation of Goethe's life that anticipate Carlyle's extension, twenty years later in the essays he wrote for the *Edinburgh Review* and other journals in the 1820s, of Goethe's cultural influence from the merely literary to ethical authority. Despite their interpretive value Crabb Robinson's essays on Goethe received no notice in his lifetime. The reasons for such neglect are fairly clear: first, the essays appeared in a journal as ephemeral as it was obscure; secondly, Crabb Robinson's workmanlike performance as a translator and critic was eclipsed by Carlyle's visionary brand of criticism. It was Crabb Robinson's translation and commentary that reflected prescient critical judgment as well as the advantages he enjoyed of being steeped in the German language and culture to a degree unknown by previous visitors to Germany. In contrast to Coleridge he had the advantage of well-connected cicerones, including members of the Brentano family, the philosopher Schelling, Böttiger, Knebel, A. W. Schlegel, and Germaine de Staël. In *The Monthly Register* essays we find Crabb Robinson writing in an original vein; here, far in advance of his more prominent contemporaries, he argues for Goethe's preeminence among German writers and draws attention to a side of Goethe's achievement hitherto ignored or underappreciated by Goethe's British critics—his achievement as a lyric poet. It was not, of course, as a mere poet but as a prophet that Carlyle admired Goethe; Arnold and Saintsbury saw him chiefly as a critic; Lewes emphasized his work in science; and Taylor saw the genius in his dramas.

Crabb Robinson's critical sensibility is well displayed in the translations and commentary published in *The Monthly Register*. His sometimes striking insights and always accurate and generally tasteful versions of Goethe's texts argue for recognizing Crabb Robinson as an important early critic of Germany's leading man of letters.

Interlude One
Goethe and the Romantic Idealization of the Artist

> "A total iconoclast, Goethe inherits everything that is wildest and most idiosyncratic in Western aesthetic culture."
>
> Harold Bloom[1]

The birth of Romanticism in British, European, and American literature can be traced to idealized representations of artists and poets in prose fiction published at the start of the "long nineteenth century." In these works a dominant trope emerges: the artist or poet as hero, sage, priest, messiah, superman, and privileged decipherer of nature's immanence and meaning. The special status, sacred vocation, and reverence due the artist for his special powers is acknowledged in many, if not all, European traditions, and in works that comprehend an enormous range of genres and sub-genres of prose fiction—fairy tales, dream visions, novellas, variations on the *Bildungsroman* as well as realistic fiction and historical novels, including Heinrich Wilhelm Wackenroder (1773–1798) and Ludwig Tieck's *Herzensergiessungen eines kunstliebenden Klosterbruders* [*Effusions of an Art-loving Friar*] (1797); William Godwin's *St. Leon* (1799); Novalis's *Heinrich von Ofterdingen* (1802); Germaine de Staël's *Corinne, ou Italie* [*Corinne, or Italy*] (1807); E.T.A. Hoffmann's "Rat Krespel" ["Attorney Krespel"] (1814–1815), "Das Fräulein von Scudéry" ["Mademoiselle Scudéry"] (1817), and "Kater Murr" ["Tomcat Murr"] (1820); Mary Shelley's *Frankenstein* (1818); Thomas Carlyle's *Wotton Reinfred* (1826–1827); Gottfried Keller's *Der grüne Heinrich* [*Green Henry*] (1854–1855); Nathaniel Hawthorne's *The Marble Faun* (1860); Fyodor Dostoyevsky's *Zapiski iz podpol'ia* [*Notes from Underground*] (1864) and *Prestuplenie i nakazanie* [*Crime and Punishment*] (1866); George Eliot's *Middlemarch* (1871); Louisa May Alcott's *The Modern Mephistopheles* (1877); J.P. Jacobsen's *Niels Lyhne* (1880); Knut Hamsum's *Sult*

[*Hunger*] (1890); and Thomas Mann's *Buddenbrooks* (1901), "Tonio Kröger" (1903), and *Der Tod in Venedig* [*Death in Venice*] (1911).

In these texts interrogating the status and function of art and the artist takes center stage. Building upon the *Sturm-und-Drang* cult of the genius, the Romantics and their post-Romantic heirs assert that the artist's authority is derived not from a clout of wealthy patrons, but from his or her individual originality, vision, and imagination. The elevated status of the artist comes, however, at the price of his or her alienation from the bourgeoisie and the philistine's work-a-day world. The protagonist of Goethe's *Wilhelm Meisters Lehrjahre* [*Wilhelm Meister's Apprenticeship*] (1795), was the original Romantic "bourgeois manqué," whose descendents include Byron's Childe Harold, Coleridge's Ancient Mariner, Hoffmann's gallery of mysterious artists, homicidal jewelers, and shadowy musicians, Wagner's Flying Dutchman, George Eliot's Will Ladislaw, Dostoevsky's Raskolnikov, Jacobsen's Niels Lyhne, and Mann's Tonio Kröger. In a certain sense, the artist's exile seems warranted for the artist is often figured as dangerous, a threat to society, as the warning in Coleridge's "Kubla Khan" (1797/1816) makes clear:

> And all should cry, Beware! Beware!
> His flashing eyes, his floating hair!
> Weave a circle around him thrice,
> And close your eyes with holy dread,
> For he on honey-dew hath fed,
> And drunk the milk of Paradise. (lines 49–54)

Responses to the alienation of the artist, to the impossibility of comfortably meshing with bourgeois society, varied according to each writer's ideology. Conservative Romantics, such as Novalis, Carlyle, and Keller, longed for the revival of an idealized, proto-fascist medieval pastoral world. By contrast, progressive Romantics, e.g. Godwin, Mary Wollstonecraft, and the Shelleys sought redemption in a future Utopia in which social and individual fragmentation would be healed. Immediately after the publication of *Wilhelm Meister*, the novel's *Bildungsroman* pattern, which valorizes the suffering of the would-be artist, was challenged by a new and ultimately dominant "anti-*Bildungsroman*" tradition in Romantic and post-Romantic prose fiction. Examples of this latter type include *St. Leon, Heinrich von Ofterdingen, Corinne, Notes from Underground, Middlemarch, Niels Lyhne, Hunger,* and "Tonio Kröger," in which the alienating experience of modernity is not validated or redeemed. Indeed, the suffering and estrangement of the artist are represented as neither purposeful nor redemptive, but as simply the cost to be borne by sensitive individuals in the modern age.

While several Romantic and post-Romantic prose narratives depict a world constructed according to an artist-friendly design, e.g., *Heinrich von Ofterdingen* and *Also Sprach Zarathustra* [*Thus Spoke Zarathustra*] (1883), other prose narratives of the period explore the vocation of the artist as an unrelieved nightmare (*St. Leon, Frankenstein, Hunger,* and *Notes from Underground*). Still others examine the conflict between artists or artistically inclined protagonists and the resistant medium of reality. In *Middlemarch*, for example, Dorothea Brooks, Will Ladislaw, and Tertius Lydgate, "the offspring of a certain spiritual grandeur ill-matched with the meanness of opportunity" in George Eliot's provincial world circa 1832, "struggl[e] amidst the conditions of an imperfect social state."[2] *Past and Present* (1843), Thomas Carlyle's contribution to the sub-genre of conservative "looking backwards" narratives, is an instructive example of the impact of nostalgia in shaping the Romantic imagination. With the publication of his idealized portrait of life among peasant artisans in pre-modern Britain Carlyle aligns himself with the chief concerns in Novalis's *Die Christenheit oder Europa* [*Christianity or Europe*] (1799) and Coleridge's *On the Constitution of the Church and State* (1830).

There are ideological and generational as well as generic distinctions in the Romantic representation of the artist. In British High Romanticism, for example, the assertion of the artist's special vocation as a visionary and healer is most closely associated with the major Romantic poets—Wordsworth, Coleridge, Byron, Shelley, Keats, and Blake. It is only later, in the early Victorian era, following the importation and dissemination of German Romantic literature, that the "problem of the artist" becomes a major concern of British novelists. This similarity becomes clear if we compare statements on the vocation of the artist and poet and on the function of art and poetry from the writings of German, British, and French writers. Because they seek to obliterate the distinction between prose and poetry, and between literature and the other arts, in the following passages the distinction between critical commentary and imaginative writing breaks down:

> Novalis: "Der Künstler seht auf dem Menschen, wie die Statue auf dem Pedestal."[3]

> Schlegel: "Was die Menschen unter andern Bildungen der Erde, das sind die Künstler unter den Menschen."[4]

> Blake: "And I know that This World Is a World of imagination & Vision. I see Every thing I paint in This World, but Every body does not see alike . . . Some See Nature all Ridicule & Deformity, & by these I shall not regulate my proportions; & Some Scarce see Nature at all. But to the Eyes of the Man of Imagination, Nature is Imagination itself. As a man is, So he Sees. As the Eye is formed, such are its Powers. You certainly Mistake, when you say that the Visions of Fancy are not to be found in This World. To Me This World is all One continued Vision of Fancy or Imagination."[5]

> Wordsworth: "[W]hat is meant by the word Poet? What is a Poet? To whom does he address himself? And what language is to be expected from him?—He is a man speaking to men: a man, it is true, endowed with more lively sensibility, more enthusiasm and tenderness, who has a greater knowledge of human nature, and a more comprehensive soul, than are supposed to be common among mankind."[6]

> Coleridge: "The poet, described in ideal perfection, brings the whole soul of man into activity, with the subordination of its faculties to each other, according to their relative worth and dignity."[7]

> Shelley: "But poets . . . are not only the authors of language and Music, or the dance and architecture, and statuary, and painting; they are the institutors of laws, and the founders of civil society, and the inventors of the arts of life, and the teachers, who draw into a certain propinquity with the beautiful and the true, that partial apprehension of the agencies of the invisible world which is called religion."[8]

Keats: "As to the poetical Character itself . . . it is not itself—it has no self—it is every thing and nothing—It has no character—it enjoys light and shade; it lives in gusto, be it foul or fair, high or low, rich or poor, mean or elevated—It has as much delight in conceiving an Iago as an Imogen. What shocks the virtuous philosopher, delights the camelion Poet. It does no harm from its relish of the dark side of things any more than from its taste for the bright one; because they both end in speculation."[9]

Vigny: "Le Poète cherche aux étoiles quelle route nous montre le doigt du Seigneur."[10]

And, finally, Keller: "Warum sollte dies nicht ein edler und schöner Beruf sein, immer und allein vor dem Werken Gottes zu sitzen, die sich noch am heutigen Tag in ihrer Unschuld und ganzen Schönheit erhalten haben, sie zu erkennen und zu verehren und ihn dadurch anzubeten, daß man sie in ihrem Frieden wiederzugeben versucht? Wenn man nur ein einfältiges Sträuchlein abzeichnet, so empfindet man eine Ehrfurcht vor jedem Zwiege, weil derselbe so gewachsen ist und nicht anders nach den Gesetzen des Schöpfers; wenn man aber erst fähig ist, einen ganzen Wald oder ein weites Feld mit seinem Himmel wahr und treu zu malen, und wenn man endlich dergleichen aus seinem Innern selbst hervorbringen kann, ohne Vorbild, Wälder, Täler, und Gebirgszüge, oder nur kleine Erdwinkel, frei und neu, und doch nicht anders, als ob sie irgendwo entstanden und sichtbar sein müßten, so dünkt mich diese Kunst eine Art wahren Nachgenußes der Schöpfung zu sein."[11]

The Importance of *Wilhelm Meister*

Friedrich Schlegel described the three major European phenomena of the early nineteenth century as the French Revolution of 1789, J. G. Fichte's *Wissenschaftslehre* [*Doctrine of Knowledge*] (1794), and Goethe's *Wilhelm Meisters Lehrjahre* [*Wilhelm Meister's Apprenticeship*] (1795–1796). Indeed, a powerful factor in the emergence of Romanticism was the varied, rich, and creative response to *Wilhelm Meister*, for and against, throughout the nineteenth century. Indeed, the importation of ideas from Germany about the artist's place in society molded the discussion of post-French Revolution discussions of this relationship in Europe, Britain, and the United States. This influence was deeply felt in New England where an independent cultural life was just starting to assert itself in the activities of the Transcendentalists Ralph Waldo Emerson and Margaret Fuller and their colleagues in Boston, Cambridge, and Concord.

Meanwhile, exiled in Switzerland the novelist Germaine de Staël, whose *Corinne* features one of the few examples of a female poet-artist protagonist in the entire Romantic canon, identified German Classicism and Romantic culture as a potentially important source of spiritual authority for the rest of Europe. In *De l'Allemagne* Staël identifies Goethe as a living classic. Romantic and Victorian writers in Britain found in Staël's idealized vision of German culture a subversive alternative to the soulless, mechanistic thinking of the Enlightenment against which the Romantics had originally rebelled. Staël's portrayal of Germany as the land of poets and thinkers gave impetus to the transformation of Goethe's public image from that of the dangerous author of *Werther* to the cultural hero who published *Wilhelm Meister*, which was embraced throughout Europe and the United States as a kind of self-help book for poets and artists. At a time when Goethe was decidedly less popular than Kotzebue, Schiller, and Wieland, Staël made the bold claim that he, and not his more prominent contemporaries, "[R]éunit tout ce qui distingué l'esprit allemand" [unites all that distinguishes the German mind] and possesses "les traits principaux du génie allemand" [the chief characteristics of the German genius].[12] Indeed, Thomas Carlyle's translation of *Wilhelm Meister* (1824) ignited the first "culture war" of the Victorian era in Britain, as writers on the left and right debated the merits of erecting German cultural idols in the Anglo-American literary landscape.

According to Carlyle, the most staunchly pro-Goethe Victorian writer before G.H. Lewes, *Werther* had given voice to "the cry of that dim, rooted pain, under which all thoughtful men of a certain age were languishing" and affirmed Goethe's cultural authority as an expression of his capacity for redemptive suffering.[13] *Wilhelm Meister*, in Carlyle's translation, appealed to British readers more than *Werther* because it suggested links between the growth of aesthetic sensibility and ethical self-awareness and thus indicated a hopeful solution to the artist's dilemma. Carlyle credits Goethe with having gone further than any other human being in his age in breaking through the paralysis of reflection and demonstrating the possibility of sensitive souls undertaking meaningful action in the modern world. Goethe's fusion of realism, wisdom literature, and lyric poetry in *Wilhelm Meister* presented an allegory of the nineteenth century that offered "a picture full of the expressiveness, of what men are striving for, and ought to strive for, in these actual days."[14] *Wilhelm Meister* thus served as a counterweight to the "wild suicidal Night-thoughts of *Werther*," the representation of artistically inclined individuals as suffering, deracinated, and casteless.[15] Goethe's realism is valuable because its "figurativeness" has a "supernatural" quality. That is, Goethe's "singularly emblematic intellect; his perpetual never-failing tendency to transform into shape, into life . . . the opinion, the feeling that may dwell in him. Goethe's figurativeness . . . manifests itself as the constructing of the inward elements of a thought, as the vital elements of it" and that this "emblematic" faculty is "the very essence of Goethe's intellect."[16] Carlyle was sufficiently impressed with Goethe's novel to use it as a model for his own *Bildungsroman*, the posthumously published *Wotton Reinfred* (1892).

Effusive Responses

The first important response to Goethe's *Wilhelm Meister* was Wackenroder and Tieck's *Herzensergiessungen eines kunstliebenden Klosterbruders* [*Effusions of an Art-loving Friar*] (1797). German Romanticism can, in fact, be said to have been born in Wackenroder and Tieck's evocation of the divinity of art and the sacred mission of the artist, which was inspired by their re-discovery of medieval and Renaissance art as well as the architecture of Nuremberg and the impressive Baroque churches they visited in Franconia. This aesthetic response was combined with a sympathetic orientation toward Roman Catholicism and a contemporary influence, the activities of a group of Austrian and German artists based in Rome. The quasi-monastic *Lukasbund* [Brotherhood of St. Luke] or Nazarenes pre-dated the Pre-Raphaelites in their efforts to revive the color, composition, and pre-perspectival simplicity of medieval and early Renaissance painting, and they included Friedrich Overbeck (1789–1869), Franz Pforr (1788–1812), Peter von Cornelius (1783–1867), and Philipp Veit (1793–1877). The Nazarenes' reaction against Neoclassicism lies at the heart of Romanticism and anticipated the central place of mediæval revivalism and the admiration of the Gothic in the latter half of the nineteenth century.[17] Wackenroder and Tieck were also deeply impressed by the Goethe cultist, novelist, travel writer, and antiquarian Karl Philipp Moritz (1756–1793), whose lectures on art history they attended at the Berlin Academy of Fine Arts. Moritz's anti-rationalistic, emotional teaching that art may be felt but not easily comprehended is evident throughout *Herzensergiessungen* and in the works of the Romantics generally.

This work's characteristically Romantic trait, the fusion of genres—essays, fictionalized autobiography, anecdotes, epistolary essays, biographical sketches, prose that verges on, at times merges with, and often gives way to verse—offered a template for Richard Wagner's conception of the *Gesammtkunstwerk* [total work of art] as manifested in the music dramas *Tristan und Isolde* [*Tristan and Isolde*] (1865), *Der Ring des Nibelungen* [*The Ring of the Nibelungs*] (1853–1874), and *Parsifal* (1882). Such striving after a universal, all-inclusive work of art is denoted as definitively Romantic in Friedrich Schlegel's *Athenäum Fragment*, No. 116:

> Die Romantische Poesie ist eine progressive Universalpoesie. Ihre Bestimmung ist nicht bloß, alle getrennten Gattungen der Poesie wieder zu vereinigen, und die Poesie mit der Philosophie und Rhetorik in Berührung zu setzen. Sie will, und soll auch Poesie und Prosa, Genialität und Kritik, Kunstpoesie und Naturpoesie bald mischen, bald verschmelzen, die Poesie lebendig und gesellig, und das Leben und die Gesellschaft poetischen machen, den Witz poetisieren, und die Formen der Kunst mit gediegnem Bildungsstoff jeder Art anfüllen und sättigen, und durch die Schwingungen des Humors beseelen. Sie umfaßt alles, was nur poetisch ist, vom größten wieder mehrere Systeme in sich enthaltenden Systeme der Kunst, bis zu dem Seufer, dem Kuß, den das dichtende Kind aushaucht in kunstlosen Gesang . . . . Nur sie kann gleich dem Epos ein Spiegel der ganzen umgebenden Welt, ein Bild Zeitalters werden . . . . Die romantische Dichtart ist noch im Werden; ja das ist ihr eigentliches Wesen, daß sie ewig nur

werden, nie vollendet sein kann ... Die romantische Dichtart ist die einzige, die mehr als Art, und gleichsam die Dichtkunst selbst ist: denn in einem gewißen Sinn ist oder soll alle Poesie romantisch sein.[18]

The mouthpiece selected by Wackenroder and Tieck—a fictitious Baroque friar indicates their deep affinity with Roman Catholicism and its rich pageantry and ceremony, in which the spiritual and the sensuous are merged. As interpreted in their revolutionary hybrid of prose fiction, in the Catholic imagination art in all forms— painting, sculpture, architecture, music, and drama—is subordinated, sympathetically, to the transmission of supernatural experience. The link between religion and art, the central concern in *Herzensergiessungen*, is clear in the following passage:

> Die Sprache der Worte ist eine große Gabe des Himmels, und es war eine ewige Wohltat des Schöpfers, daß er die Zunge des ersten Menschen löste, damit er alle Dinge, die der Höchste um ihn her in die Welt gesetzt, und alle geistigen Bilder, die er in seine Seele gelegt hatte, nennen und seinen Geist in dem mannigfältigen Spiele mit diesem Reichtum von Namen üben könnte. Durch Wörte herrschen wir über den ganzen Erdkreis; durch Wörte erhandeln wir uns mit leichter Mühe alle Schätze der Erde. Nur das Unsichtbare, das über uns schwebt, ziehen Wörte nicht in unser Gemüt herab.[19]

At this early moment in the history of the creative reception of *Wilhelm Meister*, the failure of art to serve as an adequate substitute for religion was not yet perceived. Indeed, the flocks of German converts to Roman Catholicism and their fellow travelers represent a virtual encyclopedia of Romantic practitioners in the arts.

Heinrich von Ofterdingen

Another influential early response to *Wilhelm Meister* that occupies the core of the Romantic canon is *Heinrich von Ofterdingen* (published posthumously in 1802) by Georg Philipp Friedrich von Hardenberg (1772–1801), who published under the name Novalis. During his student years in Jena, Leipzig, and Wittenberg, the writer's acquaintances included many of the architects of Romantic aesthetic ideas—Johann Gottlieb Fichte, Friedrich Schiller, Friedrich and A. W.

Schlegel, Wackenroder, and Tieck. The turning point in his life occurred in 1797 when his thirteen-year-old fiancée, Sophie von Kühn, died of tuberculosis, foreshadowing his own death from the disease in 1801.

In 1800 Novalis broke with Schiller's classicism and Goethe's realism as he sought to represent Romantic desire in a totally new, independent, and revolutionary voice. In contrast to the classical *Bildungsroman* tradition inaugurated by Goethe's *Wilhelm Meister*, in which human development appears as the highest goal. In *Heinrich von Ofterdingen* there is no developmental telos as such—no hoped-for result or valorized paradigm—only the pursuit of self-forgetting in longing, dreams, and death. The significance-laden blue flower, for which the eponymous hero of *Heinrich von Ofterdingen* yearns, takes on ultimate reality, whose hieroglyphs are indecipherable except to the vision of the dreaming poet. In contrast to Nature's "große Künstlichkeit" [great artfulness], which is everywhere visible to the naked eye, Novalis interrogates the magical, mysterious, secret nature of poetry as reconceived by the Romantics—an esoteric art, analogous to alchemy or magic:

> Dagegen ist von der Dichtkunst sonst nirgends äußerlich etwas anzutreffen. Auch schafft sie nichts mit Werkzeugen und Händen; das Auge und das Ohr vernehmen nichts davon: denn das bloße Hören der Worte ist nicht die eigentliche Wirkung dieser geheimen Kunst. Es ist alles innerlich, und wie jene Künstler die äußern Sinne mit angenehmen Empfindungen erfüllen, so erfüllt der Dichter das inwendige Heiligtum des Gemüts mit neuen, wunderbaren und gefälligen Gedanken. Er weiß jene geheimen Kräfte in uns nach Belieben zu erregen und gibt uns durch Worte eine unbekannte herrliche Welt zu vernehmen.[20]

For Heinrich, the aspiring poet, the source of meaning is love and the higher world that is hidden but can be made manifest by the poet:

> "Die Sprache," sagte Heinrich, "ist wirklich eine kleine Welt in Zeichen und Tönen. Wie der Mensch sie beherrscht, so möchte er gern die große Welt beherrschen und sich frei darin ausdrücken können. Und eben in dieser Freude das, was außer der Welt ist, in ihr zu offenbaren, das tun zu können, was eigentlich der ursprüngliche Trieb unsers Daseins ist, liegt der Ursprung der Poesie."[21]

Wotton Reinfred

The major concern of British Romantic and early Victorian prose fiction is, with few exceptions, the transformation of the Gothic, historical, picaresque, satirical, and country house tropes and themes associated with the eighteenth-century novel. In contrast to the German tradition, the British response to Goethe's *Wilhelm Meister* was, as noted above, delayed until the mid-1820s and after. The fragmentary, posthumously published *Wotton Reinfred* was written between 1826 and 1827, exactly in the middle of Thomas Carlyle's formative, decade-long engagement with German literature, and it suggests that the reception of *Wilhelm Meister* played a crucial role in the formation of late British Romanticism and early Victorian culture. A fusion of the German *Bildungsroman*, philosophical dialogue, and wisdom literature, *Wotton Reinfred* was chiefly inspired by Goethe's *Wilhelm Meister's Apprenticeship*, a translation of which Carlyle published in 1824, and Novalis's *Heinrich von Ofterdingen*, which was also the chief model for Carlyle's major work of prose fiction, *Sartor Resartus* (1834), to be published in his lifetime. There are, in addition, traces of Carlyle's distinctive synthesis of British and German Romantic aesthetics, philosophy, and nature worship, including a rudimentary expression of "natural supernaturalism." At the same time *Wotton Reinfred* is replete with Goethean homilies on the sanctity of work, renunciation, and anti-eudamonism assimilated from Goethe, ideas that are associated with the mature Carlyle.

Because Carlyle considered Enlightenment culture soul-less, ego-driven, emptily mechanistic, and his native land bereft of contemporary heroes worthy of the name, he frequently expressed a deep sense of estrangement from contemporary Britain; a lament that is also echoed in *Wotton Reinfred*. Thus for the overall blueprint underlying this rich intertextual extravaganza, Carlyle turned to Goethe, his primary literary and spiritual master, whose influence on the young Scottish writer was as pervasive and enduring as it was on Wackenroder, Tieck, Schlegel, and Novalis. The dialogues that comprise the narrative contain a concise exposition of Carlyles's aesthetics in relation to the thought of his time in Germany and Britain and constitute a defense of his appropriation and naturalization of German thought.

St. Leon and *Frankenstein*

Frankenstein (1818), Mary Shelley's science fiction parable of the suffering and persecution of a philanthropic scientist steeped in alchemy and his maligned creature, was preceded by her father's novel on a remarkably similar theme, *St. Leon: A Tale of the Sixteenth Century* (1799). In both novels the protagonists' use of alchemy becomes the perfect symbol for art and the status of the artist in the Romantic era. As a revision of Godwin's novel and an appropriation of Goethe's characterization of a desire for knowledge that was both transgressive and redemptive in *Faust* (1808/1832), *Frankenstein* illustrates the dialogic progression from Mary Shelley's appropriation of her father's discourse to the emergence of her authorial originality and thus also functions as an allegory of the author's education and literary apprenticeship. At the center of *St. Leon* is a presentation of the "education" of the protagonist Reginald de St. Leon alternately through alchemy and exile. Reginald's travels, however, embody an inversion of the Goethean *Bildungsreise* [trajectory of development]: his education is based on a process of disillusionment rather than instruction, enlightenment, and growth. Hounded by authorities from one end of Europe to the other, his freedom is purchased only by continual flight. As the bearer of a monstrous secret Reginald embarks on an endless odyssey "hated by mankind, hunted from the face of the earth, pursued by atrocious calumny, without country, without a roof, without a friend."[22]

Emulating Reginald's and Victor's search for ideal companionship, empowering knowledge and opportunities for doing some action that is "great and good," Shelley's monstrous creature also embarks on an odyssey that begins with the discovery that he lives in a hostile world, rejected by his "father," and denied the chance to procreate and to live a "normal life." His *Bildungsreise* ends with a murderous inversion of Godwinian altruism as he lashes out at Victor, destroying all those with whom he enjoys emotional intimacy in order to render his condition identical to his own. The rebellion of the creature, which proceeds from inarticulate rage to the discovery of literature and the art of discourse, invites comparisons with Mary Shelley's efforts simultaneously to assimilate and to overcome her father's and her husband's more authoritative discourse. Mary's and the creature's obsession with language, this "godlike science," that can produce golden music out of arbitrary signs and sounds, is akin to Reginald's obsession with alchemy and Victor's with the "new science."

St. Leon and *Frankenstein* are myths of misguided benevolence in which well intended but hubristic transgressions of social, religious, and scientific conventions are punished by enforced exile from human society. The ostracism of Reginald, Victor, and the creature mark them as members of the tribe of Romantic outcasts. Formally innovative in a way that reinforces their transgressive themes, *St. Leon* and *Frankenstein* are militantly anti-canonical, composite literary forms that explore the outer boundaries of the novel's possibilities as a genre and combine and appropriate such narrative sub-genres as the Gothic novel, science fiction, the *Bildungsroman*, travel and sentimental fiction.

Schopenhauer and Romantic Aestheticism

The Romantic idealization of the creative genius culminates in the artist-centered philosophical writings of Arthur Schopenhauer. Indeed, no other philosopher in the nineteenth century assigned such an integral role for art in the workings of his metaphysical system than Schopenhauer. Unlike predecessors and contemporaries such as Kant, Fichte, and Hegel, Schopenhauer does not consider art an intellectual narcotic, a deviation from the path of serious philosophical inquiry, or just a handy servant to superior masters. On the contrary, according to Schopenhauer art and the creative genius offer the most accessible means to achieving nothing less than the salvation of all existence. In contrast to the scientist, who is concerned with the phenomenal world and establishing laws for its behavior, the artist, in league with the philosopher, pursues higher, eternal truths:

> Nicht bloß die Philosophie, sondern auch die schönen Künste Arbeiten im Grunde darauf hin, daß Problem des Daseins zu Lösen . . . . Jedes Kunstwerk ist demgemäß eigentlich bemüht, uns das Leben und die Dinge so zu zeigen, wie sie in Wahrheit sind, aber, durch den Nebel objektiver und subjektiver Zufälligkeiten hindurch, nicht von Jedem unmittelbar erfaßt werden können. Diesen Nebel nimmt die Kunst hinweg . . . . Die Werke der Dichter, Bildner und darstellenden Künstler überhaupt enthalten anerkanntermaßen einen Schatz tiefer Weisheit: eben weil aus ihnen die Weisheit der Natur der Dinge selbst redet, deren Außagen sie bloß durch Verdeutlichung und reinere Wiederholung verdolmetschen. Deshalb muß aber freilich auch Jeder, der das Gedicht liest, oder das Kunstwerk betrachtet, aus eigenen Mitteln Beitragen, jene Weisheit zu Tage zu fördern.[23]

Through the action of artists, whose talent consists in perceiving and then representing not specific phenomena that exist only in the relation but the Ideas of such things, the mist distorting our vision is cleared. The Veil of Maya is torn back and the inner meaning of reality is revealed in the eternal ideas, existing outside space and time. Artistic creation or the contemplation of a work of art has the power to free the intellect from its original subservience to the will, thus allowing the intellect to rise above the trammels of everyday existence and beyond the illusory satisfactions of the world of appearances. The observer is blessed with enlightenment, momentarily relieved of attachment to the will and free to contemplate his or her relation to the world, disinterestedly, as a will-less subject of knowledge. Thus, as Nietzsche observes,

> Jener Heroismus der Wahrhaftigkeit besteht darin, eines Tages aufzuhören, sein Spielzeug zu sein. Im Werden ist Alles hohl, betrügerisch, flach und unserer Verachtung würdig; das Räthsel, welches der Mensch lösen soll, kann er nur aus dem Sein lösen, im So- und nicht Anderssein, im Unvergänglichen.[24]

Released from subservience to the senses, the subject ceases to be merely individual and becomes the pure will-less subject of

Interlude One: Goethe and the Romantic Idealization of the Artist

knowledge, the "clear eye" and mirror of "the inner nature of the world":

> Wenn man, durch die Kraft des Geistes gehoben, die Gewöhnlichen Berachtungsart der Dinge fahren läßt, aufhört, nur ihren Relationen zu einander, deren letztes Ziel immer die Relation zum eigenen Willen ist, am Leitfaden der Gestaltungen des Satzes vom Grunde, nachzugehen, also nicht mehr das Wo, das Wann, das Warum und das Wozu an den Dingen betrachtet; sondern einzig und allein das Was; auch nicht das abstrakte Denken, die Begriffe der Vernunft, das Bewußtsein einnehmen läßt; sondern, statt alles diesen, die ganze Macht seines Geistes der Anschauung hingiebt, sich ganz in diese versenkt und das ganze Bewußtsein ausfüllen läßt durch die ruhige Kontemplation des gerade gegenwärtigen natürlichen Gegenstandes, sei es eine Landschaft, ein Baum, ein Fels, ein Gebäude oder was auch immer; indem man, nach einer sinnvollen Deutschen Redensart, sich gänzlich in diesen Gegenstand *verliert*, d.h. eben sein Individuum, seinen Willen, vergißt und nur noch als reines Subjekt, als klarer Spiegel des Objekts bestehend bleibt; so daß es ist, als ob der Gegenstand allein da wäre, ohne Jemanden, der ihn wahrnimmt.[25]

In the process of gaining a remarkable new capacity for seeing into the truth of things the perceiving subject also attains

> der schmerzenslose Zustand, den Epikuros als das höchste Gut und als den Zustand der Götter pries: denn wir sind, für jenen Augenblick, des schnöden Willensdranges entledigt, wir feiern den Sabbath der Zuchthausarbeit des Wollens, das Rad des Ixion steht still.[26]

Not only does artistic contemplation yield insight into the immutable profound truths of existence, it also emancipates the individual from the tyranny of the will. Thus liberated from subservience to the will knowledge becomes pure perception, pure objectivity, pure repose. As Nietzsche states,

> *Der Schopenhauerische Mensch nimmt das freiwillige Leiden der Wahrhaftigkeit auf sich,* und dieses Leiden dient ihm, seinen Eigenwillen zu ertödten und jene völlige Umwälzung und Umkehrung seines Wesens vorzubereiten, zu der zu führen der eigentliche Sinn des Lebens ist.[27]

By making such large claims for the production and contemplation of art, Schopenhauer was naturally the artist's philosopher *par excellence*. From the mid-nineteenth century onwards, Schopenhauer found among artists and connoisseurs his most fanatical converts.

Countless artists and writers found an antidote to their own suffering and alienation as well as hope for the redemption of humankind in his prescription of art as the means to achieve victory over the will. In addition to Nietzsche and Wagner, some of Schopenhauer's admirers on the Continent included Leo Tolstoy (1828–1910), Knut Hamsun (1859–1952), Edvard Munch (1863–1944), Vyacheslav Ivanov (1866–1949), and Thomas Mann (1875–1955). In Britain Schopenhauer's following among writers and artists associated with the rise of aestheticism and Modernism included Walter Pater and Oscar Wilde. Indeed, the embrace by European Modernism of both the pose of self-conscious alienation and aspects of the aesthetic idiom of the Romantic artist suggests an essential continuity in the representation and idealization of the artist throughout the long nineteenth century.

Chapter Four
Resistance and Concealment: Goethe and the Canonical British Romantic Poets

> As for your Germans, petty pismire hosts,
> Nathans, Iphigeneias, Meisters, Fausts,
> Any two stanzas here are worth 'em all . . .
> So let your Privy Council give the wall.
> Goethe may be a baron or a graf,
> Call him a poet and you make me laugh:
> Either my judgment is entirely lost or
> Never was there so cursed an imposter.
>
> Walter Savage Landor[1]

> "Initial love for the precursor's poetry is transformed rapidly enough into revisionary strife."
>
> Harold Bloom[2]

Coleridge and Wordsworth

Coleridge's reputation as a genuine British polymath, which has, at times, been nearly commensurate with Goethe's in Germany, remained intact until the end of the nineteenth century. In his cranky compendium of preferences and prejudices, *A History of Criticism and Literary Taste in Europe*, George Saintsbury ranks Coleridge with Aristotle and Longinus as one of the greatest critics in the Western tradition. No other critic writing in English could match Coleridge's erudition, reading, and, most importantly, "pure" interest in literary form and the prerogatives of the text. Thus Saintsbury urges Coleridge upon his readers as "the critical author to be turned over day and night."[3] Similar judgments could be gleaned from critics of the Romantic period who were closer to us in time and taste like Walter Jackson Bate, Paul De Man, and Harold Bloom. Still others contributed to the renaissance that Coleridge scholarship has enjoyed since the Second War World, which has restored Coleridge's reputation as a critic of unparalleled importance.

Saintsbury's estimate of the importance of Coleridge is found among a series of portraits rendered in characteristically forceful strokes. "[John] Dryden [1631–1700]," he insists, "is great, but he is not fully formed." Bernard Le Bovier de Fontenelle (1657–1757), too, is "very great," but he unfortunately combines Dryden's shortcomings with "an almost, perhaps a quite, wilful eccentricity and capriciousness." G. E. Lessing (1729–1781), Saintsbury continues, is acknowledged as great in his way, but he has, in focusing on drama, "fixed his main attention on the least literary parts of literature." Goethe, Lessing's successor in Germany, is certainly "great, but a great pedant," since his reputation stems from confusion about the difference between knowledge and judgment. Saintsbury concedes that, among British critics in the nineteenth century, Hazlitt, too, deserves to be considered "great," but in comparison with his "master," Coleridge, he is not unfairly dismissed as "insular and parochial in range and reading, if not in spirit." Similarly, in the critical writing of Charles Augustin Sainte-Beuve (1804–1869) "we want a little more theory; some more enthusiasm; a higher and more inspiring choice of subjects." Matthew Arnold (1822–1888), a close contemporary of Saintsbury's, is dispatched most tersely of all leading critics; in his writings "the defects of Fontenelle reappear without Fontenelle's excuse of chronology."[4]

It is, perhaps, of little consequence that, while T. S. Eliot (1888–1965) furthered Saintsbury's demotion of Enlightenment and nineteenth-century critics to antiquarian curios, he does not share his predecessor's enthusiasm for Coleridge. Eliot does, however, endorse the view that the function of criticism in the Romantic period was compromised by the importation of non-literary, that is, philosophical and biographical criteria. Aside from a few other differences of opinion, among them Eliot's intense admiration for Samuel Johnson, who does not appear on Saintbury's list of "great" critics, one perceives that they share a common vision of the function of criticism as primarily analysis of formal and structural features of the text. Indeed, because Coleridge's criticism embraces disciplines on the periphery of literature and "has tended to be something less than purely literary," Eliot confesses that he never thinks of him as a *literary* critic. With Coleridge

> criticism merges into philosophy and a theory of aesthetics; with Arnold it merges into ethics and propaedeutics, and literature becomes a means towards the formation of character. In some critics, of whom Pater is a specimen, the subject-matter of criticism becomes a pretext of another kind.[5]

Any examination of the forces that shaped British criticism and letters in the nineteenth century cannot properly begin before first coming to terms with Coleridge and his engagement with German culture. Despite his acknowledged and, more crucially for his post-Fruman reputation, unacknowledged debts to Kant, Schelling, and Friedrich Schlegel, Coleridge's interest in or awareness of the relationship between German philosophy and the imaginative creations of Goethe, Schiller, and their younger contemporaries is less apparent. One must turn to a critic of minor stature, such as Crabb Robinson, for an early, turn-of-the-century critique that anticipates Carlyle's argument that the new German and "European tendency" in thought and literature, which springs "from the general condition of intellect in Europe," is dominated by Kant and Goethe.[6] Perceptively, Noel Annan has argued that Carlyle's affinity for German thought justifies a radical realignment of nineteenth-century intellectual history. Whereas "Coleridge had little talent for abstract ideas, Carlyle was a genuinely original thinker . . . . It was not until historians related Carlyle to Wagner and Nietzsche, the heirs of German transcendentalism . . . that Carlyle could be seen at once a reactionary and a romantic."[7]

Coleridge's first lengthy exercise in cultural interaction, as a translator and mediator of one of the giants of German literature, has its origins in a lecture that the novelist and playwright Henry Mackenzie (1745–1831) presented at the Royal Society of Edinburgh on 21 April 1788. Speaking on the German *Schicksalsdramen* or "dramas of fate," Mackenzie gave birth to a vogue for German plays that took Britain by storm. Over the next decade the "German invasion" of the English popular stage, led by Kotzebue and Schiller, elicited a withering reaction from critics and reviewers. In the vanguard of the xenophobic press were the acid-tongued critics writing for *The Anti-Jacobin Review,* whose hostility toward German writers anticipated the conservative cultural criticism printed in Francis Jeffrey's conservative *Edinburgh Review* in the first quarter of the nineteenth century. Somewhat ironically, Jeffrey, as Carlyle's first editor, published his corrective criticism, which ridiculed British enthusiasm for Kotzebue and sought to direct it into more worthy channels—Goethe, Schiller, and Jean Paul Richter. It was in the charged atmosphere of politicized review criticism that a Romantic "culture war" broke out (which anticipated, in essential respects, the partisanship and the ad hominem tone of the "culture war" over poststructuralist theory during the 1980s) and Crabb Robinson's essays and Coleridge's first effort at translation, of Schiller's *Wallenstein,* made their appearance.

Overcome by prevailing critical prejudices, both writers' projects fell victim to bad timing. Crabb Robinson's pieces on Kant and Goethe—which proposed a fundamental realignment of canonical boundaries—challenged what the critical establishment was ready to accept. Coleridge, conversely, entered the field too late. By the time he had agreed to translate Schiller's *Wallenstein* the popular enthusiasm for German drama—which coincided with the Napoleonic Wars—had waned, to be replaced by a reactionary phase of retrenchment in British taste which "wasted and depressed" Coleridge's spirits and "left a sense of wearisomeness and disgust."[8] In a letter published in 1800 and addressed to the influential editor of *The Monthly Review,* Coleridge sought to exculpate himself for what a hostile reviewer blamed on an egregious lapse in taste, implying that the decision to publish his translation was purely practical:

> In the review of my translation of Schiller's *Wallenstein* I am numbered among the Partizans of the German Theatre. As I am confident there is no passage in my Preface or Notes from which such an opinion can be legitimately formed: and, as the truth would not have been exceeded, if the directly contrary had been affirmed, I claim it of your justice that in your answers to Correspondents you would remove this misrepresentation. The mere circumstance of translating a manuscript play is not even evidence that I admired that one play, much less that I am a general admirer of the plays in that language.[9]

Chapter Four: Resistance and Concealment 119

A similarly plaintive note is sounded in Coleridge's Preface to the third section of the play, *The Death of Wallenstein*:

> The admirers of Schiller, who has abstracted their conception of that author from the Robbers and Cabal and Love, plays in which the main interest produced by the excitement of curiosity and in which the curiosity if excited by terrible and extraordinary incident, will not have pursued without some portion of disappointment the dramas which it has been my employment to translate.[10]

Coleridge's mea culpas had a dual purpose—to disown this particular play and to justify his enraptured description of the early Schiller, uttered to Robert Southey at Cambridge, as a "convulser of the heart" more sublime than Milton.[11] These renunciatory gestures are full of consequence for the history of British criticism because they succeeded in sealing off the Anglo-American critical tradition from an important foreign influence, which nevertheless overtook an unprepared academic establishment when Jacques Derrida and Paul De Man leaped over the barricades in the late 1960s. Coleridge's disillusionment with *Wallenstein* and Schiller eventually spread to Goethe and German culture as a whole, and his public recantations reflect private misgivings about the translation that he had undertaken. In letters to Southey, Samuel Perkins, and Josiah Wedgwood, he expressed severe dissatisfaction with the play, frustration with his task as translator, and disillusionment with the original author's achievement:

> O this Translation is indeed a Bore—never, never, never, will I be so taken in again—Newspaper writing is comparative exstacy. In this engagement of translating the prolix Plays of Schiller I made too a very, very foolish bargain . . . . [O]f their success I have no hope—for I can say with truth, that I could have written a far better play myself in half the time . . . . Have you seen my translation of the *Wallenstein*? It is a dull heavy play.[12]

Coleridge reaped neither financial gain nor encouragement to continue in this line of work. And yet, while his *Wallenstein* did not awaken any measure of "artistic or intellectual response," years later it did become commercially "a lasting success, for this translation by Coleridge went on to become the standard version throughout the nineteenth century on both sides of the Atlantic."[13] The success of Coleridge's *Wallenstein* in the 1840s and throughout the second half of the nineteenth century was largely the result of an about face in the attitudes of British critics toward Schiller's dramatic innovations and German literature as a whole. This in turn led to a renewed interest in German drama reminiscent of the cultural scene fifty years before, with a signal difference: while the German craze of the 1790s was largely restricted to the sensationalism of the stage, the 1840s witnessed the beginning of a revolution in British intellectual life in which a renewed interest in German culture was emblematic of a more widespread phenomenon. Beginning with his essays on Schiller, Goethe, and Jean Paul, and culminating in his remarkable novel, *Sartor Resartus*, Carlyle's interest in German culture was transmitted to others, notably George Eliot, Matthew Arnold, and Walter Pater. The German cultural "invasion" of Britain resembles a similar process of appropriation in France after both World Wars, which was accomplished by the irresistible prestige, mystique, and influence of Friedrich Nietzsche and Martin Heidegger.

At first restricted to enthusiasm for German literature and reflected in the attempts of George Eliot, G. H. Lewes, and F. D. Maurice, among others, to produce "novels of education" on the model of *Wilhelm Meister* and *Sartor Resartus*, the impact of German ideas would eventually extend to innovations in philosophy, theology, historiography, literary criticism, and science. For example, a revolution in British academic philosophy was announced as Transcendental Idealism, assimilated in the work of T.H. Green (1836–1882), F.H. Bradley (1846–1924), Bernard Bosanquet (1848–1923), and J.M.E. McTaggert (1866–1925), taught the British mind the art of German metaphysical speculation. In theology the impact of David Friedrich Strauß (1808–1872) and Ludwig Feuerbach (1804–1872) was felt through the translations of George Eliot, whose interest in the latter was so intense that Feuerbach's de-mythification of Christianity—the distillation of its ethical content from the ontological status of the Incarnation replacing faith in the Supernatural with love, sympathy, and "a movement of the human heart"—inspired her first experiments in depicting the hidden motivations of the human heart in *Scenes of Clerical Life* (1857) and *Adam Bede* (1859). Contributions to historical scholarship by Henry Milman (1791–1868), Connop Thirlwall (1797–1875), Julius Hare (1795–1855), Thomas Arnold (1795–1842), and Arthur Stanley (1815–1881) reflect familiarity with the positivistic methodology of Barthold Georg Niebuhr (1776–1831) and Albert Eichhorn (1856–1926). Despite a national tendency toward adopting utilitarian solutions, Britain's assimilation of German scientific and aesthetic culture becomes the central concern of both Arnold and Pater. Indeed, Arnold's acknowledgement of Goethe as "the greatest critic . . . that has ever lived," represents one of the highwater marks in the assimilation of German culture in Britain.[14] In other fields, the dominance of German ideas is also felt. In his discussion of Hegel's *Vorlesungen über die Ästhetik* [*Lectures on Aesthetics*] (1818, 1820/21, 1823, 1826, 1828/29) and K.W.F. Solger's *Vorlesungen über Ästhetik* [*Lectures on Aesthetics*] (1829), which were as fresh and challenging in their day as Carlyle's essays on Goethe, Novalis, and Jean Paul twenty-five years earlier, Lewes introduced post-Kantian aesthetics to the English-speaking world.[15]

But to return to the starkly different cultural landscape of the early nineteenth century, Coleridge's gloomy predictions for the reception of his translation of *Wallenstein* proved sadly accurate, and his embarrassment was so profound that it brought on a reverse "conversion experience."[16] Even though Coleridge, like William Taylor and Thomas Holcroft, started his literary career as a champion of German literature and thus a cultural and political insurgent, the failure of *Wallenstein* transformed him to a conservative defender of the British literary canon free of foreign influence.[17] This is the context out of which Coleridge's animus against Goethe emerged and it provides clues to his motivation for plagiarizing Kant, Fichte, Schelling, and others.[18] By illicitly appropriating the work of German authors and claiming their accomplishments for his own, Coleridge was falsely asserting that Britain was the creative center of post-Enlightenment European culture.

The same high canonical considerations inspired Coleridge and Wordsworth's journey to the German states, which was the scene of one of the greatest missed opportunities in literary history. Coleridge, in the company of William and his sister Dorothy, set sail for Germany in 1798, two years before Crabb Robinson, twelve years after Goethe's return to Weimar from Italy, and seven years before the death of Schiller—the blossom time of Weimar culture and the height of Goethe's fame as a *Dichterfürst* [poet prince]. Despite a lengthy sojourn, their contact with German writers of any note was limited to two meetings—one with the elderly Klopstock, who no longer represented the leading tendency of German culture and had just five more years to live, and another meeting with Christian Gottlob Heyne (1729–1821), the Göttingen philologist, whom Carlyle later praised as the counterpart to archeologist Johann Joachim Winckelmann (1717–1786), with whom he resuscitated the literature of antiquity in the spirit of the modern world, but whose impact on the interpretation of antiquity was ultimately far less influential than Goethe's or Schiller's creative and critical writings. Of course, one might excuse even a missed opportunity of such magnitude with the observation that the German literary world at the close of the eighteenth century was in flux. From this perspective, perhaps, Coleridge and Wordsworth's decision to meet with Klopstock (inspired, perhaps, by Goethe himself, who situates Klopstock in *Werther* at the flashpoint of Lotte's and Werther's mutual attraction) might seem as no disgrace. And yet, it is instructive to compare Coleridge and Wordsworth's obliviousness to the presence of Goethe in nearby Weimar with the awareness of Goethe's centrality in radical and Dissenting circles, as evidenced by the publication of Helen Maria Williams's novel *Julia* (1790), along with a whole host of lesser Wertheriads in the last quarter of the eighteenth century, and the near-contemporaneous presence of Crabb Robinson in Weimar. There were also countless translations of *Faust* circulating in Britain and Ireland, the reviewing activity by William Taylor, and the accompanying attacks by conservative journalists, all of which served to foreground Goethe in the collective literary psyche even as Coleridge and Wordsworth met with Klopstock. This bizarre misstep might be explained by other causes—their affinity for the older generation of German writers, and opposition to the revolutionary *avant-garde*, or, perhaps, most likely, their resistance to the dominating influence of Goethe. Travel to Germany as a vehicle of self-cultivation for Dissenters and Jacobins has not been fully appreciated until now. A pilgrimage to Weimar represented an important variant on the "Grand Tour." No mere capstone of a gentleman's education, such a journey embodied an appropriation of the German institution of the *Bildungsreise*: it is travel as an exercise in acquiring an education unavailable to Dissenters and other outsiders in existing British institutions. In appropriating German culture these pilgrims and exiled poets, critics, and novelists drank at the spring of a cultural tradition alien to their own, but it was immensely empowering. The most significant encounter on these pilgrimages was with the "other" as represented by Goethe.

It is nonetheless surpassingly strange that Taylor and Crabb Robinson knew what they were doing when they ventured to Weimar,[19] and that Holcroft wrote directly to Goethe and received a critique of his translation of *Hermann und Dorothea* in reply, while the greatest critic and the foremost poet of the Romantic generation tarried in Klopstock's garden! What might have resulted in a memorable exchange of ideas with the older poet actually never rose much above a farce. In a letter to Thomas Poole dated 20 November 1798 Coleridge described the extraordinary moment during which Wordsworth's French had to serve as the medium of communication between the author of *Der Messias* [*The Messiah*] (1773) and Coleridge, who, because of insecurity about his German, was forced to speak in Latin:

> [Klopstock] was lively, kind and courteous. He talked in French with Wordsworth—& with difficulty, spoke a few sentences to me in English.—We were with him somewhat more than an hour. He began the conversation by expressing his rapture, in a very voluble [sic] utterance, at the surrender of the French in Ireland .... The subject changed to Poetry—& I enquired, in Latin, concerning the history of German poetry .... He answered in French, & Wordsworth interpreted it to me.[20]

In Coleridge's description of this strange encounter with the writer whom he considered "the venerable Father of German poetry," Wieland and Schiller are mentioned, but Goethe, incredibly, is not. Coleridge mentions Klopstock's high regard for Wieland and his generational hatred of Schiller and Kant. The omission of Goethe is puzzling; his absence is palpable:

> Wordsworth [Coleridge, with his linguistic handicap, returns to the role of the auditor] had a long and various Conversation on Literature with Klopstock . . . . [H]e spoke in high terms of Wieland, as the greatest master of the German language. . . . He spoke with the keenest *contempt* of Schiller's Productions; and said, they could not retain their fame many years.—Of Kant he said, that he was a Mountebank & the Disgrace of Germany—an unintelligible Jargonist.—And that his New Lights were going out very fast in Germany.[21]

Apparently unknown to Coleridge, Wieland and Schiller were still active in Weimar, where they belonged to the constellation of geniuses assembled by Goethe and supported by the patronage of Grand Duke Karl August, leader of what was perhaps the smallest culturally influential state in European history.

The interview with Klopstock, as recorded by Coleridge, constitutes a strange detour, an anti-pilgrimage or farcical parody of the pilgrimages of Taylor, Lewis, Crabb Robinson, the American George Bancroft (1800–1891), and others to Weimar. Rather than acknowledge the "new gods" of culture who had taken up residence in Weimar, Coleridge and Wordsworth's visit with Klopstock represents, as a statement of cultural politics, an identification with the poetic canon represented by "old gods" of pre-Revolutionary culture.

While Coleridge boasted of plans to write a study of Goethe, Wordsworth expressed little interest in knowing Goethe in any way. But even light acquaintance with the German language, in an age of few decent translations, did not inhibit him from voicing strong opinions of Goethe's works. As James Simpson has pointed out, Wordsworth's "comments on Goethe are as virulent and unpleasant as any that one encountered in the nineteenth century" and are wholly concerned with the author's supposed moral lapses:

> There is a profligacy, an inhuman sensuality, in his works which is utterly revolting. I am not intimately acquainted with them generally. But I take up my ground on the first canto of Wilhelm Meister, and as the attorney general of human nature, I there indict him for wantonly outraging the sympathies of humanity.²²

Crabb Robinson, who respected Coleridge's learning and seemed to accept his views of Goethe with something like resignation, reacted to Wordsworth's criticism of Goethe with understandable impatience. Dining with Wordsworth and Thomas Arnold in 1835, Crabb Robinson reported afterwards that he did not enjoy the remarks that Wordsworth made about Goethe, "whom he deprecates in utter ignorance. Dr. Arnold seems to be aware of the real objections of Goethe's moral character and is likely to overrate their importance."²³ Again, Wordsworth's objections are expressed in the form of a conflict between the ethical and the aesthetic. Rumored transgressions in the former sphere were deemed extreme enough to disqualify Goethe from high rank as a writer.

By contrast with Coleridge and Wordsworth, who seemed without a cultural compass, Crabb Robinson arrived in Germany with introductions provided by Taylor, who had earlier made his own formative pilgrimage or *Bildungsreise* to Weimar. As we have seen, Crabb Robinson's subsequent friendship with the gifted Brentano siblings shaped his itinerary, his social contacts, and his reading. Additional personal encounters with leading German intellectuals encouraged Crabb Robinson to study Kant, Goethe, and Schelling long before Coleridge did the same. Indeed, while Coleridge was still preoccupied with collecting materials for a "Life of Lessing"—like Klopstock, Lessing was another literary hero from an earlier era— Crabb Robinson had already registered for Schelling's lectures at the University of Jena, an institution revitalized by Goethe and Schiller, and had become a frequent guest at the author's distinctive yellow house on the *Frauenplan* in Weimar.

Coleridge's plan for a "Life of Lessing," formulated at the precise moment when German literature and science, philosophy and history, music and scholarship were undergoing a rebirth that would wield tremendous influence throughout the century and beyond, seems as strangely anachronistic as the visit with Klopstock. In a letter to Thomas Poole dated 4 January 1799 Coleridge offered a typically exaggerated account of the work he had already done on the "Life of Lessing" (no trace of this manuscript has survived) and of recent measures undertaken to combat his resistance to working; his insight into his paralysis is fascinating and it comes many years before his total breakdown:

> The work I have planned—& I have imperiously excluded all waverings about other works—:That is the disease of my mind—it is comprehensive in its conceptions & wastes itself in the contemplations of the many things which it might do!—I am aware of the disease, & for the next three months, if I cannot cure it I will at least suspend its operation.

As the letter continues Coleridge then states his intention to combine his proposed "Life of Lessing" with "a true state of German literature, in its rise and present state."[24] Five months later, in a letter to his patron, the pottery magnate Josiah Wedgwood (1730–1795) who was sponsoring the trip to Germany, Coleridge describes his projects with typical panache and exaggeration, in a tone, partly fawning, partly bragging, reminiscent of a hastily written grant report:

> What have I done in Germany?—I have learnt the language . . . . I have read & made collections for an history of the Belles Lettres in Germany before the time of Lessing . . . [and] very large collections for a Life of Lessing;—to which I was led by the miserably bald & unsatisfying Biographies that have been hitherto given, & by my personal acquaintance with two of Lessing's Friends [Klopstock and Heyne?].[25]

Considering Coleridge's avoidance of meaningful contacts with the most famous German intellectuals, it is not surprising that he did not finish this ambitious study. It would be difficult not to determine that Coleridge's "study abroad" funding to Germany was ill spent and that on the basis of this report, the fellowship would not be renewed. As things turned out, the British public would wait nearly thirty years before Carlyle would provide an extensive and discriminating critique of German literature of the *Goethezeit*.

On 15 November 1810, a decade following Coleridge's return from Germany, Crabb Robinson quotes Coleridge, who now seems to hold an opinion of Goethe, albeit a starkly negative one: "He conceded to Goethe universal talent, but felt a want of moral life to be the defect of his poetry." Amplifying this point two years later, Coleridge, as Crabb Robinson notes following a meeting with Coleridge and Wordsworth on 29 May 1812, "denied merit to [Goethe's play] *Torquato Tasso* [first performed in 1807], and talked of the improbability of being a good poet without being a good man, adducing at the same time the immoral tendency of Goethe's works. To this I demurred."[26] It becomes apparent in further conversations with Crabb Robinson that Coleridge's attitude toward Goethe varied. On the appearance of a new edition of *Faust*, Coleridge acknowledged "the genius of Goethe in a manner he never did before." And yet, as in the past, "the want of religion and enthusiasm [code words for conservative reaction] in Goethe" remains "in Coleridge's mind an irreparable defect." Also, he faulted the beginning of *Faust* for what he considered the inadequately developed character of Mephistopheles. Because Goethe fails, in his opinion, to offer a convincing explanation for the "state of mind which led to the catastrophe," he considers the character of Faust is not *motivirt* [motivated]." Concerning Coleridge's plan to surpass Goethe by writing "a new Faust," Crabb Robinson—familiar with Coleridge's penchant for planning new projects that never came to fruition—was pretty certain that "he would never get out of vague conceptions—he would lose himself in dreams."[27]

There are, of course, important antecedents for Coleridge's overly fastidious reaction to Goethe and the long tradition in British literature of moralizing criticism, which, echoing Quintilian's profoundly influential *Institutio Oratoria*, considers literary excellence as a reflection of the personal morality of the poet. The impact of Quintilian on Coleridge was felt via Sir Thomas Elyot's *The Governour* (1531), Thomas Wilson's *Arte of Rhetorique* (1562), and Ben Jonson's *Timber: or, Discoveries upon Men and Matter* (1640), not to mention the controversy over the immorality of German writers that centered upon Goethe in the British popular press and which was led by the xenophobic critics of *The Anti-Jacobin Review*. Coleridge's perfunctory disapproval is, in fact, so close in tone to the reactionary rhetoric of the conservative press that it has a party line feel to it. At other times Coleridge's objections to Goethe were based on purely literary and aesthetic grounds, which he attempted on several occasions to clarify and to defend. For example, on 2 March 1813, Crabb Robinson describes Coleridge's attempt "to rank Goethe as a poet." Similar to the pattern of development later articulated by Carlyle, Coleridge "distinguishes the early and mature phases of Goethe's career and clearly prefers the early works." According to Crabb Robinson's transcription, Coleridge "thought Goethe had, from a sort of caprice, underrated the talent which in his youth he had so eminently displayed in his *Werther*, that of exhibiting man in a state of exalted sublimity." In contrast to his early manner, the later Goethe, Coleridge complained, "delighted to exhibit . . . purely beautiful objects, not objects of desire and passion . . . as a statuary does a succession of marble figures."[28] As a result, "Coleridge called Goethe *picturesque*."[29]

A week after he had voiced his displeasure with Goethe's sacrilegious tendencies in *Faust*, Coleridge boasted to Crabb Robinson of his intention to write "a new Faust," which he would supply a properly reverent moral tone.[30] A few years later the impulse to revise Goethe is manifested again in connection with *Zur Farbenlehre* [*Toward a Doctrine of Colors*] (1810). Clearly, envy of Goethe's many-sided achievement in literature and science, more than any real moral qualms, accounted for Coleridge's disapproval of the poet prince. Unlike Goethe, whose studies of optics, osteology, plant morphology, geology—to name just a few of his interests—yielded publications and influenced a number of Anglophone science-oriented intellectuals, including G.H. Lewes, Charles Darwin, and Henry David Thoreau (1817–1862)—Coleridge's many ambitious projects and schemes and designs generally came to nothing. During a conversation with Crabb Robinson on 4 July 1816 Coleridge "talked about Goethe's work on the theory of colors" and made the astonishing claim that "some years back," he had "discovered the same theory and would certainly have reduced it to form and published it, had not Southey diverted his attention from such studies as poetry."[31] The man from Porlock strikes again![32] A year later, in a letter to Crabb Robinson dated 4 July 1816, Coleridge, who was still apparently preoccupied with *Zur Farbenlehre* and chafing under Goethe's influence, unveiled his intention to publish a study of Goethe that, like so many of his projects (including the aborted "Life of Lessing"), never materialized:

> As this is the very work I am now taking in hand and shall send to the press within a week after my second sermon [*Lay Sermons* (1816)] is out—namely on Goethe as poet and philosopher with a biographical critical analysis of his writings with translations.[33]

For no apparent cause, after articulating bold plans and great enthusiasm for the sage of Weimar, Coleridge's attitude towards Goethe slipped back into moral disapproval. In June 1824, for instance, Crabb Robinson met Coleridge at the home of the essayist Charles Lamb (1775–1834) and recorded his conversation. In a manner reminiscent of William Taylor, who three decades earlier had placed Wieland and Schiller ahead of Goethe, Coleridge "set Goethe far below Schiller, allowing no other merit than that of exquisite taste." Indeed, he reiterated "his favorite reproach," the overemphasis on aesthetics, namely, that "Goethe wrote from an idea that a certain thing was to be in a certain style, not from the fullness of sentiment on a certain subject." Coleridge also took a swipe at the multitalented poet and cultural philosopher Johann Gottfried Herder (1744–1803), whom he called "a coxcomb" and affirmed his conviction that Goethe is "utterly unprincipled." As a contemporary of Novalis and of Clemens and Bettina Brentano, a frequent guest of Goethe's, and more deeply read in the works of Goethe than any British critic before Carlyle, Crabb Robinson disputed this characterization of Goethe as more concerned with art than morality. On the same occasion at Charles Lamb's house, Crabb Robinson met the famous preacher, Edward Irving (1792–1834). Observing that the conversation revolved around Goethe, Irving mentioned that a young friend and fellow Scot, Thomas Carlyle, had coincidentally just completed a translation of *Wilhelm Meister's Apprenticeship*.[34] This novel is the one later work of Goethe's that elicited Coleridge's approval. More than ten years previously, on 20 March 1813, Crabb Robinson found Coleridge at John Flaxman's house "enraptured" with *Wilhelm Meister*. Despite considering "the conclusion very bad" and the death of Mignon and the incidents in the castle "unworthy of the exquisite early parts," he recited "Kennst Du das Land" ["Do You Know the Land Where the Lemon Trees Bloom"] "with tears in his eyes and he praised the 'Song of the Harper' which Walter Scott told Coleridge was the original of his Minstrel in the Lay."[35]

Despite claims of authoritative familiarity with Goethe's works as well oft-repeated intentions to write the first critical study of Goethe in English, Coleridge's privately expressed misgivings concerning Goethe's alleged preoccupation with aesthetic matters which involved little more than a repetition of the charges levelled against him in Taylor's *An Historic Survey of German Poetry* (1828–1830). (These, in turn, had echoed the anti-German attacks printed in *The Anti-Jacobin Review*.) It is indeed puzzling that Goethe should have been so misunderstood and unappreciated by British contemporaries who had identified themselves as revolutionaries of the intellect and imagination.[36] Especially curious is the cause of their disapproval—Goethe's eroticism and supposed immorality. It is also puzzling that the qualities prized in Goethe by his admirers—universality, naturalism, and flouting of social conventions—are the same ones attacked as indecorous by leading British Romantics such as Coleridge, Wordsworth, Hazlitt, and De Quincey.

Shelley and Byron

Percy Bysshe Shelley (1792–1822) and George Gordon Byron (1788–1824) responded to Goethe in a receptive and creative manner that marks a startling contrast with the first generation of Romantic poets. "Scenes from the *Faust* of Goethe" (1822, 1824), translated by Shelley, reflects more than mere affinity for Goethe's drama.[37] This work also reveals the grounds for conflict between Shelley and his older contemporaries; a conflict, as described by Arnold, that pitted

Chapter Four: Resistance and Concealment   131

Shelley's passion for applying "the modern spirit in English literature" against the "Philistinism" and an "inveterate inaccessibility to ideas" which characterized British Romanticism as a whole.[38] Somewhat paradoxically, Shelley's "modern" instincts place him closer to "the main stream of modern literature" represented by Goethe and Heinrich Heine than to Wordsworth, Scott, and Keats, all of whom, in Arnold's comparison, ultimately "constitute minor currents" because "they do not apply modern ideas to life." Conversely, Shelley and Byron, will

> long be remembered, long after the inadequacy of their actual work is clearly recognized, for their passionate, Titanic effort to flow in the main stream of modern literature; their names will be greater than their writings; *stat magni nominis umbra* [he stands, the shadow of a great name].[39]

Shelley's "re-writing" of *Faust* emerged during the intensely emotional crucible that was the final year of his life. Shelley revealed his interest in the German poem in a letter to John and Maria Gisborne dated 31 July 1821 in which he ponders whether *Faust, Part I*, an edition of which was published in 1808 and which he had been reading, has exerted any discernible influence on his own most recent creations. Shelley also expresses impatience for the publication of the long-awaited conclusion of Goethe's poem, which would not appear until a decade after his death:

> I will only remind you of Faust; my desire for the conclusion of which is only exceeded by my desire to welcome you. Do you observe any traces of him in the poem I send you? Poets—the best of them, are a very chameleonic race; they take the colour not only of what they feed on, but of the very leaves under which they pass.[40]

During the Pisan winter of 1822, his last, Shelley, in another letter to Gisborne, enthuses over a set of "astonishing etchings ... from a German master," Friedrich Moritz Retsch (1779–1857). These were illustrations for the first English edition of *Faust* (1821), which has been controversially identified as the supposedly nonexistent translation by Coleridge.[41] Shelley considers the artist worthy of Goethe: "The meeting of him [Faust] and Margaret is wonderful. It makes all the pulses of my head beat—those of my heart have been quiet long ago." Shelley's disappointment, conversely, in the accompanying translation of the poem is acute. It is, in short, "miserable." He entreats his friend to "[a]sk Coleridge if [its] stupid misintelligence of the deep wisdom and harmony of the author does not open him to action."[42] Coleridge was nearly universally considered the proper man for the job, but he was not recognized as the fabricator of the anonymously published translation.

Shelley's remarks on *Faust* open with a description of the effect that the poem has on him. He felt "sensations which no other composition excites. It deepens the gloom and augments the rapidity of ideas." He considers *Faust* "an unfit study for any person who is prey to the reproaches of memory, and the delusions of an imagination not to be restrained." But the pain that results from reflecting on Goethe's poem is balanced by the "pleasure of sympathising with emotions known only to few." Putting it another way, Shelley suggests that "discontent with the less . . . supposes the sense of a just claim to the greater, and that we admirers of *Faust* are on the right road to Paradise." Shelley then compares the two works that he has been engaged in translating, *Faust* and Pedro Calderón's Spanish Faust-drama *Magico Prodigioso* (1637)—the latter was intended for Gisborne's journal: "I find a striking similarity between Faust and this drama, and if I were to acknowledge Coleridge's distinction, should say Goethe was the greatest *philosopher*, and Calderon the *greatest* poet." Shelley, however, laments the difficulties involved in translating *Faust*: "I feel how imperfect a representation, even with all the license I assume to figure to myself how Goethe would have written in English, my words convey." Apparently oblivious to Coleridge's deep anxiety with regard to Goethe, he reiterates the unintentionally ironic opinion that "no one but Coleridge is capable of this work."[43]

Shelley's last recorded comments on *Faust* contain an direct allusion to Faust's exclamation at the sight of Gretchen (line 1699) — "Verweile doch! Du bist so schön!" He describes an evening on the Bay of Spezia that was similarly charged with erotic anticipation and transgression—an allusion to Jane's status as a married woman: "[The] earth appears another world. Jane brings her guitar, and if the past and future could be obliterated, the present would content me so well that I could say with Faust to the passing moment 'Remain thou, thou art so beautiful.'"[44]

Byron's Creative Appropriation of *Faust*

Relations between Byron and Goethe were conducted through intermediaries and included an exchange of notes and a few admiring reciprocal winks: Byron's blank verse dramas *Sardanapalus* (1821) and *Werner* (1822) are both dedicated to "The Illustrious Goethe." Euphorion, the offspring of Faust's union with Helen of Troy and the symbol of reconciliation between Classicism and Romanticism (in *Faust, Part II*), is a representation of Byron, whom Goethe claimed to esteem more than any other contemporary writer. But the most important and problematic of these gestures is one that Byron vehemently denied: the revisionary appropriation that resulted in the dramatic poem *Manfred* (1817). The points of resemblance in *Manfred* (as a creative redaction) to *Faust* are, of course, obvious and undeniable. Despite the unmistakable intertextual relationship between the two texts, what is of real significance is Byron's denial of filial debt to Goethe, the father figure and the progenitor of Romantic culture. The imputed obligation was nonetheless not lost on Goethe who interpreted Byron's action as a genuine compliment. In a letter to the poet Karl Ludwig von Knebel Goethe remarks that "ein junger Amerikaner" [a young American], George Bancroft—the future educator, historian, statesman, and founder of the U.S. Naval Academy—hand-delivered a copy of *Manfred* to him in Weimar. Goethe's public acknowledgement of Byron's tribute appeared in an issue of the journal *Über Kunst und Altertum* [*On Art and Antiquity*], the gist of which is captured in the aforementioned letter to Knebel, dated 13 October 1817:

> Dieser seltsame geistreiche Dichter hat meinem Faust in sich aufgenommen und für seine Hypochondrie die seltsamste Nahrung daraus gezogen. Er hat alle Motive auf seine Weise benutzt, so daß keine mehr daßelbige ist, und gerade deshalb kann ich seinen Geist nicht genug bewundern. Diese Umbildung ist so

aus dem Ganzen, daß man darüber und über die Ähnlichkeit und Unähnlichkeit mit dem Original höchst interessante Vorlesungen halten könnte.[45]

These observations, in turn, prompted an admission (written on 25 May 1820) from Byron, who confesses to his publisher John Murray, that he was somewhat crushed and perplexed by the attribute "hypochondrisch" [hypochondriacal]. Byron hated being caught out as a "re-writer" of *Faust* and he takes Goethe's remarks—consistent with his famous remark recorded by Eckermann that "the Romantic" is "sickly"—as constituting a bad review:

> [I]f I may judge by two notes of admiration . . . and the 'hypochondrisch' are anything but favorable.—I shall regret this—for I should have been proud of Goethe's good word—[but] I shan't alter my opinion of him even though he should be savage.[46]

Like a bone that he could not stop gnawing, and as evidence of how profoundly in Coleridgean denial he was about his own "creative appropriations" from Goethe, just two weeks later, in another letter to Murray, Byron revisits Goethe's opinion of *Manfred*. He now seems reconciled to Goethe's characterization of his work's being the embodiment of "Hypochondrie," having come to the conclusion that it was a positive mark of esteem. Expanding on an earlier letter to Murray on 12 October 1817, he now seeks also self-defensively to correct Goethe's impression that *Faust* was the model for *Manfred*. Byron begins, however, by congratulating himself on coming to Goethe's attention in the first place. "Whether favorable or not," he argues, "the opinions of such a man . . . the Greatest man of Germany—perhaps of Europe . . . are always interesting." Then he distances himself, formulaically, from any presumption of indebtedness to *Faust*, albeit not very convincingly. First, Byron denies emphatically that he had even *read* the poem, "for I don't know German." What he does admit to is a transparent dodge: "Monk" Lewis did translate *Faust* to him "viva voce" in 1816 at Coligny. Byron also admits to having been "naturally much struck with it." Nonetheless, he insists, "it was the sublime landscape featuring the peaks of the *Staubach* and the *Jungfrau*—and something else [no doubt here as to what he means—a romantic attachment]—much more than Faustus that made me write Manfred." He seems to have convinced himself that it was a mere coincidence that "the first scene" in his poem and that of *Faust* are "very similar."[47] There is, at least, a beguiling charm to Byron's statements of denial, but the effort to escape his fate as a mere Bloomian "ephebe" rather than a "strong poet" in his own right is manifested in this and all of Byron's comments on *Faust*.

One of the last letters Byron wrote before his death was composed in response to a hand-written note from Goethe, a true rarity, since almost all of his correspondence was dictated to a secretary (whose painfully indecipherable hand is familiar to scholars who have worked at the Goethe-und Schiller-Archiv in Weimar). In his reply, Byron expresses his utmost respect for the writer, "who for 50 years has been the undisputed Sovereign of European literature," and reiterates his unfulfilled intention to visit Weimar:

> I could not have had a more favorable Omen or more agreeable surprise than a word from Goethe written by his own hand. —I am returning to Greece to see if I can be of any use there; if ever I come back I will pay a visit to Weimar to offer the sincere homage of one of many Millions of your admirers.[48]

Shelley and Byron, however united they were in wishing to be identified as leading British poets, reacted in markedly different ways to the challenge posed by Goethe to contemporary poets in the Anglophone world. Shelley was a willing participant in the "pre-" and "re-writing" paradigm that was sketched out in Chapter One. Byron, by contrast, took umbrage at the idea that *Manfred* was nothing but a metaphrastic encomium to *Faust*. Like Coleridge, he had taken pains to conceal any direct knowledge of Goethe's poem. But the main difference between Shelley and Byron's response to Goethe is, ultimately, this: Shelley consciously acknowledged his participation in the process of Goethean self-formation when he translated *Faust, Part One*. Despite Byron's protestations at the time that *Manfred* owed nothing Goethe's paternal text, it is impossible to ignore the resemblance between *Manfred* and *Faust, Part One*. In the end, Byron's effort to evade or skip a stage in his filial literary development—that of being a "re-writer"—must be judged a failure, if an artistically satisfying one.

What is also distinctive about Byron's relationship to Goethe is that it was not one sided; their mutual admiration was genuine and Goethe was uninhibited in sharing his enthusiasm for Byron with anyone within earshot. Compared to Coleridge and Wordsworth, then, Shelley and Byron were fully conversant with the literary fashions and the cultural leaders of the times. But their advantage was not merely a matter of twenty years' growth in Goethe's renown for, as we know, there was no more famous literary celebrity in Europe than Goethe following the publication of *Werther* in 1774. Shelley was, of course, less anxious about acknowledging Goethe's influence than Byron. He did not hesitate to recognize Goethe as a classic, a master, and a literary father figure. Byron, by contrast, was torn between honoring Goethe as a living classic and asserting his independence from the seemingly irresistible influence of the sage of Weimar. And Goethe's self-confidence was more than adequate enough to permit him to promote Byron as *the* literary phenomenon of the age.

The major difference between the first and the second-generation Romantic poets' views pertaining to Goethe is one of degrees of cultural openness, on the one hand, and degrees of cultural resistance or anxiety, on the other. Coleridge and Wordsworth avoided Goethe and the cultural Mecca that was Weimar because they were heavily invested in a construction of the literary canon, in which Klopstock played the role of the venerable but feeble anachronism and they represented what was new and strong. To acknowledge Goethe as the dominant force in contemporary European cultural life, as Holcroft, Crabb Robinson, the American visitors from Harvard, and Shelley and Byron did, would have forced Coleridge and Wordsworth to revise not only their personal narrative of literary history, but also their places in it. The assertion of such cultural myopia, especially when Weimar was just a day's carriage ride from Coleridge's rooms in Göttingen, discloses itself as nothing more, and nothing less, than an effort at maintaining their cultural autonomy. Visiting the elderly Klopstock, whose writings are cast in a totally outdated poetic idiom, involved no risk to Coleridge and Wordsworth, but they feared, no doubt with good reason, as revealed in Byron's experience with *Manfred*, that Goethe's modern voice threatened to colonize their own.

Chapter Five
Thomas Carlyle and the *Imitatio* Goethe

> "He is the man in whom for the first time there dawned the consciousness that human life is man's struggle with his intimate and individual destiny—that is, that human life is made up of the problem of itself, that its substance consists not in something that already *is* but in something which has to make itself, which, therefore, is not a *thing* but an absolute and problematical task."
>
> José Ortega y Gasset[1]

A major focus of Thomas Carlyle's formative early period is his critique of Goethe. In exchange for the perceived failure of British Romanticism to provide adequate cultural leadership, Carlyle offers an interpretation of Goethe as a cultural icon and vehicle of transcendence for adoption and emulation. The "cult of personality" that emerges in Carlyle's essays on Goethe forms the keystone in the arch of his critical and aesthetic ideology. By privileging the author's personality above the created text Carlyle's approach suggests parallels with what Ludwig Marcuse (1894–1971), the prominent exiled critic and associate of the Frankfurt School, identified as the "reactionary" element in German Romanticism.[2] Moreover, Carlyle's dismissal of politics as a vehicle for reform forms a bridge between his thought and German Romanticism. In significant ways, Carlyle's mediation of Goethe resembles the position taken by Heinrich Heine as well as and August Wilhelm Schlegel—full of awe, seeking approval, and ready to interpret Goethe as an oracle. Carlyle's "Goethe," like Heine's "Goethe" or the Schlegel brothers' "Goethe," is the product of cultural interaction and the projection of idiosyncratic personal concerns onto a broader cultural canvas.

Because Carlyle endowed the poet Goethe with the status and charisma of a prophet David Riede argues that he "never doubted that the true church of literature could be restored."[3] But it is, indeed, a curious matter that Carlyle looked to Germany rather than to Britain for redemptive cultural heroes. Therefore, before inserting Carlyle's critique of Goethe in its broad European context, it is first necessary to assess some of the key ways in which Carlyle's intellectual orientation conflicted with that of the Romantic generation in Britain and led him to turn to German writers for an alternate source of cultural authority and personal validation.

Contrasting intellectual orientations divided Carlyle from the British Romantics. These opposing ideological positions are represented by Jean-Jacques Rousseau and William Godwin, patron saints of revolutionary radicalism, on the one hand, and Goethe, who was equally skeptical of utopianism and the Jena transcendentalists, on the other.[4] Even though there are superficial parallels between Carlyle's "almost obsessive" interest in a living poet—Goethe—and John Keats's complex relationship with Wordsworth (the contemporary poet in Britain who approached Goethe in stature[5]), Carlyle had little else in common with his nearly exact contemporary. Besides Wordsworth, the literary authorities with whom Keats wrestled were the long-deceased Shakespeare and Milton. By contrast, Carlyle engaged most intensely with living or only recently deceased writers such as Schiller and Jean Paul (1763–1825).

Like Coleridge, Carlyle followed Ariadne's thread to Germany, where he found both intellectual liberation and replacements for the broken idols of Enlightenment rationalism.[6] Perhaps their shared background (before Coleridge turned to orthodox Christianity in later years) as religious outsiders in mainstream Anglican society explains their readiness to adopt an intellectual tradition that clashed so vehemently with British empiricism. Notwithstanding T. S. Eliot's view that Coleridge's omnivorous intellectual appetite diminishes his value as a critic, there is no denying the importance of the resulting cross-fertilization between British and German culture for the development of Anglo-American criticism.[7] From their contact with transcendental idealism Coleridge and Carlyle acquired philosophical depth and then, after serving their intellectual apprenticeship under German masters, they served successively as "sage" of British letters. Other Teutophiles who gained prominence in the nineteenth-century include George Eliot, G. H. Lewes, and, especially, Matthew Arnold, who quotes Goethe in nearly all of his critical essays. While Coleridge and Carlyle are of two minds concerning Goethe, they do concur in their high regard for Schiller.[8] In fact, Coleridge's ecstatic response to the former's play *The Robbers* (1781) conveys an almost illicit thrill of discovery:

> 'Tis past one o'clock in the morning—I sate down at 12 o'clock to read the "Robbers" of Schiller—I had read chill and trembling until I came to the part where Moor fires a pistol over the Robbers who are asleep—I could read no more— My God! Southey! Who is this Schiller? This Convulser of the Heart? Did he write this Tragedy amid the yelling of Fiends? . . . Why have we ever called Milton sublime?[9]

In Carlyle's biography of Schiller, his first book-length publication, one encounters sublimity, too, but the experience is recollected, so to speak, in tranquility:

> What gives him a place of his own . . . is the vastness and intense vigour of his mind; the splendour of his thoughts and imagery, and the bold vehemence of his passion for the true the sublime. He does not thrill, but he exalts us. His genius is impetuous, exuberant, majestic; and a heavenly fire gleams through all his creation. He transports us to a higher and loftier world than our own; everything around us breathes of force and solemn beauty.[10]

Despite their shared enthusiasm for Schiller, Carlyle stood apart from Coleridge because he could accept neither a resurgent Church nor an increasingly inclusive parliamentary democracy as guarantors of a British cultural rebirth. In his mind these institutions offered "only the illusion of a means, since they minister to the imagination in a diseased manner."[11] In 1823 he confides in his notebook: "my case is this: I comport myself wholly like an alien,—like a man who is not in his own country; whose own country lies perhaps a century or two distant."[12] On another occasion he observed, in a mixture of English and his adopted language, that he was "an *abgerissenes Glied*, a limb torn from the family of Man."[13] Even in later years, when fame and economic security were assured, Carlyle could still write that his work was produced by "a wild man, a man disunited from the fellowship of the world he lives in."[14] Such feelings were derived from the recognition that as an impoverished Scot, whose early career was devoted to mediating a co-extensive but competing Romantic tradition in Germany, he was twice alienated from the dominant culture where he sought to make his name as a writer.

It is indeed ironic how this consummate outsider acquired his enormous wealth of cultural capital. Sensing that the appetite of the British public to submit to a cultural and spiritual leader could not be met by the producers of domestic high culture, in its place he offered an idiosyncratic interpretation of German literature and its leading representative. Carlyle's mediation of Goethe represents an effort to solve the dilemma described by Chris Vanden Bossche as "how to author a belief to replace the faith in which he could no longer believe." The lost faith of his childhood was replaced by Goethe's redemptive cultural authority.[15] "Witnessing" for Goethe as a cultural messiah thus guided the aesthetic mission disclosed in the essays and translations that he published between 1824 and 1832.[16]

One of the chief reasons for Carlyle's affinity for Goethe was the latter's aristocratic disdain for parliamentary democracy and the capacity for meliorative legislation to correct social injustice. Carlyle's response to the Reform Bill of 1832 is fairly typical of his attitude: "Vain hope to make mankind happy by Politics!"[17] Emulating Goethe's teaching on the unavoidable presence of evil in the economy of existence, he believed that a fundamental balance between the forces of good and evil is necessary. With philosophical disinterest he observes

> that Evil and Good are everywhere like shadows and substance: inseparable (for man); yet not hostile, only opposed. There is considerable significance in this fact—perhaps the new moral principle of our Era.—It was familiar to Goethe's mind.[18]

Inspired by *Faust*, Carlyle fleshed out the ethical implications of this idea in "Characteristics," his first major essay: "Evil is precisely the dark, disordered material out of which man's Freewill has to create an edifice of order and good."[19] This pre-established condition is antithetical to faith in progress, which served as the defining issue for Victorian intellectuals such as Bentham and Mill. Carlyle believes that radical self-transformation (the product of *Bildung*, following the example of *Wilhelm Meister*) must precede any reorganization of society.[20] "Politics," he opines, "are angry, agitating, for the present little productive business: what have I to do with it? Will any Parliamentary Reform ever reform me?"[21]

In *Past and Present* (1843) Carlyle anticipates the proto-revolutionary rallying cry of the nineteenth-century Russian reform movement when he poses the question: "What is to be done, what would you have us do?"[22] In contrast to the preceding generation of dissenting writers clustered around the publisher Joseph Johnson, who saw in the French Revolution a chance for reform to catch on in Britain, Carlyle's response to the crisis takes the form of either *Entsagen* [renunciation] of action in quiescent political disengagement or in calling for the aesthetic redemption of humankind and the earth. At twenty-eight years of age Carlyle admits that "I have never yet done any one political act" and insists that "the only Reform is in *thyself*. Know this O Politician, and be moderately political."[23] In keeping with this fusion of the "New Licht" theology of his Burgher sect forebears and the Romantic impulse to resituate the source of transcendental values from a supernal realm to the human imagination, he believes that the ability to ascertain a proper course of action depends on one's willingness to listen to the voice within: "there will then be light in the inner heart of here and there a man, to discern what is just, what is commended by the Most High God, what *must* be done."[24] In addition to elements of dissenting Protestantism, there are echoes here of Emerson as well as the famous injunction of the Oracle at Delphi to "know thyself." Later, under the salubrious influence of Goethe's objectivity, Carlyle rewrites this dictum so as to reduce even further the element of egoism: better than knowing oneself is to know "the work you must do." Dismissing the likelihood of social reform being attained through modern politics, Carlyle posits a grand "Palingenesia" or rebirth of the modern world as the product of artistic vision. This idea brings together the Romantic apotheosis of the artist and the doctrines of "hero worship" and "natural supernaturalism." Presiding over this synthesis is the inspirational presence of Goethe, who is the catalytic, organizing touchstone in Carlyle's aesthetic vision.

In contrast to the futuristic utopias projected by such radical reformers as Godwin and Shelley, for Carlyle the possibility of redemption is always present: "Everywhere and Everywhen lie the materials of Art. . . . Here, even here, is the revelation of the Infinite in the Finite; a majestic Poem (tragic, comic, or epic), couldst thou but read it and recite it!"[25] The artist capable of engendering a transfiguring vision of the mundane world must be endowed with "a sense of the Invisible Existences of Nature, and be enabled as it were to read the symbols of these in the visible. . . . For is not the poorest nature a mystery . . . a type in some obscurer sense and an emanation from the Land of Wonders?"[26] Contemporary Britain lacked such a "modern spiritseer" and a genius with the "spiritual eye" to discern the potential for the artistic exploitation of modern life, which would ground culture upon everyday experiences and who would make realism the dominant representational mode. "Where, O where," he wonders, "is the Artist that can again body this forth!—Not yet born?"[27] Carlyle considered the work of the leading British Romantics deficient in the philosophical vision and moral seriousness required to redeem the modern world through the vehicle of literature. His derisive comments on the leading figures of the period are in stark contrast to his remarks on Goethe: Walter Scott's "deep recognition of the Past" lacks philosophical depth and the great historical novelist is ultimately disparaged as "the great Restaurateur of Europe."[28] Byron is merely "a Dandy of Sorrows" and Wordsworth "a genuine but a small diluted man."[29] Hazlitt, perhaps an unlikely nihilist, is the target of Carlyle's wrath because he "has discovered nothing; been able to believe nothing."[30] Carlyle's "theory of Coleridge" is based on the view that moral defects of character prevented this great intellect from achieving its full potential. "His cardinal sin" was fundamentally a lack of will power:

> He has no resolution . . . . The conversation of the man is much as I anticipated — a forest of thoughts . . . . But there is no method in his talk . . . . Poor Coleridge is like the hulk of a huge ship — his masts and sails and rudder have rotted quite away.[31]

As for the army of lesser lights seeking their fortune as journalists and reviewers in London, Carlyle considered them in contrast to German writers, who followed a higher calling, as a "rascal rout, [a] dirty rabble."[32]

A lack of confidence in the capacity of British writers to overcome what he perceived as the nihilistic tendency of the age eventually modified Carlyle's view of the efficacy of aesthetic solutions to the cultural and social crises of modernity. It is in this context that his ambivalence towards the British Romantics and his decision to look abroad for models to emulate should be viewed. In the tendency to "despise or overlook the common blessedness which Providence has laid out for all his creatures, and try to substitute for it a distilled quintessence prepared in the alembic of painters and rhymers and sweet-singers" Carlyle recognized a precursor of the *l'art pour l'art* disposition that would emerge fully-fledged in the later nineteenth century. He insists that it is impossible to depend on literature as "the sole nourishment of any true human spirit . . . . Literature is the *wine* of life. It will not, cannot, be its food."[33] Carlyle frames the opposition between ethics and aesthetics in a series of rhetorical questions: "What is Art and Poetry? Is the beautiful really higher than the good? A higher form thereof?" If one were to accept this premise then, of course, the poet must be seen not only as "a Priest but a High-Priest."[34] Upon the death of Goethe in 1832 Carlyle rejected this designation for the poet. He offered an alternative, which anticipates his own abandonment, after 1834, of literary criticism and prose fiction for biography and history: "Do I really love Poetry? I sometimes fancy, almost, not . . . . Are the True Heroic Poems of these times to be written with the ink of Science?"[35]

The heroic examples of Schiller and Goethe failed to calm Carlyle's suspicions that literature was not a matter of the highest importance. In a surprising reversal of his normally reverential attitude toward the demigods of Weimar, Carlyle concedes that "one is tired to death of his and Goethe's *palabra* about the fine arts."[36] In place of such "palabra" Carlyle prefers directly to confront the diminishing prestige and historical relevance of the arts as well as their place in modern life. In a manner that suggests parallels with Hegel's prophecy of the end of art, he inquires if "Art in the old Greek sense," that is, as the expression of the highest cultural values, is still "possible for man at this late era?"[37] The response he provides to this question helps clarify his own changing relationship to art and contains an implicit challenge to writers and artists to accept the new conditions imposed on them by the times:

> In my heterodox heart there is yearly growing up the strangest, crabbed, one-sided persuasion, that art is but a reminiscence now: that for us in these days prophecy . . . not poetry, is the thing wanted. How can we sing and paint, when we do not yet believe and see?[38]

Wilhelm Meister's Apprenticeship (1795–1796; translated by Carlyle in 1824), especially the protagonist's choice of an active vocation based on science and philanthropy, continued to play an influential part in the further development of Carlyle's ambivalent aestheticism. It finally gave way to a full-blown Arnoldian "Hebraism," which becomes the basis for a theory of cultural authority based on ethical action rather than aesthetic criteria. What did not change as a result of this transaction is, however, Carlyle's focus on the personality of charismatic individuals. He merely exchanges idols: Goethe for, successively, Oliver Cromwell and then Frederick the Great. And yet, while Carlyle sought to transcend the limitations of British Romanticism, it remains to indicate, through the critical lenses of Heinrich Heine and Ludwig Marcuse, Carlyle's appropriation of German Romanticism.

Solutions to the apparent paradox of Carlyle's reactionary Romanticism have been suggested by LaValley (1968) and Vanden Bossche (1991), but their analyses fall short because they do not draw more than perfunctory parallels with the Continental context of Carlyle's thought. One the one hand, Vanden Bossche seems surprised by the combination of primitivism, ultra-nationalism, and the construction of a cult of personality around Goethe that characterizes Carlyle's hybridic Romanticism. On the other hand, Vanden Bossche recognizes that it is an "insistence on a transcendental source of authority" in Carlyle that is "crucial to understanding why the artists who mounted the most powerful critiques of emerging industrial capitalism were nonetheless much more politically conservative than those writing in other modes of discourse."[39] (A twentieth-century example that suggests striking correspondences with Carlyle's aesthetico-political ideology is the the neo-Romantic *Georgekreis*, the cultish circle of admirers that gathered around the poet Stefan George (1868–1933), in pre-Nazi Germany.)

Heine's *Die Romantische Schule* (published in 1836) is a scathing denunciation of the anti-liberal tendencies of German Romanticism, but offers unexpected and instructive parallels to Carlyle's rejection of the British Romantics. In a bravura display of caustic wit and literary polemics, Heine quite consciously narrows his definition of Romanticism in order to attack its followers' nostalgia for medieval order, Catholic spiritualism, and radical alienation from the modern world. This ideological matrix of reactionary Romanticism stands opposed to the "Humanität, Menschen-Verbrüderung, und Cosmopolitismus" [humanism, international brotherhood, and cosmopolitanism] embodied by Lessing, Herder, Schiller, and the classical Goethe, who, in Heine's view, represent the genuine tendency of German culture.[40] Heine blames the Schlegels, Fichte, Schelling, Wackenroder, Novalis, Adam von Müller (1779–1829), and Zacharias Werner (1768–1823) for the rise of vulgar German patriotism, its calls for authoritarian government, and its religio-aesthetic mysticism. Whether it is a deliberate part of his rhetorical strategy in *Die Romantische Schule* or an unconscious reflex of the Oedipal strife between a literary "father" and his most admiring "son," Heine vacillates in his opinion of Goethe from irreverence to the highest respect. He designated the early nineteenth century as the "goethesche Kunstperiode" or the Goethean epoch of art, due to its preference for art over politics.[41] Proof of his ambivalence is displayed when at one point, Heine seems to appropriate and amplify for the benefit of his own argument Goethe's famous distinction between Classical and Romantic tendencies in literature. Throughout his essay, German Romanticism is variously described as "deutscher Wannsinn" [German lunacy], "somnabulisch kränklich" [sickly sleepwalking], "unnnatürlich" [unnatural], and the German Romantics as a group are characterized "wie die Narren eines Narrenhauses" [as fools in an asylum] who "trieb das Ding so weit wie man es nur treiben könnte, ohne von Obrigskeitswegen in ein Narrenhaus gesperrt zu werden" [push things as far as possible without being locked in a mental hospital]. Alluding to one of the most beloved literary touchstones of the period, Heine obseves that the German Romantics are "von demselben Wahnsinn befangen, der auch den edlen Manchaner zu allen seinen Narrheiten begeisterte" [afflicted with the same madness that inspired the inanities of the noble Don Quixote of La Mancha].[42] The parallels here with Goethe's rejection of Romanticism—as reported by Eckermann—as a pathological phenomenon are clear:

> "Das Klassische nenne ich das Gesunde, und das Romantische das Kranke . . . . Das meiste Neuere ist nicht romantisch weil es neu, sondern weil es schwach, kränklich und krank ist, und das Alte ist nicht classisch weil es alt, sondern weil es stark, Frisch, froh und gesund ist. Wenn wir nach solchen Qualitäten Klassisches und Romantisches unterscheiden, so werden wir bald imreinen sein."[43]

Heine's attack on German Romanticism is revisited in Marcuse's essay "Reaktionäre und progressive Romantik" ["Reactionary and Progressive Romanticism"] (1952), where it is asserted that intellectuals on the left and right are linked in their search for ways to escape from or to reform an imperfect present. In so doing they express complementary sides of Romantic ideology:

> Gemeinsam war beiden Gegen-Bewegungen die Rebellion gegen eine Gegenwart, die immer liebloser und farbloser wurde. Aus dieser Gegenwart strebten sie fort—und wegen dieses gemeinsam Fort verwechselt man bis zu diesem Tage die reaktionäre und die progressive Romantiker. Aber es unterscheidet sie, wohin sie strebten: in die Vergangenheit oder in die Zukunft. So gab es feudalistische, liberale und sozialistische Romantiker. Nach dem Wort des No-

valis: 'Alles wird romantisch, wenn man es in die Ferne rückt'—ist die Vergangenheit ebenso romantisch wie die Zukunft. Und das erklärt die Zweideutigkeit, die diesem Wort seit je eigen war.[44]

Regardless of individual political orientation, the promise of escape from the present is the catalytic element in the Romantic imagination. Nostalgia pervades the passage from Novalis quoted by Marcuse; everything observed from a distance is romanticized, whether one's vision is directed towards the feudalistic past in a gesture of recovery or towards the future with utopian aspirations. Marcuse identifies the progressives in Germany as Novalis, Hölderlin, Heine, Büchner, and Nietzsche, while the reactionary party consists of Friedrich Schlegel, Schopenhauer, and the economist Adam von Müller. Such works as the *Lyrical Ballads* (1798, 1800) by Wordsworth and Coleridge, Godwin's *Political Justice*, and Shelley's philosophical poems and his play, *Prometheus Unbound* (1820), manifested an analogous progressive tendency in Britain. Conversely, Scott's historical novels, Coleridge's *On the Constitution of Church and State* (1830), and Carlyle's *Past and Present* (1843) represent an idealized vision of the past as a lost utopia with which to challenge the legacy of 1789. Indeed, even more vivid than similar gestures in Burke's *Reflections on the Revolution in France* (1790) is Carlyle's sweeping apologia for even the most archaic institutions: "The Past had always something true."[45] Such passionate reverence for history is also analogous to the reactionary Romantic fascination for primitive cultures and the idealization of the Middle Ages by Novalis, the Schlegels, Wackenroder, and Tieck. The role played by Goethe in awakening interest in German history was combined with his appropriation of the Shakespearean style and manner that were then reawakened in Britain with the publication of Scott's translation of *Götz von Berlichingen* (1799). There is little doubt that Goethe, along with Schiller (who was professor of history at the University of Jena when Crabb Robinson matriculated there), influenced the development of Carlyle's historicism. Indeed, the characterization of Odin as a heroic divinity in *On Heroes and Hero-Worship* (1843) and the celebration of Nordic pagan culture in *The Early Kings of Norway* (1875) reflect Carlyle's conviction, shared by Goethe, that Christian civilization was in decline and ripe for replacement in the same way that the old order suffered a foreseeable conflagration during the revolutionary period in Europe.

Carlyle is, however, drawn to paganism not because of the qualities that Nietzsche admires—its "superior culture" or aesthetic virtues. On the contrary, Carlyle is fascinated by the purely ethical implications of ancient anthropomorphism as the worship of man *qua* man. While Nietzsche's interest in paganism is also ethical, he is concerned, above all, with the condition of art prior to the conquest of the ancient world by rationalism. The passing of the "pre-rational" or pre-Socratic world, in which tragedy and unreflective modes of art flourished, is symbolized in Nietzsche's *Die Geburt der Tragödie* [*The Birth of Tragedy*] (1870–1871). It is the death of Pan, the personification of nature and instinct: "'der große Pan ist tot,' so klang es jetzt wie ein schmerzlicher Klageton durch die hellenische Welt: 'die Tragödie ist tot! Die Poesie selbst ist mit ihr verlorengegangen!'" [the great Pan is dead! and so a painful wail resounded through the Hellenic world: 'tragedy is dead! Poetry itself is lost with it!]⁴⁶ While Carlyle came to the conclusion that ancient anthropomorphism was the precondition or "the germ of Christianity," Nietzsche, as perhaps the first archaeological psychologist in the West, recognized that the two ethical systems were fundamentally antagonistic, especially in their teleological explanations of the origin and purpose of human existence: "die antike Philosophie hatte den Menschen als *Zweck* der Natur im Auge" [ancient philosophy always saw humankind as the *purpose* of nature]. By contrast, "die christliche Theologie dachte die Erlösung des Menschen als Zweck der göttlichen Vorsehung" [Christian theology considered the salvation of humankind as the purpose of Divine Providence].⁴⁷ Notwithstanding Walter Pater's idealization of the "aesthetic" Goethe in *The Renaissance* (1873), Goethe was also sensitive to the radical disjunction between the two cultures—as represented by the northern and southern sensibilities—as his sensuous side was awakened during his first visit to Rome (1786–1787).

Chapter Five: Thomas Carlyle and the Imitatio Goethe

According to Marcuse's binary division of German Romanticism into right- and left-wing camps, Carlyle clearly belongs to the category of "reactionary Romantic." "Hero worship" or the cult of personality mirrors propositions elaborated by Nietzsche and Kierkegaard in order to counter the decline of authority in nineteenth-century Europe. As outlined above, one of the leading sources of the doctrine of "hero worship" was the challenge to the status quo in British literary culture offered by Carlyle's mediation of Goethe. His effort was intended to counteract the "general blindness to the spiritual lightning" manifested in "the great man." The common purpose of hero worship, the prophecy of the *Übermensch* or superman and the Kierkegaardian "dialectic of leadership" is, therefore, to give hierarchical structure and meaning to modern experience, so that "reverence and obedience done to men really great and wise" once again becomes "the vivifying influence in man's life."[48] While the hero or leader's specific vocation fluctuates, since the mode in which his genius expresses itself is dependent on historical context, his cultural function remains constant. Regardless of his specific identity, the hero as king, priest, prophet, or poet embodies what Nietzsche calls "das Wesentliche" and, as Carlyle explains, "with his free force direct out of God's own hand" he is "the lightning" and his word is "the wise healing word which all can believe in." Carlyle's insight into the impulse to worship and to obey great human beings as the most important element in man's existence corresponds to Nietzsche's insistence that

> das Wesentliche, im Himmel und auf Erden, wie es scheint, ist nochmals gesagt, daß lange und in einer Richtung gehorcht werde: dabei kommt und kam auf die Dauer immer Etwas heraus, deßentwillen es sich lohnt, auf Erden zu leben, zum Beispiel Tugend, Kunst, Musik, Tanz, Vernunft, Geistigkeit – irgend etwas Verklärendes, Raffiniertes, Tolles und Göttliches.[49]

In other words—and it is interesting to note that Nietzsche's argument is cast in the rhetoric of social anthropology as opposed to Carlyle's ecstatic language of worship—the source of art, reason, and virtue is the worship of essential being.

Nietzsche describes the *Übermensch* as an electric force that catalyzes the process of self-overcoming. The mock-biblical rhetoric of *Also Sprach Zarathustra* (1883–1891) verges more closely on a parody of Carlyle's style than the work of any other European writer: "Wo ist doch der Blitz, der euch mit seiner Zunge lecke? Wo ist der Wahnsinn, mit dem ihr geimpft werden müßtet? Seht, ich lehre euch den *Übermenschen*: der ist dieser Blitz, der ist dieser Wahnsinn!" [Where is the lightning to lick you with its tongue? Where is the madness with which you would have to be vaccinated? Behold, I teach you the superman: he is that lightning, he is that madness!][50] The *Übermensch* differs in one fundamental degree from the Carlylean hero: he is a prophecy of human aspirations rather than a real actor on the stage of history. Nor is the *Übermensch* comparable to Schopenhauer's idea of the aesthetic or ascetic saint, whose achievement of transcendence is potentially within the grasp of one and all. Following hints in this direction dropped by Schopenhauer, Charles Darwin, and Alfred Russell Wallace (1823–1913), Nietzsche posits the appearance of the *Übermensch* as the culmination of an evolutionary process. According to this scheme, humanity in its present state serves only a transitional role in history; it is at most a bridge joining separate stations along the path of spiritual growth: "Der Übermensch ist unsre nächste Stufe!" [The superman is our next step!"][51]

Kierkegaard derived his solution for cultural decadence in the nineteenth century from the paradigm of leadership and obedience provided by his mediation of antiquity. The parallels with Carlyle's "hero worship" that emerge from a comparison of the two concepts are striking:

> [T]he dialectic of antiquity tended towards leadership (the great individual and the masses—the free man and the slaves) . . . the dialectic of the present age tends towards equality, and its most logical—though mistaken—fulfillment is leveling, as the negative unity of the negative reciprocity of all individuals.[52]

For Kierkegaard, as well as Carlyle and Nietzsche, the modern democratic leveling tendency cannot guarantee the fulfillment of one's destiny. Instead of strengthening the individual, democratic institutions, which are governed by "the principle of association . . .

enervates him; it strengthens numerically, but ethically that results in a weakening."[53] The solution to the modern predicament is found in restoring a subordinate relationship to a known superior: "In the old order the officers, generals, heroes (i.e., the man of distinction, the leader within his own sphere) were *recognizable*, and every one . . . fitted picturesquely and organically into the whole, both supporting and supported by the whole."[54] Kierkegaard blames misguided humanitarianism and faulty psychology for the disappearance of the hierarchical feature in human relations: "No longer can the individual, as in former times, turn to the great for help when he grows confused." The individual can save himself from the "dizziness of unending abstraction" only if he can make "the 'leap' of enthusiasm" that would result in obedience to a great man. Reflection, instead of leading to destruction of the individual's relationship to the concrete and the essential basis of life, "becomes a noose which drags one into eternity."[55]

The "dialectic of leadership," the *Übermensch*, and Carlyle's notion of "hero worship" seek to replace Christian ethics with not simply another deity created in man's image, but with a human being endowed with divinity. For both Carlyle and Nietzsche, Goethe is either implicitly or explicitly the model for this new deity. Friedrich Schlegel anticipates Carlyle's transformation of Goethe into a hero of comprehensive cultural and ethical significance when he writes that "jeder gute Mensch wird immer mehr und mehr Gott. Gott werden, Mensch sein, sich bilden, sind Ausdrücke, die einerlei bedeuten" [every good person is becoming more and more godlike. To become God, to be human, to form oneself, are expressions that mean the same thing].[56] But Schlegel's thinly veiled expression of the traditional Christian *Weltbild* clashes with the post-Christian ethical universe of Carlyle and Nietzsche. According to the latter, it is not the "guter Mensch," the Christian or the eponymous *vir bonus*, but the intrepid individual who is able to advance ethically "jenseits von Gut und Böse" [beyond good and evil] and thus heralds the advent of the *Übermensch*. The model for Nietzsche's superior individual who shall initiate the "reevaluation of all values" is Goethe's Faust.

The consummate overreacher, Faust emerges as the symbol of the dynamism of Western civilization in *Der Untergang des Abendlandes* [*The Decline of the West*] (1923) by Oswald Spengler (1880–1936).⁵⁷ The focus of Kierkegaard's critique of Romanticism is found in the strict separation of aesthetic and ethical attitudes. This position stands in contrast to the Romantic tendency to blur distinctions between the functions of poet and priest.⁵⁸

That the reconciliation within Romanticism of these apparently contradictory impulses had taken place by mid-century was recognized by Arnold, who observed that, "the strongest part of our religion today is its unconscious poetry." Carlyle's assertion that "every man that writes is writing a new Bible" and "the true Church is the guild of Authors" anticipates the twentieth-century American poet Wallace Stevens's description of the psychological process by which art is elevated to a substitute theology.⁵⁹ As consolation in the form of belief in a transcendental realm vanishes, the creative imagination is called upon to provide a substitute for God:

> After one has abandoned a belief in God, poetry is that essence which takes its place as life's redemption.... In an age of disbelief, or, what is the same thing, in a time that is largely humanistic, in one sense or another, it is for the poet to supply the satisfactions of belief. ⁶⁰

The origin of this aestheticization of experience is found in the Romantic Period and its characteristic statement in "Ode on a Grecian Urn" (1819) by John Keats (1795–1821): "Beauty is truth, truth beauty,—that is all ye know on earth and all ye need to know" (lines 49–50). Not since the Renaissance, when poets such as Sir Philip Sidney and John Milton asserted the poet's function as *vates*, had poets taken their vocation so seriously. Goethe, as mediated by Carlyle, also stands in the background of Nietzsche's *Bildung*. He is the supreme example of the poet exercising comprehensive (not merely literary) cultural authority in the modern era. This was seen by some as the restoration of the poet's original sacred duties in human society. For Novalis, the role of the poet was interchangeable with the priest:

> Dichter und Priester waren im Anfang eins, und nur spätere Zeiten haben sie getrennt. Der echte Dichter ist aber immer Priester, so wie der echte Priester immer Dichter geblieben. Und sollte nicht die Zukunft den Alten Zustand der Dinge wieder herbeiführend?[61]

According to Pierre-Simon Ballanche (1776–1847), the French counterrevolutionary poet, not only are the functions of poet and priest essentially inseparable, but poetry is properly an elaboration, in symbolic form, of religious truth: "C'est toujours une verité religieuse que le poète est chargé de transmettre. Religion et poésie ne font qu'une seul et même chose. Le poète est le prêtre" [It's always a religious truth that the poet is responsible for transmitting. Religion and poetry are one and one and the same. The poet is the priest].[62] Accordingly, the poet and the priest possess what Friedrich Schlegel calls "das hohere Seelenorgan, wo die Lebensgeister der ganzen äußern Menschheit zusammentreffen und in welchem die innere zunächst wirkt" [the higher organ of the soul, where the life spirits of all humanity meet, and in which the inner acts first].[63] Thus the essential difference between modern culture and ancient culture is the absence of a common mythology, a body of beliefs extensively subscribed to and supported by the co-mingling of the efforts of poets and priests:

> Es fehlt, behaupte ich, unsrer Poesie an einem Mittelpunkt, wie so die Mythologie für die der Alten war, und alles Wesentliche, worin die moderne Dichtkunst der antiken nachsteht, läßt sich in die Worte zusammenfaßen: Wir haben keine Mythologie.[64]

Schlegel's call for the creation of a new mythology so as to remedy the impoverishment of modern culture—"es wird Zeit, daß wir ernsthaft dazu mitwirken sollen, eine hervorzubringen" [it is high time that we earnestly work together to bring forth such a mythology]—does not go unheeded among his heirs in the later nineteenth-century. Kierkegaard attempts to re-establish Christianity on purer, albeit nearly invisible proofs of faith, and Nietzsche responds with the annunciation of the *Übermensch*. Carlyle's solution is different in its wholly human dimension. He insists that any new mythology should be based on the biographies of superior individuals.[65] This creates the convergence of two dominant tendencies in nineteenth-century intellectual life: nostalgic historicism and "Romantic titanism."[66] Carlyle's assertion that "Biography is the only History" reflects how, in an age in which literature has taken over the function once served by religion, the lives of the poets—Goethe's in particular—become as important as hagiography in the age of faith. Carlyle's preference for biographical criticism, which is evident, above all, in the essays on Goethe, reveals the impact of the substitution of ethical values for aesthetic criteria. As evidence of this, he insists that the enigma of Shakespeare could be resolved by the acquisition of unmediated contact with his personality: "Would that I saw the Poet and knew him . . . . I could then fully understand him!"[67] Indeed, the life of the exemplary writer warrants scrutiny and that the critic is thus obliged to reveal

> all the inward springs and relations of his character. How did the world and man's life, from his particular position, represent themselves to his mind? How did coexisting circumstances modify him from without: how did he modify these from within? With what endeavors and what efficacy rule over them; with what resistance and what suffering sink under them? In one word, what and how produced was his effect on society?[68]

Here it would be instructive to compare Samuel Johnson's *Lives of the Most Eminent English Poets* (1779–1781) with Carlyle's approach in his biocritical essays on Goethe and other German writers. Johnson elaborates a critical approach that evolved over a long career, whereas Carlyle's essays on German writers appeared at the outset of his career and anticipate the major themes of his mature writings. Carlyle objected to John Gibson Lockhart's biography of Walter Scott (published in 1838–1839) because it presented a "detached catalogue of his several supposed attributes" based on an "arithmetical" calculation "instead of a delineation of the resulting character as a living unity." Comparing the investigation of character to a creative activity, Carlyle asserts the primacy of art in consolidating human character and the resistance of the personality to examination by mechanical methods: "we are yet to learn by what arts or instruments the mind could be so measured or gauged." The enumeration of faculties and characteristics, the legacy of eighteenth-century psychology, is incapable of accounting for the complex relationship between a poet's life and work. If only one were seriously to examine this relationship, instead of piling fact upon fact in the spirit of empiricism, one would "furnish a model of perfection in biography."[69]

The center of interest in Carlyle's idea of biography is a journey into the interior of an author's personality. As nature is "the living visible garment of God," the poem or work of art is merely the symbol or vesture cloaking the soul. Novalis, whom Carlyle quotes in his own translation, insists that poetry reflects the inner self: "Poesy is the representation of the spirit of the inner world in its totality. Even its medium, words, indicates this, for they are the outer revelation of that inner realm."[70] Schlegel's prescription for the renovation of modern culture was the construction of a new mythology, which, in contrast to the great outward deeds recorded by Homer, must "aus der tiefsten Tiefe des Geistes herausgebildet werden" [be brought out of the deepest depth of the soul].[71] Paradoxically, rather than directing his attention to a writer's work, Carlyle insists that his approach avoids the pitfalls of extreme subjectivity, reflection, and inwardness frequently associated with Romanticism. These qualities, as we have seen above, Goethe considered telltale signs of cultural decadence. Carlyle invokes Goethe's avowed objectivity as a corrective to the egoism of Byron, whom he deemed the chief representative of the "diseased culture" of early nineteenth-century Britain: "one is wearied of that; the healthy soul avoids that. Thou shalt look outward, not inward . . . . It is a course which leads nowhither; a course which should be avoided."[72] He urges the reader instead to meditate on Goethe's salutary example:

> Not by looking at itself, but by looking at things out of itself and ascertaining and ruling these, shall the mind become known. "One thing above all others," says Goethe once; "I have never *thought about Thinking*." What a thrift of thinking-faculty there; thrift almost of itself equal to a fortune, in these days: "habe nie ans Denken gedacht!" But how much wastefuller still is it *to feel about Feeling!* One is wearied of that; the healthy soul avoids that. Thou shalt look outward, not inward.[73]

Self-awareness of this kind fostered Schiller's distinction between "naive" and "sentimental" poets, between those whose talent is exercised unconsciously and those who are by nature highly self-conscious and self-critical; a distinction modeled after perceived temperamental contrasts between Goethe and himself. In *Über naive und sentimentalische Dichtung* [*On Naïve and Sentimental Poetry*] (1795–1796) Schiller describes the extraordinary paradox of the modern, "sentimental" poet, who, in an effort to recapture the harmony with nature and the unity of perception and reflection that characterized the "naive" poet (silently represented throughout the essay by Goethe), seeks to transcend the obstacles to literary excellence erected by self-consciousness through further reflection. According to Schiller, while the genius of the "naive" poet is to maintain original unity between his own thought and feeling as well as the unity of nature and humankind, the destiny of the "sentimental" poet is "die naive Empfinding, dem Inhalt nach, wiederherzustellen" [the restoration of the naive feeling and its substance].[74] In a similar fashion, Kierkegaard suggests that reflection is not "in itself something harmful . . . on the contrary, it is necessary to work through it in order that one's actions should be more intensive."[75]

There are important precedents in the history of European thought for what Saintsbury dismissed as "the gradual ascendency obtained by anthropology over . . . philology" in nineteenth-century criticism. None commands more attention than Herder, who articulated the central premise of the biographical method espoused by Carlyle:

> Man sollte jedes Buch als ein Abdruck einer lebendigen Menschenseele betrachten können . . . . Das Leben eines Autors ist der beste Commentar seiner Schriften, wenn er nehmlich treu und mit sich selbst Eins ist . . . . Jedes Gedicht, zumal ein ganzes, großes Gedicht, ein Werf der Seele und des Lebens, ist ein gefährlicher Verräther seines Urhebers, oft, wo dieser am wenigsten sich zu verrathen glaubte."[76]

The need to be active, Herder's criterion for genius, also corresponds to Hazlitt's "gusto," since both ideas are dependent on experience that is intense and deep. "Am Anfang war die Tat" [in the beginning was the deed], Faust's famous biblical revision, echoes the deep conviction of the priority of action over reflection. It also coincides with Fichte's teaching in *Grundlage der gesammten Wissenschaftslehre* [*Foundations of a Total Science of Knowledge*] (1794), a text with which Carlyle was more than superficially familiar, that "die Tat," the deed, signifies the self-affirmation of identity through the will. This correspondence may account for the nostalgia, expressed by many writers of the period, for primitive phases of civilization, in which, it was believed fostered a kind of genius. Carlyle's "hero worship" bears the imprint of a far less technically difficult text, Fichte's *Über das Wesen des Gelehrten und seine Erscheinungen im Gebiete der Freiheit* [*On the Nature of the Scholar*] (1805).

Another precedent for the apotheosis of the creative genius is found in Johann Kasper Lavater's *Physiognomische Fragmente zur Beförderung der Menschenkenntnis und Menschenliebe* [*Physiognomical Fragments for the Promotion of Human Knowledge and Love for Mankind*] (1775–1778). An intimate of Goethe's circle in Weimar, Lavater's distinctive fusion of pseudo-science and aphorism first appeared in Britain (as discussed in Chapter One) in Holcroft's translation (1793):

> Menschengötter! Schöpfer! Zerstörer! Offenbarer der Geheimnisse Gottes und der Menschen! Dollmetscher der Natur! Aussprecher unaussprechlicher Dinge! Propheten! Priester! Könige der Welt . . . . Offenbarer der Majestät aller Dinge: Genien.[77]

The dilemma facing the writers of the *Sturm und Drang* and their spiritual heirs in the nineteenth century—Carlyle, Nietzsche, and Kierkegaard—was one and the same:

> [H]ow to reconcile this never-satisfied urge (to give in to their infinite longings) with action, with achievement, which alone makes real personality and which necessarily imposes self-limitation (*Entsagen*); and how to justify the inevitable conflict between unrestrained subjectivism and the outer social and moral world.[78]

In *Sartor Resartus* (1833–1834), his Goethean *Bildungsroman*, Carlyle speculates on the purpose of the creative genius in the modern world: "A question arises, whether there ought to be, in a perfect society, any caste of purely speculative men? Whether all men should not be of active employment and habitude."[79] There is more than a hint of Socratic irony in this passage, perhaps even more of that Romantic doubt bordering on despair captured in Hölderlin's "Brot und Wein" (1800): "wozu Dichter in dürftiger Zeit?" [what is the purpose of poets in this spiritually impoverished age?] (stanza 7, line 14)—a question that resonates throughout the nineteenth century and beyond. Carlyle's response to what Paul Tillich considered "the decisive event" of modernity—the loss of a spiritual center in the world—involved exploitation of the dual legacy of Romanticism—art as substitute religion and the cult of the artist's personality—in order to fill the void created when Romanticism reached its culmination and failed to provide lasting ethical and spiritual authority.[80] The revelation of Goethe, who functions "immer als eine ungeteilte Einheit" [always as an undivided unity], is offered as compensation for the loss of spiritual certainty and as a paragon for all to emulate.[81] Thus Carlyle's mediation of Goethe embodies simultaneously the fulfillment and the transcendence of the cultural ambitions of British Romanticism.

Interlude Two
Cultural Identity and the Transmission of Goethe in New England

> "As wine and oil are imported to us from abroad, so must ripe understanding, and many civil virtues, be imported into our minds from foreign writings;— we shall else miscarry still, and come short in the attempt of any great enterprise."
>
> John Milton[1]

> "Every foreigner is welcome in Germany. He receives honours, which no native can hope for, and is allowed liberties, which no German dare take."
>
> George Bancroft[2]

The passage by Milton above was selected by George Ripley (1802–1880), a leading New England intellectual associated with Transcendentalism, to serve as the epigraph for all fourteen volumes of *Specimens of Foreign Standard Literature*, a series of translations that he published between 1838 and 1842. Ripley's series was intended to present selected European classics to an elite American readership. While Ripley clearly sought to embrace continental European culture as a whole, the majority of titles are German books.[3] Nineteenth-century Boston constituted what Claude Lévi-Strauss would describe as "a human community which had believed itself to be complete and in its final form," but which "suddenly learned . . . that it was not alone, that it was part of a greater whole, and that, in order to achieve self-knowledge, it must first of all contemplate its unrecognizable image in this mirror" of a foreign, German otherness.[4] Ripley's series and related efforts constitute the emergence of hermeneutic vehicles in New England for the mediation of German culture. This multifaceted project embodied a reversal of the original Puritan migration to the New World. In the small towns and villages ringing Boston a new generation of pilgrims sought cultural enrichment in German literature and the vigorous intellectual life of German universities.

While Goethe did not appear anywhere in the contemporary university curriculum, he loomed large in the cultural life of Europe and visiting Goethe in Weimar was an essential stop on their pilgrimage route.

With the cessation of the Napoleonic Wars (1795–1815) the lifting of the British blockade on continental Europe signaled the departure of the first wave of student pilgrims from Boston—Edward Everett (1794–1865), George Bancroft (1800–1891), George Ticknor (1791–1871), Joseph Green Cogswell (1786–1871), and Frederic Henry Hedge (1805–1890)—who matriculated at Göttingen or studied at other German institutions of higher learning in the years between 1815 and 1830. The second wave of students who left for Germany in the 1830s and 1840s included many future leaders in the coming generation of New England intelligentsia: John Lothrop Motley (1814–1877), George Henry Calvert (1803–1889), William Emerson (1801–1868), and Henry Wadsworth Longfellow (1807–1882). Their travel expenses, tuition, and upkeep were paid for by the Harvard Corporation, the governing body of America's first university, which sought to enhance Harvard College's academic standing virtually overnight with the training of these handpicked young men in advanced German philology and biblical exegesis.[5] At this time the institution was still little more than a glorified boarding school with cows grazing in Harvard Yard and only 2,000 books in the library as compared to the 200,000 volumes in its counterpart at the University of Göttingen. After establishing cultural ties with Germany through extensive personal contacts and the enriching experience of the Göttingen lecture halls and library, these young Americans returned to Boston and served as *Kulturträger*, ambassadors of German culture in Cambridge, Boston, and New York. There was a great irony involved in this ambitious plan as well as some false expectations. Somehow the risks of exposing Harvard's best and brightest to revolutionary German biblical scholarship were not acknowledged. Harvard President John Thornton Kirkland (in office from 1810 to 1828) and his advisers seemed unaware that once infected with this "Higher criticism" (the study of the historical origins of Christian

Interlude Two: Cultural Identity and the Transmission of Goethe

scripture), the returning students, intellectually awakened but suffering from a post-Puritan hangover, would no longer be content to teach Harvard's antiquated curriculum. Henceforward they would seek to transplant the subversively secular learning they had acquired in Germany into the intellectual soil of Harvard.

Appalled by the large disparity between the impeccable scholarly standards maintained at Göttingen and the parochial, amateurish scholarship and instruction prevailing at Harvard College, the returning students exchanged their Göttingen degrees for academic appointments in literature, languages, and theology at their alma mater and began the transformation of provincial Harvard into a modern research institution. As a result of their efforts, American education was established on an entirely new foundation.[6] Course materials were upgraded with translated German textbooks, scholarly editions, and works of literature,[7] and the Harvard College library was revamped according to this Göttingen model.[8] In 1825, with the introduction of German language instruction into the Harvard curriculum, students suddenly gained access to the latest information and the most sophisticated German technology. Despite the explosion of scientific discoveries in the early nineteenth century Harvard College and Göttingen University were in essence literate cultures, in which all significant intellectual activity occurred through the medium of the printed word. Therefore, while the adoption of German scholarly methods, library organization, and secondary school pedagogy altered the function and purpose of New England's educational institutions, the primary, most lasting cultural encounter was that of the mediation of German literature by the writers whose German studies had been fostered by Harvard's Göttingen-trained professoriate, such as Ripley, Margaret Fuller (1810–1850), and John Sullivan Dwight (1813–1893).

As displaced intellectuals, British Dissenters and Jacobins, like their American cousins in and around Cambridge, formerly the strictest Puritan society, formed the basis of "oppositional" culture in their respective countries. Bound by religious heritage and the shared experience of pilgrimage, the British mediators of German culture were, however, divided from their Boston kin by differences in class and social influence. In New England, the descendants of the Puritans were socially dominant and headed up the central institutions of local culture, the Unitarian Church and Harvard College. In Britain, by contrast, Dissenters, Scots Presbyterians, and other sectarians were politically and socially marginalized, as were women, Roman Catholics, and Jews. Nonetheless, elements of all these groups formed the nucleus of the intelligentsia in Britain.

The mediatory writings of Ripley, Fuller, and Dwight, chiefly translation and criticism, merit attention of the integral relationship between the interpretation of German literature and the intense effort underway in the first quarter of the nineteenth century to declare American cultural independence from Great Britain.[9] At the same time, the mediation of German literature emerges as a vehicle enabling the migration of women writers from the margins of cultural life to the center. Indeed, the connection between Margaret Fuller's achievement as a critic and translator of German literature and her development as one of the most important literary figures of the time has yet to be fully explored. Her criticism and translations embody a record of deep personal engagement with Goethe and the arc of her tragically brief career, In it, she discloses a pattern that is also visible in the early careers of other Anglophone women writers such as Mary Wollstonecraft, Sarah Austin, George Eliot, Edith Wharton (1862–1937), and Alice Raphael (1887–1975)—namely, a prosthetic relationship between the translation and reviewing of German literature as authors evolved from the "pre-writing" and "re-writing" phases of literary development to "writing" as the creation of original works of criticism and of the imagination.

Sarah Austin was an uncannily accomplished translator whose major contribution to the elevation of Goethe to the status of the "strong poet," with whom Anglo-American writers grappled from the 1780s to the middle of the nineteenth century. It was her translation of various first-hand accounts of encounters with Goethe entitled *Characteristics of Goethe from the German of Falk, Von Müller and others* (1833) that fed the British reading public's burgeoning appetite for any contact with the object of the cult of personality which was initiated by Carlyle just a few years earlier. In the following year Austin published a translation of Victor Cousin's *Report on the State of Public Instruction in Prussia* (1834), which exerted a great deal of influence in the debate over school reform in New England.[10] Cousin supported the central argument of the Americans returning from Germany, which was that academic standards at Harvard could be elevated only after secondary schools had first been revamped along German lines. Thus the Round Hill School experiment (1823–1831), which was led by Bancroft and Cogswell, emulated the German *humanistisches Gymnasium* [humanistic high school] and was guided by the pedagogical writings of Johann Heinrich Pestalozzi (1746–1827), Friedrich Schleiermacher (1768–1834), and Wilhelm von Humboldt (1767–1835). For the Harvardians at Göttingen and other visitors from America, excursions to the Pestalozzi school in German-speaking Zurich had become de rigueur.[11] This latter group included such eminent educators as Horace Mann (1785–1859), Henry Barnard (1811–1900), and Henry E. Dwight (1832–1908). Thus, although short lived, the Round Hill School exercised a profound influence over subsequent educational theory and praxis in the United States.[12]

In 1841 Austin published another influential text, *Fragments of German Prose Writers*, which contains extensive notes on the text and over one hundred pages of background information on the authors selected for the anthology. The notes and authors' profiles form by far the most valuable part of Austin's book. These texts embody a prescient attempt to articulate the canon of non-verse forms and the work of women writers, such as Bettina Brentano, Caroline de la Motte Fouqué (1773–1831), Ida Gräfin von Hahn-Hahn (1805–1880), Louisa Queen of Prussia (1776–1810), Rahel Varnhagen (1771–1833), and Johanna Schopenhauer (1766–1838).[13] In 1854 Austin published *Germany from 1760 to 1814*, an original study of German culture, manners, and institutions, which is comparable to George Eliot's publications on German culture, including "The Natural History of German Life" (1854), her review essay of Wilhelm Riehl. This essay articulates an early statement of the Eliot doctrines of "sympathy" and "incarnate history" and thus anticipates the major themes of her fiction. Eliot's two major translations, David Friedrich Strauß's *Life of Jesus* (1846) and Ludwig Feuerbach's *The Essence of Christianity* (1854), also contributed to the dialogue on religion that had begun in the 1820s and 1830s with the transmission of the Higher Criticism from German universities to their sister institutions in the Anglo-American world.

In 1839, just three years after its initial publication in Germany, Margaret Fuller's translation of *Eckermann's Conversations with Goethe* appeared as volume four in Ripley's *Specimens of Foreign Standard Literature*. Her translation is accompanied by the first lengthy critical biography of Goethe in any language, in which Fuller seeks to distance herself from the partisan politics of Goethe reception in the English-speaking world. It offers a vision of the proper direction in which American literary criticism would go:

> I am not fanatical as to the benefits to be derived from the study of German literature. I suppose, indeed, that there lie the life and learning of the century, and that he who does not go to these sources can have no just notion of the workings of the spirit in the European world these last fifty years or more; but my taste is often displeased by German writers, even by Goethe — of German writers the most English and the most Greek. To cultivate the tastes, we must go to another school; but I wish that we could learn from the German habits of more liberal criticism, and leave this way of judging from comparison or personal predilection.[14]

Fuller was strongly attracted to Goethe's writings, even if she occasionally expressed qualms concerning his personal morality, and she was inspired to translate Goethe's verse drama *Torquato Tasso*, which appeared in the posthumously published collection of her work, *Art, Literature and the Drama* (1869). Fuller also translated *Günderode*, the fictionalized correspondence between the German women poets Bettina von Arnim (née Brentano) and Karoline von Günderode (1780–1826). As we saw in Chapters One and Two, von Arnim was Crabb Robinson's friend and guide to the cultural scene in Germany. In the translator's preface Fuller explains why she was drawn to this unusual text:

> And not only are these letters interesting as presenting this view of the interior of German life, and of an ideal relation realized, but the high state of culture in Germany which presented to the thoughts of those women themes of poesy and philosophy as readily, as to the English or American girl come the choice of a dress, the last concert or assembly, has made them expressions of the noblest aspirations, filled them with thoughts and oftentimes deep thoughts on the great subjects.[15]

In the conclusion of the translator's preface to *Eckermann's Conversations* Fuller notes that the remarkable explosion of cultural activity in Germany over the past eighty-five years was directly related to the "transfusion of such energies as are manifested in Goethe, Kant, and Schelling, into these private lives." And she considers the emulation of Germany's great poets and philosophers

> a creation not less worthy of our admiration than the forms which the Muse has given them to bestow on the world through the immediate working of their chosen means. These are not less the children of the genius than his statue or the exposition of this method.[16]

Published in another posthumous collection of Fuller's writings, *Life Without and Life Within* (1860), is an essay simply entitled "Goethe" (1935), in which guidelines are offered for a typological interpretation of the German poet's life for readers who accepted him as their cultural savior. In an observation on *Faust* that alludes to the famous "Bruchstucke" passage in *Dichtung und Wahrheit*,[17] Fuller validates the confessional dimension of Goethe's writings:

> Faust contains the great idea of his life, as indeed there is but one great poetic idea possible to man, the progress of a soul through the various forms of existence. All his other works . . . are mere chapters to this poem . . . . Faust, had it been completed in the spirit in which it was begun, would have been the Divina Commedia of its age.[18]

Fuller's essay was to have been merely the germ of a full-scale biography of Goethe, which would have predated G. H. Lewes's *Life of Goethe* (1855), the first such biography of Goethe in any language, by two decades. The loss to American literature and to the interpretation of Goethe, when Fuller drowned in a shipwreck in 1850, is incalculable.

An intense engagement with Goethe is reflected in other volumes in Ripley's series. Published in 1839 as Volume 3 of *Specimens of Foreign Standard Literature*, *Select Minor Poems of Goethe and Schiller* was compiled by Fuller's friend John Sullivan Dwight and dedicated to Thomas Carlyle. Less restrained than Fuller about breaking a lance for Goethe in the culture wars of New England, Dwight emphasizes what Americans stood to gain from the study of German literature:

> Could Goethe and Schiller be brought near to us in some such living way, it would give a new impulse to our literature, and inspire worthier aims and methods of culture, than prevail . . . . The student of these writers looks up to them as benefactors of his whole nature. From Schiller he learns lofty aspirations, and from Goethe how to realize them . . . . The living movement, which commenced with them, has been for some time making itself felt through other conventional and lifeless literatures. It has reached us here and is welcomed. Its influences cannot but be fruitful. It speaks always to the young life of a people . . . . From the poems of Goethe and Schiller, many a young mind has caught the watchword of self-culture; let him speed it onwards.[19]

For assistance in translating his selection of one hundred and twenty poems Dwight enlisted the talents of leading mediators of German culture in New England, such as Bancroft, Fuller, Hedge, James Freeman Clarke (1810–1888), and Charles Timothy Brooks (1813–1883). While some contributors were not as deeply engaged with Goethe as Dwight and Fuller, their participation does suggest the all-pervasive interest in German culture at this time—even among rivals in the New England wars of culture and religion: William Henry Channing (1810–1884), Nathaniel Langdon Frothingham (1793–1870), and Christopher Pearse Cranch (1813–1892). The symbolic value of Dwight's text is emphasized by none other than Thomas Carlyle. In a letter acknowledging Dwight's dedication to him, he encourages further efforts at mediating Goethe in New England:

> One great acquisition you have infallibly made . . . the acquisition of a Teacher and a Prophet for yourself! Alone of men, very far beyond all other men, Goethe seems to me to have understood his Century . . . . Such a man is as a Prometheus, who in a time of midnight and specters miraculously brings fire and light out of Heaven itself.[20]

Interlude Two: Cultural Identity and the Transmission of Goethe 169

Dwight was not the first New Englander to invoke Carlyle's name as an ally in the struggle against cultural isolationism at Harvard College and in Boston literary circles. Emerson, who had gotten to know Carlyle on his journey to Britain in 1833, sought to persuade him to cross the Atlantic and lecture in the United States. In 1836 Ripley wrote directly to Carlyle and offered him a "Professorship of German Literature" in the recently founded Boston University. Sharing the disillusionment of Everett, Bancroft, Ticknor, and Cogswell—who despaired of ever fully implementing German-style reforms at Harvard—Ripley describes how the new institution will be a "true University in the European sense of the word. We greatly need this to give comprehensiveness and depth to our highest culture."[21] "[E]ager to secure such an advantage for our infant literature,"[22] Ripley stresses that the key to an American cultural renaissance is the appointment of Carlyle to a prominent chair because the Scot, along with Germaine de Staël, was recognized as the foremost interpreter of German literature for speakers of English. The connection between the mediation of German literature and the cultural mission of New England could not have been more explicit or far-reaching as it involved a cross section of the most prominent intellectuals of the region.

The evangelizing spirit of Carlyle also infused Frederic Henry Hedge's *Prose Writers of Germany* (1849). Published a year before Emerson's essay, "Goethe or the Writer" in *Representative Men*, this hefty anthology authoritatively rolls out the canon of German prose fiction and intellectual prose from the time of Martin Luther to the German Romantics. Lightly annotated and amply illustrated with authors' portraits, Hedge's anthology differs from Fuller's and Dwight's translations in that it was produced for a mass audience and was frequently reprinted over the next few decades. Hedge's roster of translators, which includes pirated reprints of contributions by Carlyle and Austin, once again demonstrates the pervasive interest among leading New England intellectuals in the importation of German literature. Such scholars consisted of the omnipresent Ripley (Schleiermacher), J. Elliot Cabot (Kant and Schelling), Parke Godwin (Goethe's *Dichtung und Wahrheit*), the Rev. J. Weiss (Schiller), Charles T. Brooks (Jean Paul's *Titan*), and George Bradford (Goethe's *Die Wahlverwandschaften* [*Elective Affinities*]). The extensive biographical and interpretive notes reveal Hedge's proselytizing bias as well as his remarkable erudition. Following Fuller and Dwight, but without the former's ambivalence and the latter's worshipful tone, Hedge offers an assessment of Goethe's qualifications as a cultural leader and confronts the conservative critics in New England, who claimed to be scandalized by Goethe's treatment of human emotions and sexuality in such works as *Wilhelm Meister* and *Elective Affinities*. He insists that the "effective moralist is not the enthusiast, but the impartial and clear-seeing witness; not he who declaims most eloquently about the truth, but he that makes me see it; who gives me a clear intuition of a moral fact." Thus Hedge identifies Goethe's "intellectual sincerity" as "the quality [which is] most essential in the communication of moral, as of all other truth."[23]

Of all the writers who participated in the mediation of German literature in New England, Hedge is perhaps the soundest in his critical and historical judgments. His credentials were impressive: four years of studying at the prestigious academy at Schulpforta (the alma mater of Fichte and Nietzsche) and other German schools was followed by service with the Unitarian Church and a distinguished career as the first professor (as opposed to mere "instructor") of German language and literature at Harvard College. His command of German philosophy and theology is displayed in essays on Leibniz, Kant, Schopenhauer, and Eduard von Hartmann (1842–1906). In 1886 his Harvard lectures on German thought and literature, were published as *Hours with German Classics*.

Importing this German culture New England answered to a deep-seated need for more cosmopolitanism, growth, and development that could only be achieved along an axis of confrontation between the familiar and the foreign self. The widespread appropriation of German cultural paradigms offered a short cut to acquiring intellectual capital by a young, culturally ambitious nation. For Ticknor, Everett, Bancroft, Cogswell, Fuller, Dwight, and Hedge, the encounter with German literature was inseparable from the quest for individual authors' laurels and the creation of a unique American cultural identity. Especially in the case of women writers, the study and transmission of German literature served as a surrogate for university training based on classical philology from which women were barred.

As potentially enriching and enabling as they proved to be, the cultural treasures brought home from Germany proved disruptive to the status quo in New England cultural circles. The educational reforms sought by returning students threatened to subvert the established hierarchies of cultural power by equipping the younger generation with potent new methodologies that facilitated cultural critique and functioned, in late-twentieth century terms, as equivalent to poststructuralist theory.[24] Even though the German literary dispensation was abundant and various, the herald of this invasion was Goethe. The evidence for this is the many publications—such as reviews in *The North American Review* and *The Christian Examiner*, Phi Beta Kappa induction addresses, Ripley's series, and other editions and anthologies—that attributed cultural leadership to him. As the principal German writer, Goethe was targeted by the old guard, since he was the chief threat to their cultural hegemony and institutional power. Thus Goethe became a litmus test for intellectual politics in New England. The rejection of Goethe and German culture by opponents of reform at Harvard College foreshadowed the opposition to French theory in the post-World War II academy. Both gestures reflect the response of a defense mechanism and embody an effort to preserve the myth of self-sufficiency of Anglo-American culture.

The threat that the German literary invasion posed to the stability of the cultural order in New England was, in fact, genuine. The ideas spawned in Weimar, Jena, and Göttingen were not the products of an increasingly mass democracy like the United States. They were, instead, nourished by aristocratic patronage mechanisms in authoritarian (and anachronistic) mini-states that were deeply invested in the assertion of German nationalism. This was in defiance of French cultural and political domination of Western Europe. It is indeed paradoxical that an American literary movement like that of Transcendentalism was in large part shaped by emulation of an ennobled cultural hero who made no secret of his indifference or even hostility to democratic political institutions. Emerson found this aspect of Goethe's identity especially difficult to reconcile with his admiration for the German's writings.[25] The code word used by hostile critics as well as ambivalent admirers was Goethe's "morality," which was, of course, deemed inseparable from his reputation as the supreme literary artist of the age. This identification suggested an awareness of a conflict between New England society, which was built on a Puritan religious and ethical foundation, and the dominant cultural movement emerging in Germany, which was modeled on the aesthetic life as personally embodied by Goethe. Connected to Goethe's artistic vision is the perception on the part of his admirers that the individual is an offshoot of the ur-individual, thus Goethe himself.

The problem confronted by Emerson and Ripley as well as Hedge and Fuller, was, again, paradoxical: how were they to engender a cultural tradition devoted to individual development based on an imported aristocratic aestheticism when the civil society of New England was founded on Puritan collectivism, Christian religious values, and egalitarian ethics? A similar paradox confronts what remains of the professoriate in today's downsized and outsourced university system, which has fallen victim to such culture wars from the 1980s and 1990s. It has perpetuated as well over three decades of politically motivated cuts to publicly funded institutions of higher learning. How is it possible to reconcile the legacy of Goethean *Bildung* and Derridean epistemology, both of which emphasized the supremacy of individual cultural development, with the adoption of a business-oriented, vocational orthodoxy among the leaders of American higher education?

Chapter Six
The Failure of Romanticism and the Triumph of Realism in *Middlemarch*: Goethe and the Literary Formation of George Eliot

> "Man könnte sagen daß da, wo die Religion künstlich vorbehalten sei den Kern der Religion zu retten" [One might say that when religion becomes artificial, it falls to art to salvage the essence of religion].
>
> Richard Wagner[1]

> "Influence is simply a transference of personality, a mode of giving away what is most precious to one's self, and its exercise produces a sense, and, it may be, a reality of loss. Every disciple takes away something from his master."
>
> Oscar Wilde[2]

> "My writing is simply a set of experiments in life...."
>
> George Eliot[3]

In 1854, on the eve of her elopement to Germany with George Henry Lewes, Marian Evans had not yet adopted her famous pen name or published her first work of fiction. What she had accomplished, however, was not insignificant. Even if, with the publication of *Middlemarch* in 1871–1872, she had not emerged as the pre-eminent novelist of the nineteenth century, her translations and reviews would have established her credentials as the most important cultural intermediary between Britain and Germany since Thomas Carlyle's heroic feats of mediation in the 1820s and 1830s.[4] First, in 1846, she published a translation of David Friedrich Strauß's *The Life of Jesus, Critically Examined* [*Das Leben Jesu, kritisch bearbeitet*] (1835–1836). The product of a fusion of Hegelian idealism and liberal materialism, *The Life of Jesus* caused a sensation when it was published in Germany a decade earlier, drawing the ire of critics on the left and right. Approaching the Gospels as historical documents whose real value is aesthetic and philosophical rather than as the product of divine revelation, Strauß's book elicited a precocious display of erudition from Eliot and reinforced her fairly recent decision to stop attending church services with her father. She earned £20 for her effort, a tidy sum at the time,[5] and the publication of *The Life of Jesus* was a triumph for the twenty-seven year old. Her publisher, John Chapman (1821–1894), was so impressed that he hired her as assistant editor of the *Westminster Review* in 1851, and despite being married, invited her to join the Chapman household. The awkwardness of this situation was remedied in 1852 by Eliot's budding friendship with the philosopher Herbert Spencer (1820–1903). But when Spencer balked at marriage, he arranged an introduction with Lewes, the married editor of the progressive newspaper *The Leader*, to which Eliot subsequently contributed numerous articles and reviews. Because Lewes had countenanced his wife's longtime affair with Thornton Leigh Hunt (1810–1873), co-editor of *The Leader*, he was, according to the laws of the time, legally prevented from seeking a divorce. In becoming attached to him, Eliot consigned herself to life as a social outcast.

In 1853, as Eliot discovered the personal happiness with Lewes that had eluded her in two abortive relationships with older mentor figures, she began translating the only major work to be published (in 1854) under her given name, *The Essence of Christianity*, a translation of the celebrated work by the German philosopher Ludwig Feuerbach (1804–1872), originally published as *Das Wesen des Christentums* in 1841. Building upon Strauß's claim that religions, myths, and rituals reveal more about the psychology and social existence of individual believers than their presumed objects of worship, Feuerbach denied the transcendence of Christianity and sought to determine the purely human significance of religious and mythical thought. Radically empirical in its methodology, the work of Feuerbach was a logical extension of Strauß's *The Life of Jesus* and the scientific researches of Alexander von Humboldt (1769–1859) and Charles Darwin (1809–1882).

At a time when even rudimentary knowledge of German was still uncommon in Britain, Eliot had acquired remarkable fluency in the language. Thus without the benefit of a university education, she had accomplished what, in a famous essay, "The Function of Criticism at the Present Time" (1864), Matthew Arnold opined that the leading British writers in the nineteenth century most emphatically had not: immersion in the larger currents of European ideas.[6] As the product of a radically different cultural tradition and literary apprenticeship from that of her male contemporaries, Eliot was an exception to the typical insularity of male writers in Britain. Having been denied the classical education that formed the intellectual training of men, and permitted only the most rudimentary schooling and superficial accomplishments, she and other leading women writers in Britain and North America—Mary Wollstonecraft, Sarah Austin, and Margaret Fuller—nonetheless acquired an intellectual tradition of their own, based not on Latin and Greek but on contemporary European authors and ideas.[7] Especially important in the formation of this feminized, alternative intellectual tradition in Britain were German writers, poets, and philosophers. No figure was more crucial in this process of appropriation and domestication than Goethe, Germany's protean answer to Shakespeare, Isaac Newton, and Darwin, who had combined achievements in literature and science. As discussed in Interlude Two, translation and other forms of literary service work comprised an alternative education as well as a vehicle of entry into the profession of letters for women writers. Mediating Goethe thus functioned as a validating cultural platform for writers on the margins, with limited or completely obstructed access to the means of literary production and the expression of political dissent. To paraphrase Nietzsche, as Harold Bloom does in *The Anxiety of Influence* (1973), "When one hasn't had a good father, it is necessary to invent one."[8] Women writers in Britain had little choice but to exchange the indifferent culture of their birth for a foreign, nurturing cultural parent. Put another way, the domestication of German culture was, for women writers, a means of acquiring cultural capital from an indifferent, even hostile dominant culture, its publishing institutions and the reading public formed by them. As Goethe intimated in a letter written to Thomas Carlyle in July 1827 that the vocation of the translator as a cultural intermediary is indeed sacred:

"so ist jeder Übersetzer ein Prophet seinem Volke" [each translator is a prophet to his own people].[9] Virtually at the same instant that Eliot's baptismal name appeared on the title page of *The Essence of Christianity*, she assumed yet another identity. In her private life with Lewes she would henceforth go by "Marian." This change of identity anticipated the most important of her metamorphoses, two years following her return from Germany, when she published the three novellas that would comprise *Scenes of Clerical Life* (1857–1858) under the pseudonym "George Eliot."

Besides making her the intellectual equal of any critic on either side of the Atlantic, Eliot's intense engagement with German ideas helped her emerge as the first true psychological novelist in English. With greater clarity than her contemporaries, she diagnosed the anxieties of the age, and her understanding of the relationship between individual human psychology and the larger philosophical and cultural currents of the time puts her in the company of the great continental psychologists, Nietzsche and Dostoevsky. And if Nietzsche gave voice to the mind of Germany, Eliot was, like Carlyle, John Ruskin (1819–1900), John Stuart Mill (1806–1873), and John Henry Newman (1801–1890), a visionary, prophet, and sage, and the first woman to attain this status in Victorian Britain. More than the male sages of the era, Eliot appeals to our twenty-first century sensibility. We appreciate her irony, her skeptical attitude toward modern electoral politics, and her unsentimental, but genuine compassion for all members of society—from the privileged classes to the downtrodden. We also admire her courage, for while Eliot recognized the ambiguous, even precarious, role of women in British society in the early nineteenth century, she nevertheless dared to flout the conventions of bourgeois morality and found happiness in a relationship outside marriage.

Consistent with the demystified theology of Strauß and Feuerbach, Eliot's first book of fiction, *Scenes of Clerical Life*, a trilogy of novellas centered on the experiences of a country parson, depicts the action of individuals seeking to lead meaningful lives in a universe devoid of transcendence. Appearing in book form in 1858, *Scenes of*

Clerical Life antedated Darwin's *On the Origin of Species* (1859) and anticipated Nietzsche's announcement of the "death of God" in *Die fröhliche Wissenschaft* [*The Joyful Wisdom*] (1882). Eliot believed that religion had failed humanity and that faith in Christian redemption must now be superseded by the sympathy-inducing powers of art. Indeed, her insistence on the redemptive nature of art presaged the aestheticism of Nietzsche, Pater, and Wilde. This and other parallels between Eliot's views and Nietzsche's are not, of course, accidental. In 1865 Nietzsche first read Strauß's *The Life of Jesus*, which had also instigated Eliot's loss of faith as well as her first significant foray into print. For both Nietzsche and Eliot art replaced religion as the bearer of meaning in a world without transcendental justification, but both of them still felt the burden of believing in something that offered assistance in overcoming the suffering and apparent meaninglessness of life. Eliot's coping mechanism was to insist on the authenticity of compassion for one's fellow humans emulative of Jesus Christ, though without supernatural magic. For his part, Nietzsche postulated the *Übermensch* or superman, a mythical being capable of embracing the truth of existence without illusions. Before the advent of this being with enhanced powers, Nietzsche understood: "We have Art in order not to perish of Truth."[10]

Eliot was so preoccupied with the challenge of defending art and culture, the source of meaning and redemption, in an era of radical reform and social agitation that, from the outset, the world portrayed in *Middlemarch* is overshadowed by the threat of machine-breaking and other forms of popular unrest. It seems remarkably prescient of Eliot that her novel, which embodies Victorian anxieties about social change, should have begun appearing serially in the same year as the outbreak of the Franco-Prussian War, which saw Western Europe plunged into chaos, and priceless cultural properties and traditions put at risk. Indeed, as if by compensation, crucial scenes in Book II are situated in the timeless world of art in Rome, the eternal city, which is safely distant from the social ferment in the fictive Middlemarch and the actual chaos in war-torn Paris. Eliot visualizes Dorothea's visit to the Vatican museums and to Naumann's atelier with uncanny historical precision and a connoisseur's appreciation for the works of art encountered in both places that are unique in British literature. Moreover, by placing Dorothea, Casaubon, and Ladislaw in Rome during the heyday of the Nazarene Brotherhood, Eliot suggests the seriousness of German aesthetic theory, with which she felt an enduring affinity and which served as the greatest single influence on Pre-Raphaelitism, the leading Victorian artistic movement. The discussions of art in the novel reveal the ideological commitments of Eliot's youth, which suggest the role that art played in German Romanticism—as a vehicle of self-realization and growth—and offer a reminder of the medieval revivalism that lies at the heart of Victorian culture. The central moment in *Middlemarch*—the fateful meeting between Dorothea and Ladislaw—takes place in the Vatican's Belvedere Courtyard, surrounded by the artistic touchstones of the novel, the *Sleeping Ariadne* and the *Laocoön* sculptures, which are remnants of antiquity. The paradigm for Dorothea's growth-inducing encounter with the city's art (chapters 20 and 21) is, of course, Goethe's famous first journey to Rome (1786–1788), which precipitated a legendary outburst of creativity and further mythologized the erotic and intellectual potential of the encounter between visitors from the sober, Protestant north and mystical, Catholic Italy.

Lewes could not have chosen a better research assistant and collaborator when he invited Eliot to accompany him to Weimar and Berlin in 1854. The pretext for their journey was to permit Lewes to research his biography of Goethe, but Germany also served as a much-needed refuge and destination for an unofficial honeymoon. Once in Weimar, the couple quickly established their collaborative work routine. In the morning, Lewes composed and Eliot polished his drafts and provided the translations from Goethe's works cited in the text. In the evening, when they did not go out, they read Shakespeare aloud together. Ironically, by leaving her posts at the *Westminster Review* and *The Leader*, and abandoning her contacts in the London literary world, Eliot acquired the wherewithal to become a

Chapter Six: The Failure of Romanticism and the Triumph of Realism 179

novelist. The transformation from Mary Ann Evans, maid-of-all-literary-hackwork, to George Eliot, literary giant, can be attributed to what Virginia Woolf called "the great liberation which had come to her with personal happiness."[11] Indeed, it was in Weimar, in the shadow of Goethe, a fellow transgressor of bourgeois morality, that Eliot achieved sexual and emotional fulfillment and embarked on her career as a writer of original fiction. This pilgrimage to the epicenter of German culture, more than any other episode in her life, was decisive in shaping her destiny. Weimar offered Eliot the chance to come into close proximity with the greatest cultural figures of the day, to escape the treadmill of translating and reviewing, and to explore new avenues of self-development. In the process, she discovered unknown reserves of self-confidence and ambition that inspired the radical reconstruction of her identity.

In Weimar and Berlin Eliot and Lewes were welcomed in the best houses and salons, where they established lasting friendships with leading German cultural celebrities, including Ottilie von Goethe (1796–1872), the writer's daughter-in-law, the composer Franz Liszt (1811–1886), and the writers Johann Peter Eckermann (1792–1854), who had served as Goethe's secretary, and Karl Varnhagen von Ense (1785–1858), the widower of the prominent salonière and author, Rahel Varnhagen (1771–1833). Eliot's travel journal records her surprise at being openly received in polite society in Germany, something she could never expect on their return to London. The burghers of Weimar, they learned, were incredibly tolerant of irregular personal relations. Goethe and Christiane Vulpius (1765–1816), mother of Goethe's only child, August, lived together for several years before marrying in 1806. While still married to other people, Liszt and the Princess Sayn-Wittgenstein openly cohabited. Of German manners and morals Eliot wrote at the time that "the Germans, to counterbalance their want of taste and politeness, are at least free from the bigotry and exclusiveness of their more refined cousins" in Britain.[12] What one must keep in mind, however, is that Eliot's "female honor" had already been compromised when she made the fateful trip to Weimar with her married lover. Her reputation had been imperiled twice before—first, when she joined the Chapman ménage and, later, during her aggressive pursuit of Herbert Spencer, who was relieved to fob her off on Lewes. There is no evading the fact that living and traveling with a married man condemned her to social death, which it was possible to avoid in socially liberal Germany.

The sacrifice of friends and family who turned their back on her at the news of her flight to Weimar was undoubtedly great, but Eliot may have come to deem this loss worthwhile, because something miraculous occurred in Germany. For it was in Weimar, where she forfeited her reputation and good name for the sake of love, that Eliot morphed from a drudge, anonymously translating and reviewing, to a writer who would produce some of the century's greatest novels. Weimar, as it turns out, was a shape-shifting place where identities were emended, altered, and exchanged. Goethe had managed a similar trick, metamorphosing from the *Sturm-und-Drang* movement as the author of *Werther*,[13] the ultimate adolescent primal scream, to emerge as Europe's last true polymath and the nineteenth century's pre-eminent man of letters. In contrast to Eliot's native Britain, which was, as Johnson and Keats lamented, a conspicuously poor mother to her literary offspring, Germany was the incubator of genius, who nurtured her poets and tolerated their foibles.[14]

Other changes in identity would follow: Eliot returned to London and insisted that visitors refer to her as "Mrs. Lewes." In later years, after Lewes' death, she married a long-time admirer (John Cross) and changed her legal surname from Evans to Cross. But the most important exchange of identities took place in print. When they departed for Weimar, Lewes was by far the better-known writer. In Britain, following the publication of *Scenes of Clerical Life* (1858), Eliot instantly became the more famous of the two. And yet, by incorporating Lewes's Christian name into her pseudonym, she seemed to insist on a conflation and sharing of their identities in print that she was not permitted in real life.

Of all the geniuses based in Weimar or whose ghostly presence could still be felt in the picturesque town, Goethe exercised the most

Chapter Six: The Failure of Romanticism and the Triumph of Realism

far-reaching influence on Eliot's fiction, and with *Middlemarch* she returned to her roots, the intellectual atmosphere and concerns of her "Weimar period." The best clues to Eliot's emulation of Goethe in *Middlemarch* is displayed first by using *Wilhelm Meister* by Goethe as a template for her own novel. Secondly, the character Will Ladislaw in *Middlemarch* is similar to his namesake and persona as Wil(helm) Meister. In Weimar Eliot experienced firsthand the idealization of the artist, where untitled and penniless Ladislaws could become genuine rather than alienated Shelleys and Byrons. In *Middlemarch* Eliot addresses the characteristic dilemma confronted by the *Bildungsroman*: to represent the development of a complex personality in the midst of a typically modern crisis. This is while the old values are becoming vitiated in an increasingly industrial and democratic age. Following Goethe, Eliot poses the problem to be confronted by her protagonists: can a man or woman be the architect of his or her own experience? Can circumstances be altered to allow for the realization of epic ambitions? Can Dorothea Brooke, Tertius Lydgate, or Will Ladislaw bridge the divide between what is given and what can be achieved by sheer will, desire, or fantasy?

Ultimately, *Middlemarch* embodies a rejection of the definition of *Bildung* established in *Wilhelm Meister*, where we see the formation of the protagonist up to the moment when he ceases to be egoistic and becomes socially-centered and begins to shape the self for altruistic purposes. For example, Wilhelm ultimately gives up the wandering life of an itinerant actor to become a doctor. But in the world of *Middlemarch* such growth is not attainable. What has gone wrong? Why is it impossible for Dorothea to emulate St. Theresa of Avila? The mere selection of St. Theresa as the novel's emblem or dedicatee, an example of thought and feeling translated into significant action, anticipates Dorothea's ultimate failure and suggests that the novel is, in fact, an anti-*Bildungsroman*. The implication is, of course, that the epic life is no longer possible. Dorothea's "spiritual grandeur [is] ill-matched with the meanness of opportunity" ("Prelude") afforded in the nineteenth century. As indicated in the novel's denouement, all that is possible is withdrawal from society. Dorothea's flaw is her "romanticism," her inclination to dream an epic life and vocation, even though the conditions for such a life are no longer present. Clinging to such an ideal vision, in defiance of social reality, leads inevitably to tragedy.

Even though Dorothea finds love and happiness with Will, choosing him over a more socially appropriate suitor, her choice does not, despite her epic vocation, lead to success in reforming the social reality of *Middlemarch*. As with Casaubon, in choosing Will, she has, in fact, chosen badly, for Will is fundamentally an artist and a dreamer, not a practical man of action. Dorothea's happy life with Will is only possible because of her personal wealth, which makes the prospect of the social ostracism that she risks by marrying an "Italian with white mice" tolerable. Dorothea's growth is thus not in the direction of forming realistic expectations of the world or accepting the world as the necessary arena of human action. Her growth is actually inhibited rather than aided by her wealth, which is not the agent of social reform, but the chief obstacle to change in pre-reform Britain.

Initially, it seems that Dorothea's task is identical to Wilhelm Meister's: to discover the validity of the reality of this world, reconciling the poetry of the heart and the outer conditions of life as they find their way in a murky moral universe. But this course of action, the conventional arc of the *Bildungsroman* plotline, turns out to be an utter impossibility. As a result, Dorothea does not alter Middlemarch society, rather it changes her, obliterating her idealism and thwarting her epic ambitions. Instead of affording Dorothea with opportunities for self-realization in altruistic schemes, Middlemarch has clipped her wings, just as surely as it has corrupted the novel's Icarus figure, Ladislaw, by turning him into a fortune hunter. The possibility of finding personal happiness in a conventional marriage, if not heroic martyrdom, was an option Eliot herself never was given. The conclusion of *Middlemarch* therefore reflects a fantasy of the author, who could not overcome her status as a pariah within British society.

Chapter Six: The Failure of Romanticism and the Triumph of Realism

In *Middlemarch* Eliot offers a critique of the existing social order, starting with a withering satire of the practice of marrying off young virgins to physically and emotionally unfit older husbands. Since marriage is the medium in which a woman acquires legal status, property, and an identity, Dorothea Brooke fantasizes about a marriage that would give her life meaning. She then leaps into marriage with Casaubon because she imagines that it would be like marrying one of her heroes, Milton or Pascal. And thus because of her inexperience and for ludicrously idealized motivations Dorothea marries the wrong person. The endorsement of this marriage by Middlemarch society is akin to sacrificing virgins to the Minotaur or letting a dragon carry them off to its lair. In this microcosm of late Romantic and early Victorian Britain neither good intentions nor good deeds are rewarded, only adherence to the narrowest standard of moral, religious, and social decorum. Aside from this, the purpose of life is found in accumulating wealth and defending Middlemarch values from interlopers like Lydgate and Ladislaw. Excluding Mary Garth's parents, whose marriage reads like a memorial to Eliot's parents, the marriages in *Middlemarch* are shams, entered upon under illusions (Dorothea and Casaubon, Tertius Lydgate and Rosamond Vincy) or false pretenses such as the Bulstrodes. Class and legal obstacles stand in the way of the novel's only marriages between compatible individuals, i.e. Dorothea and Ladislaw, and Mary Garth and Fred Vincy.

If Dorothea's marriage vocation takes on "the aspect of error" or "illusion" as she struggles for a meaningful life "amidst the conditions of an imperfect social state," Lydgate, the physician (the vocation ultimately chosen by Goethe's Wilhelm Meister), marries the wrong person because of the "spots of commonness" in his character, which blinds him to a partner that is required for his life's work. His own lack of self-knowledge and failure to recognize the conditions necessary for the accomplishment of his goals mirror Dorothea's own shortcomings. Both find that their altruistic plans are derailed by the imperfect choice of a spouse. The resulting compromise of Lydgate's high vocation as medical reformer and scientist by such vulgar concerns for a pretty wife and first-rate furniture prompts an escape in opium-taking, gambling, and complicity in Bulstrode's murder of Raffles. Lydgate learns, in his disappointment in Rosamond, that his fantasy of bourgeois home life is incompatible with his ambitions to reform medical practice in Middlemarch and to discover "the origin of all tissues." Sadly, he learns that his present life will be wasted, a sacrifice to vanity and insufficient self-knowledge. Just as Dorothea cannot decipher the pointlessness of Casaubon's pursuit of "the key to all mythologies" (a Feuerbachian goal without the benefit of Hegelian methodology), Lydgate is unable to see behind the mask of Rosamond's pleasing and superficial character and accomplishments. Lydgate's tragedy, unlike Dorothea's, which owes so much to society's limitations on women, is largely caused by a fatal inability to "get his mind clear" in his emotional life and social relations.

Given all the trouble caused by defective marriages in the novel, perhaps the unintended hero of *Middlemarch* is Fred Vincy, who crosses class lines to wed Mary Garth. Committed to life rather than a dead institution, he turns his back on the Church to pursue an occupation—estate manager—déclassé though it may be, that truly suits his temperament. In the end Fred is the only major character who has not compromised his ideals or his true vocation. Mary Garth, who is of plain looks but clear vision, is not burdened by vanity or illusions of any kind. She is admired by Camden Farebrother, the bachelor clergyman, who is the novel's core of sanity. She sacrifices Fred's inheritance in order to save his honor and, ultimately, their happiness together. This "poor brown spot," who obviously lacks the advantages of a superior education enjoyed by Fred and Lydgate, and whose formal education is inferior even to both Rosamond's and Dorothea's, is the ethical heart of the novel and the closest thing to a self-portrait to appear in George Eliot's fiction since Maggie Tulliver, the protagonist in *The Mill on the Floss* (1860), which was published more than a decade prior.

In depicting the social reality of the imaginary Middlemarch, George Eliot differs from her fellow practitioners of the realistic novel (e.g., Charles Dickens, William Makepeace Thackeray, and Thomas Hardy), whose protagonists are consistently represented as choosing between clear, well-defined moral alternatives within an unquestioned socio-moral reality. *Middlemarch*, in contrast, depicts the socio-moral reality in the close-knit provincial town that is in a state of transition to a new stage of development. The pressure for reform is imposed on the town from the outside—by threats of politically motivated violence and outbreaks of disease, massive unemployment, and the incursion of railroads. Progress in the reform of society matters because the attention of the narrator is focused on the "here and now." The Divine is an illusion, if a useful illusion, according to Strauß, Feuerbach, and Nietzsche. Even in St. Theresa's epic simile the religious content is removed. Her symbolic significance, as a pursuer of waking dreams, is all that remains.

The setting of Eliot's previous works of fiction—*Scenes of Clerical Life* (1857–1858), *Adam Bede* (1859), *The Mill on the Floss* (1860), *Silas Marner* (1861), and *Felix Holt, The Radical* (1866) is rural Britain—a pastoral world, static and paternalistic, with little religious or social ferment. In *Middlemarch* Eliot leaves the nostalgic world of her childhood behind. Her subject is provincial society caught in the grip of reform and incipient industrialization. Economic development threatens to obliterate all traces of the edenic world that she knew as a girl. The anxiety manifested in the novel concerning the First Reform Bill of 1832 is a projection of her private reservations about the Second Reform Bill of the 1860s[15]. Eliot was not alone in speculating that the proposed massive expansion of the franchise could mean the end of traditional cultural values.

Fear of the masses also inspired Arnold, Carlyle, and Mill, who, in related ways, expressed the "Hellenism and Hebraism" dichotomy in their assessments of contemporary Britain—the seemingly irreconcilable conflict between pagan aestheticism and puritanical utility. The incarnation of "Hebraism" in *Middlemarch* is, of course, Casaubon, whose pursuit of "the key to all mythologies" is stymied precisely because of his ignorance of German, the medium of cutting-edge historical scholarship, the language of culture in the nineteenth century, and the vehicle, for Carlyle, Arnold, Pater (in *Studies in the History of the Renaissance*, 1873), and Eliot, of liberation from British philistinism and insularity. Indeed, one of the most telling incidents in the novel occurs when, in chapter 20, when Casaubon leaves Dorothea at the entrance to the Vatican Museum, turning his back on the art within in order to bury himself in documents for which he lacks the methodological tools necessary to interpret them in a scholarly useful way. Moreover, Eliot's scorn for the alliance between evangelical Christianity and the bourgeoisie in her presentation of Bulstrode and Featherstone foreshadows Max Weber's critique of the same in *Die Protestantische Ethik und der Geist des Kapitalismus* [*The Protestant Ethic and the Spirit of Capitalism*] (1904–1905).

In *Middlemarch* the author's interest shifts from the individual to society. This change of emphasis is reflected in the published title of the novel as opposed to its working title, which was "Dorothea." This broader focus stands in sharp contrast to the practice of other nineteenth-century novelists, including Jane Austen (*Emma*), Charlotte Brontë (*Jane Eyre* and *Shirley*), Anne Brontë (*Agnes Grey*), Charles Dickens (*David Copperfield*, *Oliver Twist*, *Nicholas Nickleby*, *Martin Chuzzlewit*, *Barnaby Rudge*, *Dombey and Son*, *Little Dorrit*, and *The Mystery of Edwin Drood*), William Makepeace Thackeray (*The Luck of Barry Lyndon*, *The History of Pendennis*, *The History of Henry Esmond*, and *Denis Duval*), and even Eliot's usual procedure. Aside from *The Mill on the Floss*, all of her works of fiction are named after their protagonists—"Amos Barton," *Adam Bede*, *Felix Holt*, *Silas Marner*, *Romola*, and *Daniel Deronda*. The novel's subtitle is also quite revealing—"A Study of Provincial Life," which suggests the impact of Gustave Flaubert (1821–1882), who claimed that the novelist must be as precise as a scientist. In addition, the influence of Honoré Balzac's novels of provincial life and Wilhelm Riehl's cultural histories (which Eliot reviewed while staying in Weimar) is visible as the role of the narrator, which has evolved from novelist Henry Fielding's "historian" to Riehl's proto-anthropologist, is now extended to include the function of detached scientific observer.[16] In her analysis of

Lydgate's scientific imagination, the narrator seems to be describing Eliot's method in writing *Middlemarch*, which is analysis that leads to observation of moral, social, and medical phenomena.

Another element of the new social reality that is explored in *Middlemarch* is the emergence of the intelligentsia. Represented by Will Ladislaw, this new class is severed from power and alienated from respectable society. In contrast to Dorothea, Will Ladislaw, a figure who walks straight out of German Romanticism into the harsh light of a realistic novel, is the true, classical *Bildungsroman* protagonist and Eliot's homage to Goethe's *Wilhelm Meister*. Unlike Dorothea or Lydgate, whose vocations are well established, Ladislaw's remains in formation. He is still seeking the proper outlet for his talents, and his experimentation runs the gamut from pursuing art in Rome to dabbling in local politics as Mr. Brooke's campaign manager and press attaché. His development is, however, interrupted by his falling in love with Dorothea, contributing to her schemes of improvement, and embarking on a journey of family life in a bourgeois setting. As a consequence, Ladislaw exchanges the questing lifestyle of a bohemian for the determined, settled existence of a bourgeois, a fate incompatible with his previous identity in the novel "as a kind of Shelley" or "a Byronic hero."

Ladislaw anticipates the modernist tradition of representing the artist or artistic type in conflict with his environment. His appearance places *Middlemarch* squarely in the middle of an entire century's idealization of the artist. He is a cultural outsider set apart from the native Middlemarchers by his artistic temperament and his foreign blood. As a musician's son and partly of Slavic extraction, he is the direct forbear of Tadzio in Thomas Mann's "Death in Venice" (1912), who is, in fact, a Pole, and also of Clavdia Chauchat, another mysterious Slav, in Mann's *Der Zauberberg* [*The Magic Mountain*] (1924). Ladislaw is "an Italian with white mice," like the sinister but brilliant Count Fosco in Wilke Collins's *The Woman in White* (1862), and an artist *manqué* like Mann's Tonio Kröger, whose mother's family is associated with a Gypsy caravan. Ladislaw belongs to the gallery of Romantic archetypes and allegorical figures representing the artist's homelessness in the modern world: Goethe's *Faust* (1806/1832), Byron's *Childe Harold* (1812–1817) and *Manfred* (1816), Richard Wagner's *Der fliegende Holländer* (1841) [*The Flying Dutchman*], Keller's *Der grüne Heinrich* (1854–1855) [*Green Henry*], Dostoevsky's Raskolnikov in *Crime and Punishment* (1866), Hamsun's unnamed protagonist in *Hunger* (1890), Mann's Aschenbach in "Death in Venice" (1912), James Joyce's *A Portrait of an Artist as a Young Man* (1914–1915), and Leverkühn in Mann's *Doktor Faustus* (1947). Indeed, Wagner's comment on his opera *Lohengrin* (1850) could easily be applied to *Middlemarch*: "hier nun treffe ich auf den Hauptpunkt des Tragischen in der Situation des wahren Künstlers zum Leben der Gegenwart" [it is here that I touch upon the heart of the tragedy in the situation of the true artist living in the present].[17]

Even though *Middlemarch* is strewn with the broken dreams of its protagonists, Eliot depicts her imperfect strivers after social justice, scientific greatness, and ideal beauty with gentle, sympathetic irony. The failure of Dorothea, Lydgate, and Ladislaw to realize their ideals in a world without transcendence is actually the strongest evidence of their humanity. In Eliot's universe, as in Goethe's, striving in and of itself is a virtue; the only real transgression consists in apathy, the absence of passion and a defining vision of the self. This is the enduring achievement of *Middlemarch*: to represent the plight of talented women and outsiders whose capacity for meaningful action is restricted by sexism, narrow-mindedness, and xenophobia. And Dorothea Brooke, the novel's endearingly zealous heroine, is a universal emblem of the fate of the noble individual immured in a provincial society in arduous transition to modernity.

Postlude
De-mythologizing Goethe: George Saintsbury and the Assertion of British Cultural Autonomy

> "[Goethe] was always 'in touch' with life and fact: there was 'no nonsense about him,' to use an excellent vernacular phrase which, if somewhat double-edged, has a keen and heavily backed edge on the favourable side. . . . . [T]he most apparently dreamy parts of his loftiest and greatest things, such as in the second part of *Faust* are always, like natural and healthy dreams, merely sublimations of actual facts—experienced or capable of being experienced."
>
> George Saintsbury[1]

The appearance of literary historian Dorothy Richardson Jones's *King of Critics* signaled a renewed interest in the career of George Saintsbury, the Victorian critic whose domination of the literary world extended into the first quarter of the twentieth century.[2] While replete with revealing anecdotes of literary politics and intimate glimpses of Saintsbury's busy career, Jones's book is strictly a biography which does not address the question of the lasting value of his achievement. In 1895, with his appointment to the Regius Chair of Rhetoric and English Literature at the University of Edinburgh, the successful journalist made an unorthodox transition to academia. Whatever disadvantages he faced as an English, non-academic dark horse in an illustrious field of Scottish applicants were overcome by the reputation he had made in nearly two decades of writing journalism for the *Manchester Guardian*, the *Daily News*, the *Pall Mall Gazette*, and the *St. James Gazette*. In addition to this large body of work, Saintsbury spent twelve years (from 1883 to 1895) as Assistant Editor of the *Saturday Review*, where he charted an independent course for the newspaper that often led to conflict with the government of Prime Minister William Gladstone (1809–1898). At the same time, he continued to produce a steady stream of articles and reviews that, if collected, would fill many volumes.[3]

Saintsbury's highly subjective, impressionistic technique is not likely to find much sympathy with readers in the twenty-first century. But during his twenty-year tenure in the Regius Chair he published several influential critical studies, literary histories, and authoritative critical editions that signaled a shift in focus from the Romantic and Victorian periods to the Renaissance and Restoration.[4] His most ambitious project, *A History of Criticism and Literary Taste in Europe from the Earliest Texts to the Present Day* (1900–1904), was intended as the first "survey of critical theory and practice from ancient Greek to modern times," and in the third volume he examines the legacy of the nineteenth-century.[5] Despite the impressive bulk and range of his output, the importance of Saintsbury's critical judgments is not generally appreciated at the present time, even though his reconfiguring of the canon anticipates, in broad strokes, the revolution in taste popularly associated with T. S. Eliot in the decade following World War I.[6] The discussion in this final chapter is intended to fill a lacuna in this rich field of inquiry: to examine Saintsbury's reappraisal of Goethe, whom Matthew Arnold considered "the greatest critic, perhaps, that has ever lived," and who was the poet, novelist, and critic whose spirit haunted British and American cultural life throughout the nineteenth century.[7] As perhaps the major stimulus to the Romantic impulse following the deaths of Byron and Shelley and the decline of Wordsworth and Coleridge, Goethe and his followers among Victorian critics, who appropriated the tone and methodology of German criticism, emerged as the chief target of cultural conservatives in Britain and the United States. While admiring Goethe's attachment to "actual facts," Saintsbury nonetheless exemplifies the conservative reaction against the search for transcendental values in art.

Saintsbury's critique of Goethe's influence begins with an attack on what is arguably the most remarkable concentration of literary activity during the transition from the eighteenth to the nineteenth century. He insists that the achievements of the *Goethezeit* are vitiated by didacticism:

> The whole of German literature from 1750–1830 is a sort of Seminar—a kind of enormous and multifarious Higher Education movement, with much more than half-consciousness, by persons often of great talent and sometimes of great genius.[8]

Goethe becomes symbolic of this period's perceived pedagogical zeal, and Saintsbury takes issue with Carlyle, Arnold, Lewes, and George Eliot, who strongly identified with Goethe's emphasis on personality, conduct, and character. But Saintsbury's intended rebuke to Victorian critics is delivered indirectly, since the focus of his critique is on Goethe and his status as a cultural icon in Britain.[9] The verdict offered on Goethe's reputation—that "he has too much the character of a superstition, now rather stale"—signals not simply the cyclical pattern of assimilation and rejection that characterizes Anglo-German literary relations from the French Revolution to World War II.[10] Situated on the threshold of Modernism, Saintsbury's critique of Goethe anticipates a radical shift in critical norms. Distancing himself from the "didactic" concerns of German critics and their British admirers, Saintsbury rejects "the gradual ascendancy obtained by Anthropology [his term for a preoccupation with character] over ... philology" in criticism and urges that renewed attention be focused on poetic features of texts.[11] Demythologizing Goethe's reputation as a critic is the first step in the rewriting of the canon that is outlined in the final volume of *A History of Criticism and Literary Taste in Europe*. This revision of the canon served as the prelude to other, more authoritative efforts at de-coupling Romanticism from the contemporary currents in late-nineteenth century literature, such as the anti-Romantic tendency embodied in Eliot's criticism.

Saintsbury turns to Goethe with a variation on the poet's famous remark in *Dichtung und Wahrheit* [*Poetry and Truth*] that his entire *oeuvre* embodies a great confession: "In a certain sense the whole six and thirty volumes of Goethe's work, with the *Letters* and *Conversations* added, may be said to be a record of his criticism."[12] Saintsbury's irreverence is as much in evidence as his humor, since his critique of Goethe commences with one of the most celebrated episodes in nineteenth-century German literature—the section on *Hamlet* in

Wilhelm Meisters Lehrjahre (Books III and V). In the following passage from Carlyle's translation, the protagonist describes to Jarno, his mentor in intellectual matters, his enthusiastic response to Shakespeare: "I cannot recollect that any book, any man, any incident of my life, has produced such important effects on me, as the precious works, to which by your kindness I have been directed." Shakespeare provides the inspiration "to quicken my footsteps forward into the actual world, to mingle in the flood of destinies that is suspended over it." If he should prove successful in a life devoted to theater, he would then like "to draw a few cups from the great ocean of true nature, and to distribute them from off the stage among the thirsting people of my native land."[13] While Crabb Robinson quibbled about details in the translation, Carlyle appropriated Goethe's text so thoroughly that his *Wilhelm Meister* surpasses the utilitarian purpose of mere historical translation. The resulting English text enjoys the status of a work of literature in its own right.[14]

Despite the genuine rhetorical power of the passages cited above, there is no solid evidence of close textual analysis or "the practical criticism" that Saintsbury, following Coleridge, considers the primary obligation of the critic.[15] According to this standard, the *Hamlet* passages in *Wilhelm Meister* do not really qualify as criticism. Thus Saintsbury sets in motion an inquiry into "Goethe's actual position as a critic" and, by implication, the position of British critics responsible for creating his reputation, such as Carlyle, Arnold, George Eliot, and G. H. Lewes.[16] Ultimately, this dispute over the perceived duties of the critic and their interpretative scope can be applied to literary texts. Saintsbury first damns with faint praise and then proceeds to illuminate what he considers glaring deficiencies:

> Goethe handles—with extraordinary and for the most part unerring insight—the characters, the situations, the conduct of the play. But there he stops dead. Of its magnificent poetical expression—of those phrases and passages which, read hundreds of times through the years, produce as much effect on the fit reader as at first, and more—he says nothing.[17]

This claim is accurate; Goethe evinces little interest in the "poetical expression" found in *Hamlet*. But his silence on these matters is outweighed by his sensitivity to Shakespeare's "wisdom." Wilhelm explains to Jarno that

> all the anticipations I have ever had regarding man and his destiny, which have accompanied me from youth upwards, often unobserved by myself, I find developed and fulfilled in Shakespeare's writings. It seems as if he cleared up every one of our enigmas to us.[18]

Goethe's apparent indifference to "poetical expression" also suggests the vices of the critical approach adopted by Carlyle, Arnold, and Lewes in Victorian Britain: "He likes to consider 'poetry' rather than 'poesy,' poets rather than poetry; and in poets he is always considering the not strictly poetical qualities . . . . Character, conduct, personality (the second construed in a liberal way), these things are what Goethe is always harping on."[19] Saintsbury argues that there is an essential continuity of opinion from Goethe's *Sturm und Drang* views to his last remarks recorded shortly before his death:

> "Shakespeare und Keine [sic] Ende" tells the same story: nearly all, if not all, the scattered references from the Frankfort speech of 1771, when he was just of age, to the last remark to Eckermann sixty years later, tell the same. It is at least a curious one. One begins to wonder whether the person who wrote Shakespeare was, not Bacon, but, say, Wieland.[20]

Saintsbury does not seem aware of Goethe's overall design in *Wilhelm Meister*. The reflections on Shakespeare and *Hamlet* do not constitute a critical treatise but reflect the protagonist's *Bildung* and his response to the life experienced on his travels. They serve an integral function in the novel and only with certain reservations, may be detached from the context in which they are found. Saintsbury also does not indicate that Goethe's response to Shakespeare is part of a larger project of forging a cultural relationship, to which Herder, Tieck, and A.W. Schlegel, made significant contributions. In addition to the translation of Shakespeare on which he collaborated with Schlegel, Tieck wrote extensive commentary, including *Briefe über Shakespeare* [*Letters on Shakespeare*] (1800), *Altenglisches Theater* [*Old English Theater*] (1811), and *Shakespeares Vorschule* [*Shakespeare's Preschool*] (1823–1829). In Herder's "Shakespear," which forms part of the influential *Sturm und Drang* manifesto *Von deutscher Art und Kunst* [*Concerning German Style and Art*] (1773), the claim is put forward that the Shakespearean drama is an expression of Britain's national genius. Goethe's contribution to the collection, "Zum Schäkespears Tag" [*On the Occasion of Shakespeare Day*] was originally delivered to the public on the first German jubilee in honor of Shakespeare held on 4 October 1771. In this early address Goethe explicitly identifies the playwright as a rallying-point in the revolt of the *Sturm und Drang* against the tyranny of French Classicism in the realm of literary taste and conventions.[21]

In the interest of interpretive fidelity it is necessary to offer a more balanced reading of Goethe's critique of Shakespeare than what we find in Saintsbury's treatment. "Zum Schäkespears Tag" is certainly full of rhetorical flourishes that are typical of the *Sturm und Drang* ("Und ich rufe Natur! Natur! nichts so Natur als Schäkespears Menschen!" [I cry nature! nature! There is nothing so natural as Shakespeare's personages!]). But the text also contains Goethe's most cogent articulation of his affinity with Shakespeare's moral universe—a universe in which goodness and evil are held in perpetual, disinterested balance. Goethe's cosmology scandalized British readers in the first decades of the nineteenth century, but enthralled Carlyle: "was wir bös nennen, ist nur die andre Seite vom Guten, die so notwendig zu seiner Existenz und in das Ganze gehört, als Zona torrida brennen und Lappland einfrieren muß, daß es einen gemäßigten Himmelstrich gebe" [What we call evil is actually only the other side of goodness. It is essential to the latter's existence and belongs to the totality of things. Similarly, according to the climatic dictates of heaven, the *zona torrida* must be hot and Lapland must freeze].[22]

In contrast to the thoroughly rhapsodic tone of this early piece, a later treatise, "Shakespeare und kein Ende" ["Shakespeare without an Ending"] (1815), is sober in tone and directly addresses the linguistic texture and literary qualities of Shakespeare's works. For example, Goethe insists that the playwright's poetic diction must be heard to be appreciated fully because "durchs lebendige Wort Shakespeare wirkt" [Shakespeare makes his impact by means of the living or spoken word]. Further on, Goethe offers a comment on Shakespeare's Roman characters and his disdain for costume, which echoes a passage in Samuel Johnson's "Preface to Shakespeare" (1765):

> Niemand hat das materielle Kostum mehr verachtet als er; er kennt recht gut das innere Menschenkostum, und hier gleichen sich alle. Man sagt, er habe die Römer vortrefflich dargestellt; ich finde es nicht; es sind lauter eingefleischte Engländer, aber freilich Menschen sind es, Menschen von Grund aus, und denen paßt wohl auch die römische Toga.[23]

Saintsbury chooses to ignore the presence of other similarly rich insights into Shakespeare's realism, stagecraft, and psychological acuity, and insists that Goethe's comments on Shakespeare offer nothing more than "a sort of running accompaniment of Goethe's thought, for all periods of his life." Concerning the diverse matter contained in such works as *Sprüche in Prosa: Maximen und Reflexionen* [*Proverbs in Prose: Maxims and Reflections*] (1833) and "the parallel verse jottings," *Zahme Xenien* [*Gentle Reminders*], Saintsbury remarks that

> no one . . . can read far in either of these divisions, much less in both of them, without perceiving the very strong, we might almost call it the overbearing, practical and ethical tendency, even of those passages which apparently bear more closely on literature.[24]

What offends his critical sensibility in these passages is Goethe's marked tendency toward generalization, which has direct bearing on his assessment of Goethe's literary output and reputation as a critic. As for the "very numerous literary reviews and notices which fill nearly two volumes" of Goethe's works, it is essential reading for *Germanisten*:

> [T]hey have not quite the importance which they might be expected to have, and very often, when they are at their best, that best comes to little or nothing more than we find condensed and quintessenced in a maxim of the *Sprüche* or a sentence of the *Conversations*.[25]

Even Goethe's criticism of specific works of literature, whether aphoristic or expository texts, displays an irrepressible ethical tendency. Saintsbury does concede that the German poet generally displays a quality in his critical writing that is also the salient feature of Johnson's criticism. This is the "common-sense judgment which is perhaps Goethe's chief claim as a critic."[26] Employing a Johnsonian turn of phrase, he also concedes that Goethe "was a man soaked in literature."[27] In an effort to account for the reason why Goethe was "exalted to the skies,", which was "owing mainly to the efforts of a large number of men from Carlyle onwards," he suggests that it has to do with being rooted in the eighteenth century:

> Goethe possessed, to an extraordinary degree, and later perhaps than any one else, that singular wisdom which has been more than once animadverted upon as the property ... of the eighteenth century. He was, for half its length and for nearly two-thirds of his own life, a man of its own: and he never escaped, or wished to escape, entirely from its influence.

Like Aristotle, Goethe is not "rash in his opinions, but he is more inadequate than Aristotle." While "we can nowadays allow for and discard Aristotle's rashness, and find abundance of the eternal left in him ... we cannot quite do this with Goethe." Those of Aristotle's insights that remain after the culling process have not only stood the test of time, they no longer give off an obvious air of antiquity. This cannot be said of even the best of Goethe's critical judgments. "We must always" say of him that "'this was the cleverest man of 1770–1830.'"[28] Saintsbury identifies the essential quality of this epoch, as expressed in Goethe's lyric poem "Prometheus," as an attachment to the concreteness of human experience. He is "always 'in touch' with life and fact." Even "the most apparently dreamy parts" of his writings, such as *Faust, Part II*, "are always, like natural and healthy dreams, merely sublimations of actual facts—experienced or capable of being experienced."[29]

Although Saintsbury admires without reservation Goethe the poet and dramatist, "for the critical Goethe" he feels "very much less." While acknowledging Goethe's influence "as a valuable popularizer of a critical attitude, useful as an alternative to that of Neoclassicism ... [and] a great revelation to Englishmen seventy, eighty, even a hundred years ago,"[30] Saintsbury insists that Goethe exercised a negative influence in Britain by giving impetus to biographical criticism. Symptomatic of Goethe's cult following decried by Saintsbury is John Morley's homage to the German poet as the founder of

> that new faith which is as yet without any universally recognized label, but whose heaven as an ever-closer harmony between the consciousness of man and all the natural forces of the universe; whose history is culture, and whose deity is a certain high composure of the human heart.[31]

Saintsbury's reappraisal of Goethe reveals confusion about origins and affiliations because he insists on linking Goethe to the Romantics. Indeed, he considers Goethe responsible for creating what he calls a "modified Romanticism" allied with science, which was, for its time, a typically German phenomenon.[32] Schiller may be responsible for Saintsbury's association of Goethe with Romanticism. In *Über naive und sentimentalische* Dichtung [*On Naïve and Sentimental Poetry*] (1795) Schiller suggests that *Iphigenie auf Tauris* (1779/1786), a drama of Goethe's classical phase, displays unconscious affinities with Romanticism. Although Walter Savage Landor, along with Schiller, praised *Iphigenie* for embodying the most exquisite statement of the classical spirit to appear since antiquity,[33] Goethe himself insisted that "durch das Vorwalten der Empfindung" [through the predominance of sentiment] the drama "keineswegs so klassisch und im antiken Sinn sei, als man vielleicht glauben möchte" [was by no means so classical and so much in the antique spirit as some people supposed]. Goethe was so thoroughly enthralled by Schiller's insight into his work that the older poet was willing to admit that "er bewies mir, daß ich selber, wider Willen, romantisch sei" [he proved to me that I, against my will, was Romantic].[34]

The distinction of being "Romantic" in the sense implied in Schiller's essay has more to do with insight into Goethe's personality than with his historically affirmable affiliation with either German Classicism or Romanticism. Schiller suggests that Goethe, in contrast to the "sentimental" poets of the modern world, a category to which he assigns himself, is "naive" (or natural or primal or unselfconscious) and thus an anachronism of world-historical importance. "Naive" as a descriptive term suggests a complicated network of ideas whose complexity is lost in Saintsbury's labeling of Goethe as a "Romantic." According to Schiller's dialectical scheme, the "naive" Goethe represents several tendencies identified with Romanticism: the victory of nature over art, the dominance of intuition over purposeful modes of creation, organic form versus cookie-cutter conventions, inner necessity as opposed to compulsion applied from the outside, and moral greatness that paradoxically transcends the violence and dynamism in nature. Schiller ultimately identifies the "naive" with genius and the perfection of being that is inborn and cannot be cultivated. In this sense, Goethe accepts Schiller's definition of the "naive" as coinciding in large part with the "Romantic":

> Naiv muß jedes wahre Genie sein, oder es ist keines. Seine Naivetät allein macht es zu Genie.... Nur dem Genie ist es gegeben, außerhalb des Bekannten noch immer zu Hause zu sein und die Natur zu erweitern, ohne über sie hinauszusehen.[35]

In a conversation with Eckermann on 2 April 1829 Goethe famously condemns Romanticism as "kränklich" [diseased or pathological]. The "Gesunde Natur" [healthy nature] praised by Schiller and which he believes is personified by Goethe, is also comparable to what Goethe praises as "das Gesunde," the "klassisch" or classical:

> Das klassische nenne ich das Gesunde und das Romantische das Kranke.... Das meiste Neuere ist nicht romantisch, weil es neu, sondern weil es schwach, kränklich und krank ist, und das Alte ist nicht klassisch, weil es alt, sondern weil es stark, frisch, froh und gesund ist. Wenn wir nach solchen Qualitäten, Klassisches und Romantisches unterscheiden, so werden wir bald im reinen sein.[36]

Apart from offering scattered praise for Goethe's common sense, realism, and unsentimental attachment to experience, Saintsbury avoids any serious discussion of the "classical" Goethe—besides *Iphigenia auf Tauris*, this is the Goethe of the *Römische Elegien* [*Roman Elegies*] (1788–1790), *Winckelmann und sein Jahrhundert*

[*Winckelmann and his Century*] (1805), the *Italienische Reise* [*Italian Journeys*] (1816–1817), and "Die neue Melusine" ["The New Melusine"] (1817). Despite Goethe's genuine and energetic efforts to distance himself from Romanticism politically, philosophically, and artistically, Saintsbury's attitude dominates British criticism. In a position that prefigures Modernist and twentieth-century critics, Saintsbury focuses almost without exception on the "Romantic" author of *Werther* and *Faust*, "Zum Schäkespears Tag," and "Von deutscher Baukunst" ["Of German Architecture"] (1773) and sees these early works as disproportionately representative of Goethe's achievement.

Another case of constructive misreading is similarly instructive. In "Goethe as Sage" Eliot confesses that he has long "been irritated" by the German man of letters, and yet he is convinced that "it seems right and necessary that he should have believed what he did and behaved as he did."[37] Even though Eliot admits feeling discomfort with Goethe and German culture generally, there are several interesting correspondences between German thought and Eliot's methods of historical argument and illustration. For example, there is the resemblance between Eliot's idea of the "dissociation of sensibility" at the onset of the age of "reflective" poetry and Schiller's distinction between "naive" and "sentimentalische" poets. These dualisms find their parallels in Goethe's positing of ages of faith and unbelief, in Hegel's dialectic, and in the factors contributing to Hugo von Hofmannsthal's prescient observation—in the "Chandos-Brief" ["Chandos Letter"] (1902), in which a fictional poet tries to explain to his patron—Sir Francis Bacon (1561–1626)—why he has lost the ability to write—that a division between thought and feeling created a language crisis that undermined literary production in the modern era:

> Mir erschien damals in einer Art von andauernder Trunkenheit das ganze Dasein als eine große Einheit: geistige und körperliche Welt schien mir keinen Gegensatz zu bilden, ebensowenig höfisches und tierisches Wesen, Kunst und Unkunst, Einsamkeit und Gesellschaft; in allem fühlte ich Natur, in den Verirrungen des Wahnsinns ebensowohl wie in den äußersten Verfeinerungen eines spanischen Zeremoniells; in den Tölpelhaftigkeiten junger Bauern nicht minder als in den süßesten Allegorien; und in aller Natur fühlte ich mich selber; wenn ich auf meiner Jagdhütte die schäumende laue Milch in mich hineintrank, die

> ein struppiges Mensch einer schönen sanftäugigen Kuh aus dem strotzenden Euter in einen Holzeimer niedermolk, so war mir das nichts anderes, als wenn ich, in der dem Fenster eingebauten Bank meines Studio sitzend, aus einem Folianten süße und schäumende Nahrung des Geistes in mich sog.[38]

Even Eliot's efforts to disengage from this tradition, to cover his tracks in what might be seen as a conscious or unconscious misreading, actually draw attention to the presence of German thought in his intellectual development and suggest that Goethe is the strong poet to whom he relates as an "ephebe." Indeed, Goethe is "the central problem" in the anxiety-ridden literary histories written by Saintsbury and Eliot; they relate to him as the Romantics related to Milton—in a state of conflict distinguished, in Bloomian terms, by "self-saving caricature and distortion, of perverse, willful revisionism without which modern poetry as such could not exist."[39] Eliot's act of asserting his intellectual autonomy from historical predecessors or rivals nonetheless reveals intellectual instincts chiefly identified with the nineteenth century. The process that most directly reveals his cultural patrimony also illustrates Goethe's dictum that "in art personality is everything":

> "Allerdings . . . ist in der Kunst und Poesie die Persönlichkeit alles; doch hat es unter den Kritikern und Kunstrichtern der neuesten Zeit schwache Personagen gegeben, die dieses nicht zugestehen, und die eine große Persönlichkeit, bei einem Werke der Poesie oder Kunst, nur also eine Art von geringer Zugabe wollen betrachtet wissen . . . . Aber freilich, um eine große Persönlichkeit zu empfinden und zu ehren, muß man wiederum selber etwas sein."[40]

To counter the "anthropological" tendency of Goethe's criticism ("in art and poetry personality is everything") Saintsbury rewrites the German canon, selecting Novalis to serve as a more salutary example for contemporary poets writing in English. He cites the "astonishing beauty and profundity" as well as a courageous willingness to critique Goethe in Novalis's *Fragmente:*

> Here . . . is that remarkable judgment of Goethe's work in general, and of *Wilhelm Meister* in particular, of which Carlyle bravely gave the gist, though it certainly did not coincide with his own opinion, and which remains almost a pattern of independent and solid judgment, unspoilt by any petulance or jealously

of youth, from a young man of letters on the living leader of his country's literature.⁴¹

On the basis of Novalis's perceived devotion to intrinsic criticism Saintsbury raises him above the Schlegels and Tieck and exalts him as "the greatest critic [in Germany] . . . though he wrote the least criticism. Indeed, there is a sense in which one might, without absurdity, call Novalis the greatest critic of Germany."⁴² This is unexpected and lavish praise in view of Novalis's religious and political agenda (German nationalism combined with medieval Roman Catholic revivalism), which serves as the subtext for his criticism. What is arguably his most important treatise, *Die Christenheit oder Europa* [*Christianity or Europe*] (1799), culminates in a vision of European culture marked by nostalgia for the social and symbolic unity of monastic life and feudalism. Despite Saintsbury's extravagant praise for Novalis, the latter's differences with Goethe—shared by all the *Frühromantiker*—signify less a break with the tradition embodied by Goethe than efforts to establish artistic independence from the Olympian gods of Weimar. The dispute between Goethe and the Romantics actually suggests an ironic inversion of Bloom's anxiety paradigm, in which the older generation seeks to liberate itself from the homage offered by the younger generation.

In the interests of "practical criticism" Saintsbury also presses his case against Schiller, whose remarks on Shakespeare disappointed him because they "are always informing from the ethical-aesthetic side; they hardly even attempt the literary."⁴³ Indifferent to the text, Schiller's criticism elicits a customarily harsh judgment:

> These passages might have been written by a man who was only acquainted with a prose translation of the piece into a language other than its own. This may seem a little staggering; but it's true.⁴⁴

In *On Naïve and Sentimental Poetry* Schiller violates the critic's obligation to perform *explication de texte,* Saintsbury's litmus test for critical competence and he considers it even "dangerous" that "when Schiller wrote this essay. . . he had not read [Aristotle's] Poetics" and he suspects that "nearly all his literary citations are of a general and second-hand character," since there is "nowhere any direct evidence of 'contact' with the texts." Saintsbury wonders if Schiller even knew "at first hand and in the originals, besides the antients [sic], Shakespeare and Milton, Dante and Ariosto, Rabelais and Molière," and because of insufficient proof of textual "contact" Schiller is dismissed, along with Goethe: "I must once more say that Schiller does not seem to me a great critic, or even a good one."[45]

Echoing the criticisms of William Taylor, Coleridge, and De Quincey, Saintsbury also expresses concern over Schiller's personal character as revealed in the drama *The Robbers* (1781), whose charismatic protagonist Karl Moor is synonymous for violent rebellion. In the process of making this identification between Schiller and his creation, Saintsbury gets tangled in the identical ethical snare that he, and Eliot after him, tried but failed to avoid. Conflating the views expressed in the controversial drama with those of its author, Saintsbury comes away convinced that "Schiller, with all his talent, all his genius, was something of a prig: and a prig is capable of almost any discreditable act."[46] Such intense discomfort with the personality of Schiller allows Saintsbury to fall prey to the biographical fallacy.

Saintsbury's critique of Goethe was fueled by a reaction against a tendency identified with German critics to search for transcendental values in art. His disapproval of Victorian critics, especially Carlyle, is based on their assimilation or emulation of this tendency. Indeed, through the early eighteen-thirties the most conspicuous part of Carlyle's literary output reveals the substitution of a response to German literature for conventional religion; he, too, is one of the "displaced persons" who give European culture in the nineteenth century its aesthetic and ethical contours.[47] Saintsbury's position is defined through a reappraisal of Goethe's authority and he offers an alternative to Goethe, the German Romantic poet Novalis. He does this even while choosing to ignore the nostalgic religious nationalism in the latter's critical writings. Saintsbury's objective is clear: Goethe the icon must first be smashed before inroads can be made on the influence that he exerted in Victorian Britain. His ultimate aim in taking on Goethe is to attack and reduce the authority and influence of pro-Goethean or pro-Romantic British critics and he does so by forcefully asserting Coleridge's (as well as his own) vision of high culture that privileges an Anglocentric standard as well as associated formal conventions. At the same time, Saintsbury seeks to erase Carlyle's identification of Goethe as the inheritor of the British Romantics' cultural authority, which was built on the foundation of nearly four decades' work in appropriating Goethe that was associated with the pioneering translation and reviewing activities of Taylor, Holcroft, Crabb Robinson, and Carlyle. Anticipating central concerns of the New Criticism, Saintsbury insists that the work of the critic must not be burdened by a need to seek justification from ethics or by investigation of the author's personality. Demythologizing Goethe's reputation as a critic is thus the first step in an extensive process of reforming the critical canon that is outlined in the third volume of *A History of Criticism and Literary Taste in Europe*.

Bibliography

Adam, Thomas and Gisela Mettele, ed. *Two Boston Brahmins in Goethe's Germany: The Travel Journals of Anna and George Ticknor*. Lanshaw, Maryland: Lexington Books, 2009.

Alford, R.G. "Goethe's Earliest Critics in England." *Publications of the English Goethe Society* 7 (1898): 8–24.

Annan, Noel. *Leslie Stephen: The Godless Victorian*. New York: Random House, 1984.

Arnold, Matthew. *Culture and Anarchy*. Ed. J. Dover Wilson. Cambridge: Cambridge University Press, 1960.

———. *Lectures and Essays in Criticism. Complete Prose Works of Matthew Arnold*. vol. 2. Ed. R.H. Super. Ann Arbor: University of Michgan Press, 1962.

———. "Ecce, Convertimur et Gentes." *English Literature and Irish Politics. Complete Prose Works of Matthew Arnold*. vol. 9. Ed. R.H. Super. Ann Arbor: University of Michigan Press, 1973. 1–19.

Ashton, Rosemary. *The German Idea: Four English Writers and the Reception of German Thought, 1800–1860*. Cambridge: Cambridge University Press, 1980.

Austin, Sara. *Characteristics of Goethe: from the German of* [Johannes Daniel] *Falk* [1768–1826], [Friedrich] *von Müller* [1779–1849], *Etc. with notes, original and translated, illustrative of German literature*. 3 volumes. London: Effingham Wilson, 1833.

———, trans. *Fragments from German Prose Writers illustrated with Notes*. London: John Murray, 1841.

———, trans. *Fragments from German Prose Writers with Biographical Sketches of the Authors*. New York: D. Appleton and Company, 1841.

———. *Germany, from 1760 to 1814, or, Sketches of German Life From the Decay of the Empire to the Expulsion of the French*. London: Longman, Brown, Green, and Longmans, 1854.

Baine, Rodney M. *Thomas. Holcroft and the Revolutionary Novel*. Athens: University of Georgia Press, 1965.

Bahr, Ehrhard. *Weimar on the Pacific: German Exile Culture in Los Angeles and the Crisis of Modernism*. Berkeley: University of California Press, 2007.

Ballanche, Pierre-Simon. *Orphée. Oevres complètes, vol. 5.* Geneva: Slatkine, 1967.

Bancroft, George. Letter to J. T. Kirkland, President of Harvard College. 22 February 1819. Autograph File. The Houghton Library, Harvard University.

Bate, Walter Jackson, ed. *Selected Writings of Edmund Burke.* New York: The Modern Library, 1947.

_____. *Coleridge.* Cambridge: Harvard University Press, 1987 [1970].

_____. *The Burden of the Past and the English Poet.* Cambridge: The Belknap Press, 1991 [1970].

Beebee, Thomas O. "Introduction: Departures, Emanations, Intersections." *German Literature as World Literature.* Ed. Thomas O. Beebee. London and New York: Bloomsbury, 2014. 1–22.

Bell, David. "Goethe's Orientalism." *Goethe and the English-Speaking World: Essays from the Cambridge Symposium for His 250th Anniversary.* Ed. Nicholas Boyle and John Guthrie. Rochester, New York: Camden House, 2002. 199–212.

Behler, Diana I. "Henry Crabb Robinson as a Mediator of Lessing and Herder to England." *Lessing Yearbook* 7. Detroit: Wayne State Press, 1975. 105–126.

_____. "Henry Crabb Robinson as Mediator of Early German Romanticism to England." *Arcadia* 13. Berlin and New York: De Gruyter, 1977. 117–155.

_____. "Henry Crabb Robinson: A British Acquaintance of Wieland and His Advocate in England." *Christoph Martin Wieland: Nordamerikanische Forschungsbeiträge zur 250. Wiederkehr seines Geburtstages 1983.* Ed. Hansjörg Schelle. Tübingen: Max Niemeyer Verlag, 1984. 539–556.

_____. "Goethezeit und westliche Denktradition: Der Gegensatz von Idealismus und Sensualismus im Spiegel Henry Crabb Robinsons." *Deutscher Literatur in der Weltliteratur: Kulturnation statt politischer Nation?* Ed. Franz Norbert Mennemeier and Conrad Wiedemann. Tübingen: Max Niemeyer Verlag, 1986. 21–26.

Benjamin, Walter. *Einbahnstrasse.* Ed. Karl-Maria Guth. Berlin: Verlag der Contumax, 2016 [1928].

Berman, Antoine. *The Experience of the Foreign*. Albany, New York: State University of New York Press, 1992.

Blake, William. "Letter to Dr. Trusler." *The Oxford Authors. William Blake*. Ed. Michael Mason. New York: Oxford University Press, 1988.

Bloom, Harold. *The Anxiety of Influence: A Theory of Poetry*. New York: Oxford University Press, 2nd edition, 1997 [1973].

———. *A Map of Misreading*. New York: Oxford University Press, 2nd edition, 2003 [1975].

———. *The Western Canon: The Books and School of Ages*. New York: Harcourt Brace, 1994.

Boening, John. "Pioneers and Precedents: The 'Importation of German' and the Emergence of Periodical Criticism in England." *Internationales Archiv für Sozialgeschichte der deutschen Literatur* VII (1982): 65–86.

Bossche Vanden, R. Chris. *Carlyle and the Search for Authority*. Columbus, Ohio: Ohio State University Press, 1991.

Bruford, W. H. "Goethe and Some Victorian Humanists." *Publications of the English Goethe Society*. New Series 18 (1949): 34–67.

Buckler, William, ed. *Passages from the Prose Writings of Matthew Arnold*. New York: New York University Press, 1963.

Burwick, Frederick and James M. McCusick, ed. *Faustus. From the German of Goethe Translated by Samuel Taylor Coleridge*. Oxford: Oxford University Press, 2007.

Butler, Marilyn, ed. *Burke, Paine, Godwin, and the Revolution Controversy*. Cambridge: Cambridge University Press, 1984.

Byron, George Gordon, Lord. *Byron's Letters and Journals*. Vol VII: "Between two worlds," 1820. Ed. Leslie Marchand. Cambridge: The Belknap Press, 1978.

Carlyle, Thomas. *The Works Thomas Carlyle (Centenary Edition)*. Ed. Henry Duff Traill. 30 volumes. London: Chapman and Hall, 1896–1899.

———. Unpublished Letter to John Sullivan Dwight. 14 March 1839. The Amy Lowell Autograph Collection, the Houghton Library, Harvard University.

———. *Letters of Thomas Carlyle, 1826–1836*. Ed. Charles Eliot Norton. London and New York: Macmillan, 1889.

———. *Two Notebooks*. Ed. Charles Eliot Norton. New York: The Groilier Club, 1898.

———. *Collected Letters of Thomas and Jane Welsh Carlyle*. Volumes 2 and 3. Ed. C.R. Sanders and K. J. Fielding. Durham, North Carolina: Duke University Press, 1970.

———. *Sartor Resartus: The Life and Opinions of Herr Teufelsdröckh*. Ed. Rodger L. Tarr and Mark Engel. Los Angeles and Berkeley: University of California Press, 2000.

Christensen, Merton A. "Taylor of Norwich and the Higher Criticism." *Journal of the History of Ideas* 20: 179–194.

Clive, John. *Scotch Reviewers: The Edinburgh Review, 1802–1815*. Cambridge: Harvard University Press, 1957.

Coleridge, Samuel Taylor. *The Collected Works of Samuel Taylor Coleridge*. General ed. Kathleen Coburn. 23 volumes. London: Routledge and Kegan Paul; Princeton: Princeton University Press, 1969–2016.

———. *The Letters of Samuel Taylor Coleridge*. 2 volumes, Ed. E.H. Coleridge. London: William Heinemann, 1895.

———. *Biographia Epistolaris*. 2 volumes. Ed. A. Turnbull. London: G. Bell and Sons, 1911.

———. *The Complete Poetical Works of Samuel Taylor Coleridge*. 2 volumes. Ed. E.H. Coleridge. Oxford: The Clarendon Press, 1912.

———. *Collected Letters of Samuel Taylor Coleridge*. 6 volumes. Ed. E. L. Griggs. Oxford: The Clarendon Press, 1956–1971.

———. *Biographia Literaria*. 2 volumes. Ed. James Engell and Walter Jackson Bate. Princeton: Princeton University Press, 1983.

Corfield, Penelope J. and Chris Evans, ed. *Youth and Revolution in the 1790s: Letters of William Pattison, Thomas Amyot, and Henry Crabb Robinson*. Stroud: Alan Sutton, 1996.

Crabb Robinson, Henry. "[Three] Letters on the Philosophy of Kant." *The Monthly Register and Encyclopedian Magazine* (August 1802, November 1802, April 1803).

———. "[Five] Letters on German Literature." *The Monthly Register and Encyclopedian Magazine* (August 1802–April 1803).

———. *Diary, Reminiscences, and Correspondence*. 2 volumes. Ed. Thomas Sadler. London and New York: Macmillan, 1872.

_____. *The Correspondence of Henry Crabb Robinson with the Wordsworth Circle*. 2 volumes. Ed. Edith J. Morley. Oxford: The Clarenon Press, 1927.

_____. *Henry Crabb Robinson in Germany 1800–1805: Extracts from his Correspondence*. Ed. Edith J. Morley. London: Oxford University Press, 1929.

_____. *Henry Crabb Robinson on Books and their Writers*. 3 volumes. Ed. Edith J Morley. London: J. M. Dent, 1938.

_____. *Essays on Kant, Schelling, and German Aesthetics*. Ed. James Vigus. London: MHRA, 2010.

Crewe, Cordula. *The Nazarenes: Romantic Avant-Garde and the Art of the Concept*. University Park: Penn State University Press, 2015.

Davis, Garold N. *German Thought and Culture in England 1700–1760*. Chapel Hill: University of North Carolina Press, 1969.

De Quincey, Thomas. "Goethe's Wilhelm Meister's Apprenticeship." *London Magazine* 10 (1824): 189–197.

_____. *The Collected Writings of Thomas De Quincey*. Volume 11. Ed. David Masson. London: A.C. Black, 1897.

Dilthey, Wilhelm. *Das Erlebnis und die Dichtung: Lessing, Goethe, Novalis, Hölderlin: Vier Aufsätze*. Dritte Erweiterte Auflage (Leipzig: B. G. Teubner, 1910).

_____. *Poetry and Experience. Volume V Selected Works*. Ed. and trans. Rudolf A. Makreel and Fritjof Rodi. Princeton: Princeton University Press, 1986.

Doderer, Klaus. "Das englische und französische Bild von der deutschen Romantik." *Begriffsbestimmung der Romantik*. Ed. Helmut Prang. Darmstadt: Wissenschaftliche Buchgesellschaft, 1968. 386–412.

Dwight, John Sullivan, ed. *Select Minor Poems of Goehe and Schiller*. Boston: Hilliard, Gray, and Company, 1839.

Eckermann, Johann Peter. *Gespräche mit Goethe in den letzten Jahren seines Lebens*. Ed. Regine Otto. Munich: C.H. Beck, 1984.

Eliot George, [Marian Evans], trans. *The Life of Jesus, critically examined*. By Dr. David Friedrich Strauß. 3 volumes. London: John Chapman, 1846.

_____. [Marian Evans], trans. *The Essence of Christianity*. By Luwig Feuerbach. London: John Chapman, 1854.

———. [Marian Evans] "The Morality of Wilhelm Meister." *The Leader* (21 July 1955): 703.

———. "German Wit: Heinrich Heine." *Westminster Review* 65 (January 1856): 1–33.

———. "The Natural History of German Life." Review of Wilhelm Riehl's *Die bürgerliche Gesellschaft* [*Bourgeois Society*] (1851) and *Land und Leute* [*Nation and People*] (1853). *Westminster Review* 66 (July 1856): 28–44.

———. "Recollections of Berlin 1854–1855." *The Journals of George Eliot*. Ed. Margaret Harris and Judith Johnston. Cambridge: Cambridge University Press, 1998.

———. *Middlemarch*. Ed. Gregory Maertz. Peterbourough: Broadview Editions, 2004.

———. *Selections from George Eliot's Letters*. Ed. Gordon S. Haight. New Haven and London: Yale University Press, 1985.

Eliot, T.S. "Johnson as Critic and Poet" [1944] and "Goethe as Sage" [1955]. *On Poetry and Poets*. New York: Farrar, Straus and Giroux, 2009 [1957]. 184–222; 240–264.

Engell, James. *The Creative Imagination: Enlightenment to Romanticism*. Cambridge: Harvard University Press, 1981.

———. "Coleridge and German Idealism: First Postulates, Final Causes." *The Coleridge Connection: Essays for Thomas McFarland*. Ed Richard Gravil and Molly Lefebure. London: Macmillan, 1990. 153–177.

Ferrier, James F. "The Plagiarisms of S. T. Coleridge." *Blackwood's Edinburgh Magazine* 47, No. 293 (March 1840): 287–299.

Firchow, Peter Edgerly. *The Death of the German Cousin*. London and Toronto: Associated University Presses, 1986.

Forster, John. *Walter Savage Landor*. Oxford: The Clarendon Press, 1875.

Frank, Mitchell Benjamin. *Romantic Painting Redefined: Nazarene Tradition and the Narratives of Romanticism*. Farnham, UK: Ashgate Publishing, 2001.

Froude, James Anthony. *Thomas Carlyle: A History of the First Forty Years of His Life, 1795–1835*. 2 volumes. London: Longman, Green, 1882.

Fruman, Norman. *Coleridge, the Damaged Archangel*. New York: George Braziller, 1971.

Furst, Lilian R. "Mme de Staël's *De l'Allemagne*: A Misleading Intermediary" and "Two Versions of Schiller's *Wallenstein*." *The Contours Of European Romanticism*. London: Macmillan, 1979. 56–73; 94–108.

_____. *European Romanticism: Self-Definition*. London and New York: Methuen, 1980.

Gadamer, Hans-Georg. "Goethe and Philosophy." *Literature and Philosophy in Dialogue*. Ed. and trans. Robert H. Paslick. Albany: State University of New York Press, 1994. 1–20.

John Gage, ed. and trans. *Goethe on Art*. Berkeley and Los Angeles: University of California Press, 1980.

Gilchrist, Alexander. *Life of William Blake*. London: J. M. Dent and Sons, 2nd edition, 1945 [1880].

Godwin, William. *Memoirs of the Author of A Vindication of the Rights of Woman* (1798). Ed. Pamela Clemit and Gina Luria Walker. Peterborough: Broadview Press, 2001.

_____. *St. Leon: A Tale of the Sixteenth Century*. 4 volumes. London: G. G. J. and J. Robinson, 1799.

_____. *Things As They Are; or, the Adventures of Caleb Williams* (1794). Ed. and intro. Maurice Hindle. Hammondsworth: Penguin Books, 1988.

Goethe, Johann Wolfgang von. *Faust: A Tragedy*. Translated in the original metre by Bayard Taylor. Boston and New York: Houghton Mifflin Company, 1870.

_____. *Goethes Gespräche, 6. Band, 1827 und 1828*. Ed. Woldemar Freiherr von Biedermann. Leipzig: Biedermann, 1890.

_____. *Goethes Gespräche, 7. Band, 1829 und 1830*. Ed. Woldemar Freiherr von Biedermann. Leipzig: Biedermann, 1890.

_____. *Gedankausgabe der Werke, Briefe und Gespräche. Briefe der Jahre 1786–1814*. Band 19. Ed. Ernst Beutler. Zurich und Stuttgart: Artemis Verlag, 1949.

_____. *Dichtung und Wahrheit, Zweiter Teil, 7. Buch. Goethes Werke, Band XI, Autobiographische Schriften I*. Munich: C.H. Beck, fourteenth printing, 2002 [1981]).

_____. *Dichtung und Wahrheit*. Ed. Walter Hettche. Stuttgart: Reclam, 1991.

Good, James M. "William Taylor, Robert Southey, and the Word 'Autobiography'." *The Wordsworth Circle* 12 (Spring 1981): 125–127.

Goodden, Angelica. *Madame de Staël: The Dangerous Exile*. Oxford and New York: Oxford University Press, 2008.

Gregory, Allene. *The French Revolution and the English Novel*. New York and London: G.P. Putnam's Sons, 1915.

Guillory, John. *Cultural Capital: The Problem of Literary Canon Formation*. Chicago: University of Chicago Press, 1993.

Günther, Horst, ed. *Goethe: Schriften zur Weltliteratur*. Franfurt: Insel Verlag, 1987.

Gundolf, Friedrich. *Goethe*. Berlin: Verlag Bondi, 1916.

Gutke, Karl S. "Destination Goethe: Travelling Englishmen in Weimar." *Goethe and the English-Speaking World: Essays from the Cambridge Symposium for His 250th Anniversary*. Ed. Nicholas Boyle and John Guthrie. Rochester, New York: Camden House, 2002). 111–142.

Hartmann, Geoffrey. *Criticism in the Wilderness*. New Haven: Yale University Press, 1980.

Harrold, C.F. *Carlyle and German Thought, 1819–1834*. New Haven: Yale University Press, 1934.

Hazlitt, William. "Mme de Staël's Account of German Philosphy and Literature." *Morning Chronicle* 3 and 17 February; 3 March; and 8 April 1814.

———. *The Memoirs of the late Thomas Holcroft*. *The Complete Works of William Hazlitt*. Ed. P.P. Howe. London: J. M. Dent and Sons Ltd., 1932; reprint New York: AMS Press 1967.

———. "Mr. Jeffery." *The Complete Works of William Hazlitt*. Ed. P. P. Howe. London: J.M. Dent, 1930–1934.

Hedge, Frederic Henry. *Prose Writers of Germany*. Philadelphia: Carey and Hart, 1849.

Heine, Heinrich. *Sämtliche Werke*. Ed. Manfred Windfuhr. 2 volumes. Hamburg: Hoffmann und Campe, 1975.

Heller, Erich, "Goethe and the Scientific Truth." *The Disinherited Mind: Essays in Modern German Literature and Thought*. New York and London: Harcourt Brace Jovanovich, 1975 [1952]. 4–34.

———. "In Two Minds about Schiller." *The Artist's Journey into the Interior, and Other Essays*. New York and London: Harcourt Brace Jovanovich, 1975 [1965]. 45–72.

―――――. *The Importance of Nietzsche*. Chicago: University of Chicago Press, 1988.

Herder, Johann Gottfried von. *Vom Erkennen und Empfinden der Menschlichen Seele. Sämtliche Werke*. 8 volumes. Ed. B. Suphan, 2008.

Hohendahl, Peter Uwe. *The Institution of Criticism*. Ithaca: Cornell University Press, 1982.

Holcroft, Thomas, trans. *The Life of Baron Frederic Trenck, Containing His Adventure, His Cruel and Excessive Sufferings During Ten Years Imprisonment at the Fortress of Magdeburg By Command of the Late King of Prussia, also anecdotes, historical, political, and personal*. 3 volumes. London: G. G. J. and J. Robinson, 1788.

―――――. *Love's Frailties*. Covent Garden: Shepperson and Reynolds, 1794.

―――――, trans. Count Leopold Stolberg. *Travels through Germany, Switzerland, Italy, and Sicily*. London: G. G. J. and J. Robinson, 1796.

―――――, trans. Johann Wolfgang von Goethe, *Hermann and Dorothea*. London: T. N. Longman and O. Rees, 1801.

―――――. *Travels from Hamburg, through Westphalia, Holland, and the Netherlands, to Paris*. 2 volumes. London: G. G. J. and J. Robinson, 1804.

―――――. *Memoirs of Bryan Perdue; a Novel*. 3 volumes. London: Longman, Hurst, Rees, and Orme, 1805.

Holquist, Michael. *Dialogism: Bakthin and His World*. London: Routledge, 1990.

Hunnekuhl, Philipp. "Reconstructing the Voice of the Mediator: Henry Crabb Robinson's Literary Criticism." *Informal Romanticism*. Ed. James Vigus. Trier: Wissenschaftlicher Verlag Trier, 2012. 61–76.

―――――. "Hazlitt and Crabb Robinson: The Common Pursuit." *The Hazlitt Review* 6 (2013): 13–34.

―――――. "Beyond Whist Sobriety: the Lambs, Crabb Robinson, and their Discourse on Literature." *The Charles Lamb Bulletin*, New Series 158 (Autumn 2013): 126–138.

Isbell, John Claiborne. *The Birth of European Romanticism: Truth and Propaganda in Staël's De l'Allemagne*. Cambridge: Cambridge University Press, 1994.

Johnson, Herschel C. "Goethe's Influence on Carlyle." *Studies in English Language and Literature* 26, No. 3 (March 1986): 29–44.

Jones, Dorothy Richardson. *King of Critics: George Saintsbury, 1845–1933: Critic, Journalist, Historian, Professor.* Ann Arbor: University of Michigan Press, 1992.

Keats, John. *The Letters of John Keats.* 2 volumes. Ed. Hyder E. Rollins. Cambridge: Harvard University Press, 1958.

Keller, Gottfried. *Der grüne Heinrich.* Ed. Peter Goldhammer. Berlin and Weimar: Aufbau-Verlag, 1986.

———. *Green Henry.* Trans. A. M. Holt. New York and London: Riverrun Press, 1985.

Kelly, Gary. *The English Jacobin Novel 1780–1805.* Oxford: The Clarendon Press, 1976.

Kiely, Robert. *The Romantic Novel in England.* Cambridge: Harvard University Press, 1972.

Kierkegaard, Søren. *The Present Age: On the Death of Rebellion.* Trans. Alexander Dru. Introduction by Walter Kaufmann. New York: Harper Perennial Modern Classics, 2010 [1962].

Kipperman, Mark. *Beyond Enchantment: German Idealism and English Romantic Poetry.* Philadelphia: University of Pennsylvania Press, 1980.

Landor, Walter Savage. *The Poetical Works Walter Savage Landor.* 3 volumes. Ed. Stephen Wheeler. Oxford: The Clarendon Press, 1937.

Lavater, Johann Casper. *Physiognomische Fragmente zur Beförderung der Menschenkenntnis und Menschenliebe.* 4 Bände. Leipzig: Winterthur, 1775–1778.

Lamb, Charles. *The Letters of Charles Lamb.* Ed. Alfred Ainger. London: Macmillan and Co., 1888.

La Valley, Albert. *Carlyle and the Idea of the Modern.* New Haven: Yale University Press, 1968.

Lévi-Strauss, Claude. *Triste Tropiques.* New York: Atheneum Books, 1974.

Lewes, George Henry. *The Life and Works of Goethe, with Sketches of His Age and Contemporaries from Published and Unpublished Sources.* 2 volumes. London: David Nutt, 1857.

Lewis, Matthew Gregory. *The Life and Correspondence of M. G. Lewis, with many pieces in prose and verse never before published.* Ed. Margaret Baron-Wilson. London: H. Colburn, 1839.

Lowry, Howard Foster, ed. *The Letters of Matthew Arnold to A. H. Clough.* Oxford: Oxford University Press, repr. 1968 [1932].

McFarland, Thomas. *Coleridge and the Pantheist Tradition.* Oxford: The Clarendon Press, 1969.

McGann, Jerome J. *The Beauty of Inflections: Literary Investigations in Historical Method and Theory.* Oxford: The Clarendon Press, 1988.

Maertz, Gregory, ed. *Cultural Interactions in the Romantic Age: Essays in Comparative Literature.* Albany, New York: State University Press of New York, 1998.

Malraux, André. *Les Voix du silence.* Paris: Gallimard, 1951.

Mander, John. *Our German Cousins: Anglo-German Relations in the 19th and 20th Centuries.* London: John Murray, 1974.

Mann, Thomas. "Freud und die Zukunft" [1936]. *Gesammelte Werke in dreizehn Bänden. Band 9: Reden und Aufsätze. Teil 1.* Frankfurt: Fischer Verlag, 1974. 478–501.

Mann, Thomas. "Freud and the Future." *Essays of Three Decades.* Trans. H.T. Lowe-Porter. New York: Alfred A. Knopf, 1948 [1937]. 411–428.

Marcuse, Ludwig. "Reaktionäre und progressive Romantik." *Monatshefte* 44, No. 4/5 (April–May 1952): 195–201. Reprinted in *Begriffsbestimmung der Romantik.* Ed. Helmut Prang. Darmstadt: Wissenschaftliche Buchgesellschaft, 1968. 377–385.

———. *Briefe von und an Ludwig Marcuse.* Ed. Harold von Hofe. Zürich: Diogenes Verlag, 1975.

Marquardt, Hertha. *Henry Crabb Robinson und seine deutschen Freunde: Brücke zwischen England und Deutschland im Zeitalter der Romantik.* 2 Bände. Göttingen: Vandenhoeck und Ruprecht, 1964, 1967.

Mason, Eudo. *The Mind of Henry Fuseli.* London: Routledge and Kegan Paul, 1951.

Mauer, Michael. *Aufklärung und Anglophilie in Deutschland.* Göttingen and Zurich: Vandenhoeck und Ruprecht, 1987.

Meyers, Jeffrey. *Edgar Allan Poe: His Life and Legacy.* New York: Cooper Square Press, 1992.

Milton, John. *History of Britain*, vol. III (1670), *The Prose Works of John Milton*. Ed. R.W. Griswold. Philadelphia: John W. Moore, 1847.

More, Hannah. *Strictures on the Modern System of Female Education with a View of the Principles and Conduct Prevalent among Women of Rank and Fortune*. London: A. Straban, 1801.

Morgan, Bayard Quincy and A.R. Hohlfeld, ed. *German Literature in British Magazines, 1750–1860*. Madison: University of Wisconsin Press, 1949.

Mueller-Vollmer, Kurt. "Staël's Germany and the Beginings of an American National Literature." *Germaine de Staël: Crossing the Borders*. Ed. Madelyn Gutwirth New Brunswick: Rutgers University Press, 1991. 141–158.

Nash, Gerald D. *The American West Transformed: The Impact of the Second World War*. Lincoln and London: The University of Nebraska Press, 1985.

Nicholls, Angus. *Goethe's Concept of the Demonic After the Ancients*. Rochester, New York: Camden House, 2006.

Nietzsche, Friedrich. "Schopenhauer als Erzieher." *Unzeitgemässe Betrachtungen*. 2 Bände. Leipzig: C.G. Neumann Verlag, 1899.

_____. *Also Sprach Zarathustra. Band 6. Werke*. Leipzig: Alfred Körner, 1910.

_____. *Gesammelte Werke*, Musarion-Ausgabe. Munich, 1922–1929. Band XIX, Fragment 882, 229.

_____. *Schopenhauer as Educator*. Trans. James W. Hillesheim and Malcolm R. Simpson. South Bend: Regnery/Gateway, 1965.

_____. *Umwertung aller Werte*. Ed. Friedrich Würzbach. Munich: Deutscher Taschenbuch Verlag, 1977.

_____. *Jenseits von Gut und Böse: Vorspiel einer Philosophie der Zukunft*. Stuttgart: Reclam, 1988.

_____. *Die Geburt der Tragödie aus dem Geiste der Musik*. Ed. Günther Wohlfart. Stuttgart: Reclam, 2007.

Norman, Frederick. *Henry Crabb Robinson and Goethe*. 2 volumes. London: Published for the English Goethe Society by A. Moring, 1930–1931.

Norton, Charles Eliot, ed and trans. *Correspondence between Goethe and Carlyle*. New York: Cooper Square, repr. 1970 [1887].

Novalis (Friedrich von Hardenberg). *Fragmente des Jahres 1798. Gesammelte Werke*. 3 Bände. Ed. Carl Seelig. Herrliberg and Zurich: Buhl-Verlag, 1946.

———. *Henry von Ofterdingen*. Trans. Palmer Hilty. New York: Unger, 1964.

———. *Heinrich von Ofterdingen. Werke in einem Band*. Ed. Hans-Joachim Mahl and Richard Samuel. Munich and Vienna: Carl Hanser Verlag, 1981.

Nye, Russel Blaine. *The Cultural Life of the New Nation, 1776–1830*. New York: Harper and Bros., 1960.

O'Keeffe, Paul. *A Genius for Failure: The Life of Benjamin Robert Haydon*. London: The Bodley Head, 2011.

Oppel, Horst. *Englisch-deutsche Literaturbeiziehungen*. Berlin: Eric Schmidt Verlag, 1971.

Orel, Harold. *Victorian Literary Critics: George Henry Lewes, Walter Bagehot, Richard Holt Hutton, Leslie Stephen, Andrew Lang, George Saintsbury and Edmund Gosse*. New York: St. Martin's Press, 1984.

Ortega y Gasset, José. "In Search of Goethe from Within." *The Dehumanization of Art and Other Essays on Art, Culture, and Literature*. Princeton: Princeton University Press, 1968 [1948]. 131–174.

Ossoli, Sarah Margaret Fuller, trans. *Conversations of Goethe in the Last Years of His Life. Translated from the German of Eckermann* (1839). Boston: James Munroe and Company, 1852.

Ossoli, Margaret Fuller. *Life Within and Without*. Ed. Arthur B. Fuller. Boston: Brown, Taggard and Chase, 1860.

Ossoli, Margaret Fuller and Minna Wesselhoft, trans. *Correspondence of Fräulein Gunderode and Bettine von Arnim*. Boston: T. O. H. P. Burnham, 1861.

Oxenford, John. "Iconoclasm in German Philosophy." *Westminster Review*, New Series (April 1853): 388–407.

Pascal, Roy. *The German Sturm und Drang*. Manchester: Manchester University Press, 1953.

Paul, Charles Kegan. *William Godwin: His Friends and Contemporaries*. 2 volumes. London: Henry S. King & Co., 1876.

Pizer, John. "Goethe's 'World Literature' Paradigm and Contemporary Cultural Globalizaton." *Comparative Literature* 52, No. 3 (Summer 2000): 213–227.

Praz, Mario. *The Romantic Agony*. Trans. Angus Davidson. New York: Oxford University Press, second edition, 1978 [1951].

Proper, C. B. A. *Social Elements in English Prose Fiction between 1771–1832*. New York: Haskell House, 1965 [1929].

Richter, Simon and Richard Block, ed. *Goethe's Ghosts: Reading and the Persistence of Literature*. Rochester, New York: Camden House, 2012.

Riede, David. "Transgression, Authority, and the Church of Literature in Carlyle." *Victorian Connections*. Ed. Jerome J. McGann. Charlottesville: University Press of Virginia, 1989. 99–130.

Ripley, George. Letter to Thomas Carlyle, 29 December 1836. Autograph File. The Houghton Library, Harvard University.

Robberds. J. W. *A Memoir of the Late William Taylor of Norwich*. London: John Murray, 1843.

Röder-Bolton, Gerlinde. *George Eliot in Germany, 1854–1855: "Cherished Memories."* Aldershot: Ashgate, 2006.

Roper, Derek. *Reviewing before the Edinburgh, 1788–1802*. Newark: The University of Delaware Press, 1978.

Sade, Marquis de. *Les infortunes de la vertu*. Introduction by Jean Paulhan. Paris: Jean-Jacques Pauvert, 1959.

———. *The Complete Justine, Philosophy in the Bedroom, and other Writings*. Trans. Richard Seaver and Austryn Wainhouse. New York: Grove Press, 1965.

Safranski, Rüdiger. *Goethe: Kunstwerk der Lebens*. Frankfurt: Fischer Taschenbuch, 2015.

Said, Edward W. *The World, the Text, and the Critic*. Cambridge: Harvard University Press, 1984.

Saintsbury, George. *A History of Criticism and Literary Taste in Europe.* 3 volumes. Edinburgh and London: William Blackwood and Sons, 1900–1904.

Sanborn, F. B., ed. *The Life and Genius of Goethe: Lectures of the Concord School of Philosophy*. Boston: Ticknor and Company, 1886.

Santayana, George. *Three Philosophical Poets: Lucretius, Dante, and Goethe.* 1910. Harvard Studies in Comparative Literature. Volume 1. New York: Cooper Square Publishers, 1970.

Schiller, Friedrich von. *Über naive und sentimentalische Dichtung.* Ed. Karl-Maria Guth. Berlin: Verlag der Contumax, 2016.

Schirmer, Walter. *Der Einfluß der deutschen Literatur auf die englische im 19. Jahrhundert.* Halle/Salle: M. Niemeyer, 1947.

Schlegel, Friedrich. "Gespräch über die Poesie." *Kritische Schriften.* Ed. Wolfdietrich Rasch. Munich: Paul Hauser, 1971.

———. "Athenäum Fragment, No. 262." *Charakteristiken und Kritiken I (1796–1801).* Ed. Hans Eichner. Munich: Ferdinand Schöningh, 1976.

———. "Ideen, No. 43." *Werke in Zwei Bände.* Ed. Wolfgang Hecht. Berlin and Weimar: Aufbau-Verlag, 1980.

Schopenhauer, Arthur. *Die Welt als Wille und Vorstellung.* 2 Bände. Ed. Werner Brede. Munich: Carl Hauser Verlag, 1977.

———. *The World as Will and Representation.* 2 volumes. Trans. E. F. J. Payne. New York: Dover, 1966.

Shaffer, E. S. "The 'Confessions' of Goethe and Coleridge: Goethe's 'Bekenntnisse einer Schönen Seele' and Coleridge's *Confessions of an Inquiring Spirit.*" *Goethe and the English-Speaking World: Essays from the Cambridge Symposium for His 250th Anniversary.* Ed. Nicholas Boyle and John Guthrie. Rochester, New York: Camden House, 2002), 145–158.

Sharpe, Leslie, ed. *The Cambridge Companion to Goethe.* Cambridge: Cambridge University Press, 2002.

Shelley, Percy Bysshe. *Letters of Percy Bysshe Shelley.* 3 volumes. Ed. Roger Ingpen. London: Sir Isaac Pitman and Sons, 1909.

———. "A Defense of Poetry." *Shelley's Poetry and Prose.* Ed. Neil Fraistat and Donald H. Reiman New York and London: W.W. Norton, 2nd edition, 2002.

Simpson, James. "*The Authority of Culture*: Some Reflections on the Reception of a Classic." *Goethe and the English-Speaking World: Essays from the Cambridge Symposium for His 250th Anniversary.* Ed. Nicholas Boyle and John Guthrie. Rochester, New York: Camden House, 2002. 185–198.

Staël, Germaine de. *De l'Allemagne*. Ed. Simone Balayé. 2 volumes. Paris: Garnier-Flammarion, 1968.

Smith, D. Nichol. "George Saintsbury." *Dictionary of National Biography, 1931–1940, 5th Supplement.* Ed. L. G. Wickham Legg. Oxford: Oxford University Press, 1949.

Stallbaumer, Virgil R. "Thomas Hocroft as a Novelist." *ELH* 15 No. 3 (1948): 194–218.

Stark, Susanne. *'Behind Inverted Commas': Translation and Anglo-German Cultural Relations in the Nineteenth-Century.* Clevedon: Multilingual Matters Ltd., 1999.

Stevens, Wallace. "Two or Three Ideas." *Opus Posthumous*. Ed. Milton J. Bates. New York: Vintage Books, 1989 [1957]. 257–266.

Stelzig, Eugene. "A Cultural Tourist in Romantic Germany: Henry Crabb Robinson as Nineteenth-Century Life Writer." *Biography* 28 (2005): 515–533.

———. "Henry Crabb Robinson as Staël's Philosophical Informant." *Prism(s): Essays in Romanticism* 15 (2007): 113–128.

———. *Henry Crabb Robinson in Germany: A Study in Nineteenth-Century Life Writing.* Lewisburg: Bucknell University Press, 2010.

Stockhorst, Stefanie. "Gelehrte Geselligkeit und europäischer Kulturtransfer. Zur Deutung des produktiven Zusammentreffens von Henry Crabb Robinson und Mme de Staël in Weimar." *"Weimar ist ja unser Athen." Mit Seume in Weimar: Vorträge des Colloquiums zu Johann Gottfried Seume in Oßmannstedt 2007.* Ed. Jörg Drews and Gabi Pahnke (Bielefeld: Aisthesis, 2010). 119–140.

———. "Das klassische Weimar aus englischer Sicht. Zum Funktionswandel des Reisens um 1800 am Beispiel von Charles Gore und Henry Crabb Robinson." *Reisen um 1800*. Ed. Helmut Peitsch. Munich: Peter Lang, 2012. 31–51.

———. "Vermittlungstrategien und transnationale Kanonbildung. Zur britischen Kotzebue-Rezeption am Beispiel von William Taylor and Henry Crabb Robinson." *Angermion* 8, No. 1 (December 2015): 35–60.

Stockley, Violet. *German Literature as Known in England 1750–1830*. London: Routledge, 1929.

Stolberg, Count Leopold. *Travels through Germany, Switzerland, Italy, and Sicily.* Trans. Thomas Holcroft. London: G.G. J. and J. Robinson, 1796.

Strauss, Claude-Lévi. *Triste Tropiques*. Paris: Plon, 1951.

Streuli, Wilhelm. *Thomas Carlyle als Vermittler Deutscher Literatur und Deutschen Geistes*. Zürich: Druck und Verlag von Friedrich Schulthess, 1895.

Swale, Martin and Erika Swale. *Reading Goethe: A Critical Introduction to the Literary Work*. Rochester, New York: Camden House, 2007.

Taine, Hippolyte. *Histoire de la littérature Anglaise*. 4 volumes. Paris: L. Hachette, 1863–1864.

Taylor, William. *An Historic Survey of German Poetry*. 2 volumes. London: Treutel and Wurtz, 1828–1830.

Thompkins, J. M. S. *The Popular Novel in England, 1770–1800*. Lincoln: University of Nebraska Press, 1961.

Tillich, Paul. *The Courage to Be*. New Haven: Yale University Press, 2000 [1952].

Van Cromphout, Gustaaf. *Emerson's Modernity and the Example of Goethe*. Colombia, Missouri: University of Missouri Press. 1990.

Vanden Bossche, Chris R. *Carlyle and the Search for Authority*. Columbus, Ohio: Ohio State University Press, 1991.

Vigny, Alfred de. *Stello, Oevres complètes*. Ed. F. Baldensperger. Paris: Gallimard, Édition Pleide, 1950.

Wackenroder, Wilhelm Heinrich and Ludwig Tieck. *Herzensergiessungen eines kunstliebenden Klosterbruders*. Ed. A. Gillies. Oxford: Basil Blackwell, 1948.

Wackenroder, Wilhelm Heinrich and Ludwig Tieck. *Outpourings of an Art-Loving Friar*. Trans. Edward Mornin. New York: Unger, 1975.

Wagner, Richard. "Eine Mittheilung an meine Freunde" ["A Communiqué to My Friends"] (1851). *Gesammelte Schriften und Dichtungen*, 4. Band. Leipzig: Verlag von E.W. Fritzsch, 1872.

———. "Religion und Kunst" ["Religion and Art"] (1880). *Gesammelte Schriften und Dichtungen*. Dritte Auflage, 9. Band. Leipzig: Verlag von E.W. Fritzsch, 1898.

Walz, John A. *German Influence in American Education and Culture*. Philadelphia: Carl Schurz Memorial Foundation, 1936.

Waterhouse, Gilbert. *The Literary Relations of England and Germany in the Seventeenth Century*. New York: Haskell House, 1966 [1914].

Wellbery, David E. *The Spectacular Moment: Goethe's Early Lyric and the Beginnings of Romanticism*. Stanford: Stanford University Press, 1996.

Wellek, René. *Immanuel Kant in England*. Princeton: Princeton University Press, 1930.

———. *A History of Modern Criticism*. 2 volumes. Cambridge: Cambridge University Press, 1955.

———. *Confrontations: Studies in the Intellectual and Literary Relations Between Germany, England, and the United States During the Nineteenth Century*. Princeton: Princeton University Press, 1965.

Werner, Anja. *The Transatlantic World of Higher Education: Americans at German Universities, 1776–1914*. New York and Oxford: Berghahn Books, 2013.

Whelan, Timothy. "Henry Crabb Robinson and Godwinism." *The Wordsworth Circle* 33 (Spring 2002): 58–69.

Wilde, Oscar. "The Portrait of Mr. W.H." *Blackwood's Edinburgh Magazine* 146 (July 1889): 1–21.

Williams, John R. *The Life of Goethe: A Critical Biography*. Hoboken, New Jersey: Wiley-Blackwell, 2001.

Willoughby, L. A. *The Romantic Movement in Germany*. London: Oxford University Press, 1930.

Witz, Ernst. *Die literarische Tätigkeit des Malers J. H. Füssli*. Unpublished diss., University of Basle, 1922.

Woolf, Virginia. "George Eliot." *Times Literary Supplement* 18 (20 November 1919): 657–658.

Wordsworth, William. "Preface." *Lyrical Ballads*. Ed. R. I. Brett and A. R. Jones. London and New York: Oxford University Press, 1968.

Notes

Notes Acknowledgements

1. Walter Benjamin, *Einbahnstrasse*, ed. Karl-Maria Guth, Berlin: Verlag der Contumax, 2016 [1928]: 7: "A visit to Goethe's house . . . . The curator requests us to sign the visitor's book . . . . As I draw near and turn the pages, I find that my name has already been signed in the big, unwieldy letters of a child's handwriting."

Notes Preface

1. Harold Bloom, *The Western Canon: The Books and School of the Ages* (New York: Harcourt Brace, 1994), 204, 215.

Notes Prelude

1. 30 March 1824, *Goethes Gespräche, 5. Band, 1824–1826*, ed. Woldemar Freiherr von Biedermann (Leipzig: Biedermann, 1890), 59: "After all, the personal character of the writer is what defines his importance in the eyes of the public, not the subtlety of his talents."
2. Rosemary Ashton, *The German Idea: Four English Writers and the Reception of German Thought, 1800–1860* (Cambridge: Cambridge University Press, 1980), 80, 90, 106.
3. *Correspondence between Goethe and Carlyle*, ed. and trans. Charles Eliot Norton (New York, 1970), 18–19, 26: "The Koran says: 'God has given to each people a prophet in his own tongue!' Thus each translator is a prophet to his people."
4. Chris R. Vanden Bossche, *Carlyle and the Search for Authority* (Columbus: Ohio State University Press, 1991), 29.
5. Klaus Doderer, "Das englische und französische Bild von der deutschen Romantik" (1955), *Begriffsbestimmung der Romantik*, ed. Helmut Prang (Darmstadt: Wissenschaftlicher Buchgesellschaft, 1968), 387.
6. Such border crossing is a characteristic feature of Romanticism. See *Cultural Interactions in the Romantic Age*, ed. Gregory Maertz (Albany, New York: State University of New York Press, 1998).
7. Wilhelm Dilthey, *Das Erlebnis und die Dichtung: Lessing, Goethe, Novalis, Hölderlin: Vier Aufsätze*. Dritte Erweiterte Auflage (Leipzig: B.G. Teubner, 1910). The

translation is by Rudolf A. Makreel and Frithjof Rodi in Wilhelm Dilthey, *Selected Works, Vol. V, Poetry and Experience* (Princeton: Princeton University Press, 1986), 237–238: "Poetry is the representation and expression of life. It expresses lived experience and represents the external reality of life . . . . What a lyric poem or a story shows us—and what it fails to show us—can be explained on this basis. But life-values are related on the basis of the totality of life itself, and these relations give meaning to persons, things, situations, and events. Thus the poet addresses himself to what is significant . . . . Surely the primary and most decisive feature of Goethe's work is that it grows out of an extraordinary energy of lived experience . . . . His moods transform everything real, his passions intensify the meaning and form of situations and things beyond the realm of the usual, and his restless creative drive changes everything around him into form and image."

8 Rudolf A. Makreel, *Dilthey* (Princeton: Princeton University Press, 1975), 152–153.

9 *The Works of Thomas Carlyle*, 30 volumes, ed. H.D. Traill (London: Chapman and Hall), vol. 26, 208.

10 George Saintsbury, *A History of Criticism and Literary Taste in Europe* (Edinburgh and London: William Blackwood and Sons, 1900–1904), vol. 3, 495.

11 13 February 1831, *Goethes Gespräche, 8. Band, 1831–1832 und Nachträge*, ed. Woldemar Freiherr von Beidermann (Leipzig: Biedermann, 1890), 15: "Personality is everything in art and poetry, yet there are many weak personages among the modern critics who do not admit this, but look upon a great personality in a work of poetry or art merely as a kind of trifling appendage. However, to feel and respect a great personality one must be something oneself. All who denied the sublime to Euripides were either poor wretches incapable of comprehending such sublimity, or shameless charlatans who by presumption wished to make more of themselves—and really did make more of themselves than they were."

12 *Goethes Gespräche, 5. Band, 1824–1826*, 116: "By the way he spoke of Dante with the most reverence, and he considered the word talent insufficient to describe him, but called him rather a nature, as if thus wishing to express something more comprehensive, more acutely sensitive, of deeper insight, and wider scope."

13 *Goethes Gespräche, 5. Band, 1824–1826*, 147–148: "He is a great talent, a natural talent, and in terms of genuine poetic power, Byron has never been superseded by anyone. In view of external circumstances and clear perception of past conditions he is as great as Shakespeare."

14 James Anthony Froude, *Thomas Carlyle: A History of the First Forty Years of His Life, 1795–1835* (London, 1882), vol. 1, 132–133. Hereafter cited as *Life of Carlyle, 1795–1832*.

15 Carlyle expressed his displeasure with the task of translating *Wilhelm Meister* in letters to Jane Welsh on 18 September 1823 and to James Johnson on 21 September 1823. See *Collected Letters of Thomas and Jane Welsh Carlyle*, ed. C. R. Sanders

and K. J. Fielding (Durham, North Carolina: Duke University Press, 1970), vol. 2, 434, 437.
16 *The Works of Thomas Carlyle*, vol. 26, 430. For an informed discussion of the political significance of Goethe's reception in Britain, see James Simpson, "The Authority of Culture: Some Reflections on the Reception of a Classic," Nicholas Boyle and John Guthrie, ed., *Goethe and the English-Speaking World: Essays from the Cambridge Symposium for his 250th Anniversary* (Rochester, New York: Camden House, 2002), 185–198.
17 *Life of Carlyle, 1795–1835*, vol. 1, 300–301. For more on the wave of British visitors to Weimar see Karl S. Gutke, "Destination Goethe: Travelling Englishmen in Weimar," in Boyle and Guthrie, ed., *Goethe and the English-Speaking World*, 111–142.
18 Letter of 20 August 1827 in *Correspondence between Goethe and Carlyle*, 34.
19 W. H. Bruford, "Goethe and Some Victorian Humanists," *Publications of the English Goethe Society*, New Series XVIII (1949), 36.
20 Contemporaries whom Goethe persuaded to join him in the service of *Grossherzog* Karl August included Schiller, Herder, Hamann, and Wieland.
21 The dispute over the supposed and real impact of Staël's propaganda on behalf of German literature in Britain and American has a long history. An authoritative discussion of her problematic mediation of German literature is found in Lilian R. Furst's "Madame de Staël's *De l'Allemagne*: A Misleading Intermediary," *The Contours of European Romanticism* (London: Macmillan, 1979), 56–73. More generous assessments of Staël's influence include Kurt Mueller-Vollmer's "Staël's *Germany* and the Beginnings of an American National Literature," *Germaine de Staël: Crossing the Borders*, ed. Madelyn Gutwirth, et al. (New Brunswick: Rutgers University Press, 1991), 141–158, and John Claiborne Isbell's *The Birth of European Romanticism: Truth and Propaganda in Staël's De l'Allemagne* (Cambridge: Cambridge University Press, 1994). For an important recent study that examines the transgressive elements in Staël's literary career and personal life, see Angelica Goodden, *Madame de Staël: The Dangerous Exile* (Oxford and New York: Oxford University Press, 2008).
22 Walter Schirmer, *Der Einfluß der deutschen Literatur auf die englische im 19. Jahrhundert* (Halle/Salle: M. Niemeyer, 1947), 39.
23 Doderer, "Das englische und französische Bild von der deutschen Romantik," 397.
24 Germaine de Staël, *De l'Allemagne* (Paris: Garnier-Flammarion, 1968), vol. 1, 189.
25 René Wellek, *A History of Modern Criticism* (Cambridge University Press, 1955), vol. 2, 224.
26 *The Works of Thomas Carlyle*, vol. 27, 476.
27 Jerome J. McGann, *The Beauty of Inflections: Literary Investigations in Historical Method and Theory* (Oxford: The Clarendon Press, 1988), 137–138.
28 Furst, "Madame de Staël's *De l'Allemagne*: A Misleading Intermediary," 56.
29 Thomas Carlyle, *Two Notebooks*, ed. Charles Eliot Norton (New York: The Grolier Club, 1898), 65.

30 James Anthony Froude, *Thomas Carlyle: A History of His Life in London, 1833–1881* (London: Longmans, Green, 1884), vol. 1, 96.
31 Peter Uwe Hohendahl, *The Institution of Criticism* (Ithaca: Cornell University Press, 1982), 66.
32 Furst, "Madame de Staël's *De l'Allemagne*: A Misleading Intermediary," 58.
33 Heinrich Heine, *Sämtliche Werke*, ed. Manfred Windfuhr (Hamburg: Hoffmann & Campe, 1979), vol. 1, 148. The implication here is that Goethe preferred aesthetic to political solutions to the problems of modernity.
34 Heine, *Sämtliche Werke*, vol. 1, 148.
35 *The Works of Thomas Carlyle*, vol. 26, 207–208.
36 *The Works of Thomas Carlyle*, vol. 26, 208.
37 *The Works of Thomas Carlyle*, vol. 26, 435.
38 *Passages from the Prose Writings of Matthew Arnold*, ed. William Buckler (New York: New York University Press, 1963), 28, 29. Ashton notes that "Arnold modelled his idea of culture and *Weltliteratur* partly on Goethe's and quoted Goethe in almost every essay he wrote" (*The German Idea*, 20).
39 Goethe to Carlyle, 1 January 1828, *Correspondence between Goethe and Carlyle*, 37–38, 42: "But now I wish to know from you what may be the merit of Tasso as an English translation? It will greatly oblige me if you will inform and enlighten me as to this, because it is precisely the bearing of an original to a translation, which most clearly indicates the relations of nation to nation, and which one must especially know and estimate for the furtherance of the prevailing, predominant and universal World literature."
40 Carlyle, *Two Notebooks*, 128.
41 See, for example, Walter Jackson Bate, *The Burden of the Past and the English Poet* (New York: W.W. Norton, 1972), Harold Bloom, *The Anxiety of Influence: A Theory of Poetry* (London and New York: Oxford University Press, 2nd edition, 1997 [1973]), William St. Clair, *The Godwins and the Shelleys* (New York: W.W. Norton, 1989), John Bowlby, *Charles Darwin* (New York: W.W. Norton, 1990), and Claire Tomalin, *John Dickens* (New York: Penguin Books, 2012).
42 Hippolyte Taine, *Histoire de la littérature Anglaise* (Paris: Hachette, 1863–1864), vol. 3, 277.
43 Letter to Josiah Wedgwood, *Collected Letters of S. T. Coleridge*, ed. Earl Leslie Griggs (Oxford: Oxford University Press, 1958), vol. 4, 698–699.
44 Saintsbury, vol. 3, 497.
45 *Diary, Reminiscences and Correspondence of Henry Crabb Robinson*, 2 volumes, ed. Thomas Sadler (London and New York: Macmillan, 1872), vol. 1, 202.
46 *Diary, Reminiscences and Correspondence*, vol. 1, 206–207.
47 "Letters on German Literature," *The Monthly Register and Encyclopedian Magazine* (August-April 1802–1803).
48 Cited in Norman, vol. 2, 58.
49 *Life of Carlyle, 1795–1835*, vol. 1, 222.
50 *The Works of Thomas Carlyle*, vol. 26, 430.
51 *The Works of Thomas Carlyle*, vol. 5, 1.

52 *The Works of Thomas Carlyle*, vol. 26, 208
53 *The Works of Thomas Carlyle*, vol. 27, 430.
54 *The Works of Thomas Carlyle*, vol. 26, 276.
55 *The Works of Thomas Carlyle*, vol. 26, 237.
56 Cited in Bruford, "Goethe and Some Victorian Humanists," 49.
57 *The Works of Thomas Carlyle*, vol. 26, 66.
58 *The Works of Thomas Carlyle*, vol. 27, 434–435.
59 *The Works of Thomas Carlyle*, vol. 27, 440–441.
60 *The Works of Thomas Carlyle*, vol. 27, 426.
61 *The Works of Thomas Carlyle*, vol. 27, 440.
62 *The Works of Thomas Carlyle*, vol. 26, 199.
63 *The Works of Thomas Carlyle*, vol. 26, 199.
64 *The Works of Thomas Carlyle*, vol. 27, 434.
65 *The Works of Thomas Carlyle*, vol. 27, 438.
66 *Dichtung und Wahrheit*, Zweiter Teil, 7. Buch, *Goethes Werke, Band XI, Autobiographische Schriften I* (Munich: C.H. Beck, fourteenth printing, 2002 [1981]), 283.
67 Samuel Taylor Coleridge, *Biographia Literaria*, ed. James Engell and Walter Jackson Bate (Princeton: Princeton University Press, 1983), vol. 2, 5.
68 *The Works of Thomas Carlyle*, vol. 27, 431, 435.
69 *The Works of Thomas Carlyle*, vol. 26, 210.
70 *The Works of Thomas Carlyle*, vol. 26, 215.
71 *The Works of Thomas Carlyle*, vol. 26, 216–217.
72 *The Works of Thomas Carlyle*, vol. 26, 217.
73 *The Works of Thomas Carlyle*, vol. 27, 427.
74 Thomas Carlyle, *Sartor Resartus: The Life and Opinions of Herr Teufelsdröckh*, ed. Rodger L. Tarr and Mark Engel (Los Angeles and Berkeley: University of California Press, 2000), 143.
75 *Life of Carlyle, 1795–1835*, vol. 1, 66.
76 *The Works of Thomas Carlyle*, vol. 26, 224.
77 *The Works of Thomas Carlyle*, vol. 27, 431. For an astute treatment of Goethe's mediation of "alien worlds," including the Anglo-Saxon lands, see David Bell, "Goethe's Orientalism," Boyle and Guthrie, ed., *Goethe and the English-Speaking World*, 199–212.
78 *The Works of Thomas Carlyle*, vol. 26, 232–233.
79 *The Works of Thomas Carlyle*, vol. 26, 234.
80 *The Works of Thomas Carlyle*, vol. 26, 242–243
81 *The Works of Thomas Carlyle*, vol. 26, 269.
82 *The Letters of John Keats*, ed. Hyder E. Rollins (Cambridge: Harvard University Press, 1958), vol. 1, 67.
83 *The Works of Thomas Carlyle*, vol. 27, 438.
84 *Sartor Resartus*, 178, 43, 182, 175.
85 *The Works of Thomas Carlyle*, vol. 27, 431.

Notes Chapter One

1. Harold Bloom, *The Anxiety of Influence: A Theory of Poetry* (New York: Oxford University Press, second edition, 2003 [1997]), 56.
2. Erich Heller, *The Disinherited Mind: Essays on Modern German Literature and Thought* (New York and London: Harcourt Brace Jovanovich, 1975), 32.
3. The scholarship on the transmission of German culture in late eighteenth-century England is limited. One of the earliest authoritative investigations of this specific relationship is John Boening's article, "Pioneers and Precedents: The 'Importation of German' and the Emergence of Periodical Criticism in England," *Internationales Archiv für Sozialgeschichte der deutschen Literatur* VII (1982): 65–87. The emphasis in Boening's article is on the innovative character of William Taylor's career as a reviewer for *The Monthly Review* and on the emergence of a class of professional literary critics in Britain that can be traced to the criticism of German literature in the reviews.
4. See especially Miriam L. Wallace, *Revolutionary Subjects in the English 'Jacobin' Novel, 1790–1805* (Lewisburg: Bucknell University Press, 2009); Allene Gregory, *The French Revolution and the English Novel* (New York and London: G.P. Putnam's Sons, 1915); C.B.A. Proper, *Social Elements in English Prose Fiction between 1771–1832* (New York: Haskell House, 1965 [1929]); Virgil R. Stallbaumer, "Thomas Holcroft as a Novelist," *ELH* XV (1948): 194–218; J. M. S. Thompkins, *The Popular Novel in England, 1770–1800* (Lincoln and London: University of Nebraska Press, 1961); Rodney M. Baine, *Thomas Holcroft and the Revolutionary Novel* (Athens: University of Georgia Press, 1965); and Gary Kelly, *The English Jacobin Novel 1780–1805* (Oxford: The Clarendon Press, 1976). For details on Holcroft's biography the main sources are *The Memoirs of the late Thomas Holcroft* (completed in 1810 and published in 1816) in *The Complete Works of William Hazlitt*, ed. P. P. Howe (London: J. M. Dent & Sons Ltd., 1932; rpt., New York: AMS Press, 1967); Charles Kegan Paul's *William Godwin: His Friends and Contemporaries* (London: Henry S. King & Co., 1876); and *Letters of Charles Lamb*, ed. Alfred Ainger (London: Macmillan and Co., 1888).
5. Preface to Frederic Leopold Count Stolberg, *Travels through Germany, Switzerland, Italy, and Sicily*, trans. Thomas Holcroft (London: G. G. J. and J. Robinson, 1796), vol. 1, iv.
6. Evidence of the affinity between German literature and radicalism is seen in Godwin's interest in *Werther* (which he was reading at the time of Wollstonecraft's death), in Mary Shelley's inclusion of Goethe's novel among the books read by Victor Frankenstein's monstrous autodidact, in P. B. Shelley's fragmentary translation of *Faust*, and in Coleridge's intense engagement with German culture as revealed in *Biographia Literaria* (1817).
7. For an example from the early nineteenth century, in 1828 Carlyle applied for appointment to a professorship at St. Andrew's University on the strength of

his reviews and translations of German literature. Goethe served as one of Carlyle's referees.

8   See James Simpson, "*The Authority of Culture*: Some Reflections on the Reception of a Classic," *Goethe and the English-Speaking World*, 185–198.
9   Charles Kegan Paul, *William Godwin: His Friends and Contemporaries*, vol. 1, 64–65.
10 Charles Kegan Paul, *William Godwin: His Friends and Contemporaries*, vol. 1, 357: "In my 31st year [1787] I became acquainted with Mr. Thomas Holcroft, and it was probably in consequence of our mutual conversations that I became two years after an unbeliever, and in my 36th year an atheist.
11 William Godwin, *Things as They Are; or, the Adventures of Caleb Williams*, ed. and intro. Maurice Hindle (Hammondsworth: Penguin Books, 1988), 4.
12 William Godwin, *Caleb Williams*, 3.
13 Marilyn Butler, ed., *Burke, Paine, Godwin, and the Revolution Controversy* (Cambridge: Cambridge University Press, 1989), 170.
14 Count Reginald De St. Leon, *St. Godwin: A Tale of the Sixteenth, Seventeenth, and Eighteenth Century* (London: Printed for J. Wright, Piccadilly, 1800).
15 Thomas Holcroft, *Love's Frailties* (Covent Garden: Shepperson and Reynolds, 1794), 29.
16 While Baine (1965), Kelly (1976), and Wallace (2014) make giant strides in clarifying the relationship between art and politics in Holcroft's novels, no recent scholarship explores the connection examined in this chapter.
17 Thomas Holcroft, *Memoirs of Bryan Perdue; a Novel* (London: Longman, Hunt, Rees, and Orme, 1805), vol. 1, iii.
18 *Selected Writings of Edmund Burke*, ed. Walter Jackson Bate (New York: Modern Library, 1947), 390.
19 Matthew Arnold, *Culture and Anarchy*, ed. J. Dover Wilson (Cambridge: Cambridge University Pres, 1960), 204.
20 Edward Said, *The World, the Text, and the Critic* (Cambridge: Harvard University Press, 1983), 11.
21 Goethe acknowledged that the achievement of Carlyle and his contemporaries (Scott, Gillies, Lockhart, and Wilson, among others) in transmitting German literature was prima facie evidence of the presence of a widespread European movement culminating in the emergence of a global, cosmopolitan aesthetic. Concerning original sources, see the entry made on 15 July 1827 in Johann Peter Eckermann, *Gespräche mit Goethe in den letzten Jahren seines Lebens* (Leipzig: Brockhaus, 1885), vol. 1, 254–257; and *The Correspondence between Goethe and Carlyle*, ed. Charles Norton Eliot (Boston, 1887; rpt. New York: Cooper Square Publishers, Inc., 1970), especially the letters from Goethe to Carlyle dated 20 July 1827 and 15 June 1828 (13–27; 91–115). For recent useful scholarship on this matter, see Thomas O. Beebee, "Introduction: Departures, Emanations, Intersections" in *German Literature as World Literature*, ed. Thomas O. Beebee (London

and New York: Bloomsbury, 2014), 1–22; and John Pizer, "Goethe's 'World Literature' Paradigm and Contemporary Cultural Globalization," *Comparative Literature* 52, No. 3 (Summer, 2000): 213–227.

22 For a thorough discussion of Anglo-German relations in the eighteenth century, see Garold N. Davis, *German Thought and Culture in England 1700–1760* (Chapel Hill: University of North Carolina Press, 1969), 64–80. For the intriguing story of the presence of English culture in Germany at a slightly earlier period, see Gilbert Waterhouse, *The Literary Relations of England and Germany in the Seventeenth Century* (Leipzig, 1914; rpt. New York: Haskell House, 1966).

23 Alexander Gilchrist, *Life of William Blake* (2nd edition, 1880; rpt. London: J. M. Dent & Sons Ltd., 1945), 294.

24 Davis, *German Thought and Culture in England 1700–1760*, 11–44.

25 Michael Maurer, *Aufklärung und Anglophilie in Deutschland* (Göttingen und Zürich: Vandenhoeck und Ruprecht, 1987). See especially pages 41–106.

26 See Ernst Witz, *Die literarische Tätigkeit des Malers J. H. Füßli* (Unpublished diss., University of Basel, 1922): "It is owing to Fuseli's influence that *The Analytical Review* (1788–1798) devoted so much attention to German literature, in which he still took a lively interest." Quoted in Eudo Mason, *The Mind of Henry Fuseli* (London: Routledge & Kegan Paul, 1951), 18. In fact, in *The Analytical* for April 1791 it is conceded that German literature has been "shamefully neglected in this country" (IX: 569).

27 This review appeared in August 1798, vol. 28: 170, 175. Fuseli comments on the peculiar character of Goethe's achievement: "The merits of invention . . . Goethe enjoys in common with many of his contemporaries. The distinguishing excellence of this celebrated writer is the display of exquisite enthusiastic passion. His pencil, dipped in the bow of heaven, sometimes exhibits a strength and brilliancy of colouring that dazzles 'the mind's eye'; and sometimes . . . displays the softest shade, the most delicate and tender touches . . . . Goethe is entitled to no vulgar merit for the judgment which his displays in the choice of his subjects: aware that his powers are most successfully applied when the softer sensibilities of our nature are to be excited, when tenderness and pity are to be called forth, he avoids all intricacy of plot, and generally selects for the foundation of his drama some simple and affecting story of domestic life, which may come home to the bosom of us all."

28 In Chapter 5 of William Godwin's *Memoirs of the Author of "The Rights of Woman"* (1798; rpt. Hammondsworth: Penguin, 1987) we read that Wollstonecraft "new-modelled and abridged" this work from an earlier translation (226). Charles Kegan Paul in *William Godwin: his friend and contemporaries* (London: Henry S. King & Co., 1876) quotes a Johnson note left in manuscript: "A translation from the Dutch of 'Young Grandison' was put into her hands, which she almost re-wrote" (I, 193). *De kleine Grandison* was a product of the Grandison craze on the Continent that emerged in the wake of Samuel Richardson's *The History of Sir Charles Grandison* (1754).

Notes   231

29 Margaret Fuller's involvement with German literature was encouraged by the Harvard Germanophiles George Ripley (1802–1880) and Frederic Henry Hedge (1805–1890). She published translations of Eckermann's *Conversations with Goethe* (1839), Bettina Brentano's *Günderode* (1842), and Goethe's *Tasso* (published posthumously in 1860). Her biographical and critical essay, "Goethe," formed the core of her planned full-length biography which, had it been completed, would have predated G. H. Lewes's *Life and Works of Goethe* (1855). Sarah Austin (1793–1867) is best remembered for two major translations—*Characteristics of Goethe from the German of Falk, Von Müller, Etc.* (3 volumes, 1833) and *Fragments from German Prose Writers* (1841). Her *Germany, from 1760 to 1814, or, Sketches of German Life From the Decay of the Empire to the Expulsion of the French* (1854) is a compilation of reviews of memoirs by Johanna Schopenhauer (1766–1838), Karl Heinrich Ritter von Lang (1764–1835), Karl Lebrecht Immermann (1796–1840), Johann Georg Jacobi (1740–1814), Henrik Steffens (1773–1845), Adelbert von Chamisso (1781–1838), and Karl August Varnhagen von Ense (1785–1858). The major essays, reviews, and translations published by George Eliot include "German Wit: Heinrich Heine" (1856), "The Natural History of German Life" (1856), "The Morality of *Wilhelm Meister*" (1855), David Friedrich Strauß's *Life of Jesus* (1846), Ludwig Feuerbach's *The Essence of Christianity* (1854).

30 An expenditure of £90 in 1790 would be worth approximately the equivalent of £9,606 in 2017 (see Measuringworth.com).

31 As a boy of seventeen Lewis met Goethe, "the celebrated author of *Werter* [sic]" in Weimar in 1792. Reporting this event to his mother, he warned her that "you must not be surprised if I shoot myself one of these mornings." Letter dated 30 July 1792, *The Life and Correspondence of M. G. Lewis*, ed. Margaret Baron-Wilson (London: Henry Colburn Publisher, 1839), quoted in Violet Stockley, *German Literature as Known in England 1750–1830* (Port Washington, New York: Kennikat Press, 1969 [1929]), 295.

32 *The Monthly Magazine* (IX, 1800), cited in Stockley, *German Literature as Known in England 1750–1830*, 27.

33 Stockley, *German Literature as Known in England 1750–1830*, 28.

34 *Johann Caspar Lavater Correspondence* (Electronic Enlightenment Project, 2008), vol. 13, 427.

35 The career of Stolberg (1750–1819), who was a friend of Goethe, formed a bridge between the *Sturm und Drang* of the 1770s and *fin-de-siécle* German Romanticism. He was a translator of Homer (1778), Plato (1796/1797), Ossian (1806), and a prominent member of the "Göttinger Dichterkreis" led by Ludwig Christian Heinrich Hölty (1748–1776).

36 Trenck's Life, translated by Holcroft and subtitled "HIS ADVENTURES and CRUEL and EXCESSIVE SUFFERINGS DURING AN IMPRISONMENT OF TEN YEARS in the fortress of Magdeburg, by command of the late King of Prussia," surely inspired Godwin's bleak portrayal of St. Leon's confinement in Bethlem Gabor's castle in *St. Leon* (1799), vol. 3. Holcroft's translation has been reprinted in multiple editions as recently as 2016 (see Amazon.com).

37 Stolberg, *Travels*, vi, vii.
38 Michael Holquist, *Dialogism: Bakhtin and his World* (London: Routledge, 1990), 33.
39 Johann Wolfgang von Goethe, *Briefe der Jahre 1786–1814* in *Gedenkausgabe der Werke, Briefe und Gespräche*. Band 19, ed. Ernst Beutler (Zürich: Artemis Verlag, 1949), vol. 19, 409–410: "Indem ich die mir mitgeteilte Übersetzung von Hermann und Dorothea mit Dank zurücksende erlauben Sie mir, wertgeschätzer Herr, einige Betrachtungen. Man kann wie es mir scheint, nach zweierlei Maximen übersetzen, einmal wenn man seiner Nation den reinen Begriff eines fremden Autors überliefern, fremde Zustände derselben anschaulich machen will, wobei man sich denn genau an das Original bindet; man kann aber auch ein solches fremdes Werk als eine Art Stoff behandeln, indem man es, nach eignen Empfindungen und Überzeugungen, dergestalt verändert, daß es unserer Nation näher gebracht und von ihr gleichsam als ein Originalwerk aufgenommen werden könne. In dem letzten Falle scheinen Sie sich zu befinden. Sie haben zwar im ganzen den Gang meines Gedichtes beibehalten, aber durchaus, soviel ich beurteilen kann, die dramatisch charakteristischen, läßlichen Äußerungen meiner Personen strenger, auffallender, didaktischer überliefert, und die gemächliche epische Bewegung in einen ernsteren gemeßnern Schritt verwandelt. Nach meiner wenigen Einsicht in die englische Literatur darf ich schließen daß Sie hierbei den Charakter Ihrer Nation vor Augen gehabt, und es ist mir um so angenehmer eine völlige Aufklärung hierüber in der Vorrede und den Noten, welche Sie Ihrer Arbeit beizufügen gedenken, nächstens zu erhalten. Übrigens kann ich die meisten Abweichungen vom Original aus meinem gefaßten Standpunkte ziemlich beurteilen, nur vermag ich nicht einzusehen warum Sie die Stelle, vom hundertsechsundzwanzigsten Vers Ihrer Übersetzungen an, bis zum hundertzweiundvierzigsten, auf den ehemaligen Brand des Städtchens gedeutet, da, im Original, dieser längst vergangenen Begebenheit nur im Vorbeigehen erwähnt und eigentlich die Beschreibung des Zuges der Ausgewanderten durch diese Stelle fortgesetzt wird. Doch erhalte ich wohl auch hierüber einige Belehrung und ergreife vielleicht irgend eine Gelegenheit über die vier, nunmehr von mir liegenden, Übersetzungen meines Gedichtes öffentlich meine Gedanken zu sagen. Der ich recht wohl zu leben wünsche und mich zu geneigtem Andenken empfehle."
40 Johann Wolfgang von Goethe, *Hermann and Dorothea*, trans. Thomas Holcroft (London: T. N. Longman and O. Rees, 1801), xii, 181.
41 *Hermann und Dorothea*, trans. Holcroft, 180. Holcroft makes the same point in his Preface to Stolberg's *Travels*: "Imagination . . . holds a looser rein; her track is aerial; and, though dazzling, closes instantly upon the view. To trace her capricious course in an exact line is impossible; and those who translate poetry must not pore over the words of the author, but imbibe his feelings, animate themselves with the same fires, and soar on the same daring wing" (ix).
42 Wilhelm Dilthey, *Das Erlebnis und die Dichtung* (Göttingen: Vandenhoeck & Ruprecht, 1965), 125–126: "[T]he broad foundation for a poetic life's work of a

totally new kind required that his personality be fully integrated. As a result, Goethe's place is not among the great scientists, philosophers, or statesmen, but rather he is to be found beside Aeschylus, Dante, and Shakespeare." Indeed, the question of Goethe's "real" vocation is the focus of a classic examination of his career. See José Ortega y Gasset, "In Search of Goethe from Within: Letter to a German," trans. Willard R. Trask, *The Dehumanization of Art and Other Essays on Art, Culture, and Literature* (Princeton: Princeton University Press, [1948]), 131–174: "Goethe is perpetually preoccupied with his life, simply because life *is* preoccupation with itself. His understanding of this fact makes him the first of our contemporaries, if you like, the first of the Romantics. Because that is what, under its literary-historical significations, Romanticism means: the preconceptual discovery that life is not reality which encounters a greater or lesser number of problems, but that it consists exclusively in the problem of itself" (146–148).

43   Saintsbury, vol. 3, 497.
44   William Taylor, *An Historic Survey of German Poetry*, 3 volumes (London: Treutel and Würtz, 1828–1830), vol. 2, 102.
45   Taylor, vol. 3, 102–103.
46   Taylor, vol. 3, 376–377.
47   Taylor, vol. 3, 362.
48   Taylor, vol. 3, 349.
49   Taylor, vol. 3, 376.
50   Arthur Schopenhauer, *Die Welt als Wille und Vorstellung*, ed. Werner Brede (Munich: Carl Hauser Verlag, 1977), Bk. 3, Par. 48, 304.
51   Taylor, *Historic Survey of German Poetry*, vol. 3, 376.
52   This is a more accurate designation than "nation," which, in the modern sense, does not come into existence until nearly forty years after Goethe's death
53   Taylor, *Historic Survey of German Poetry*, vol. 3, 376.
54   Cited Norman, vol. 1, 64.
55   Cited in Norman, vol. 1, 70.
56   Taylor, vol. 2, 102.
57   Taylor, vol. 2, 102–103.
58   *The Ladies Monthly Museum, or Polite Repository of Amusement and Instruction*, vol. 1, 477.
59   *The Anti-Jacobin Review and Magazine; and Protestant Advocate; or, Monthly Political and Literary Censor* (3: 207). In *German Literature in British Magazines 1750–1860* (Madison: University of Wisconsin Press, 1949), the editors Morgan and Hohlfeld comment: "Severest of the all magazines in its criticism, it was largely responsible for the reaction against German literature in 1800" (116).
60   *The Gentlemen's Magazine, or Monthly Intelligencer* 69, No. 2: 833.
61   *The Anti-Jacobin Review* 3: 207.
62   *The Anti-Jacobin Review* 4: viff. "Philosophism" is *The Anti-Jacobin Review*'s main pejorative term for transcendental idealism, especially as presented in Johann Gottlieb Fichte's *Wissenschaftslehre* [*The Doctrine of Science*] (1794–1795).

63   Hannah More, *Strictures on the Modern System of Female Education with a View of the Principles and Conduct Prevalent among Women of Rank and Fortune* (London: A. Straban, 1801), vol. 1, 41.

64   Taylor was not alone in failing to recognize that Goethe's writings represented a radical new departure in taste and sensibility. One must not forget that while in Germany during 1799–1800, Coleridge anachronistically beat a path to Klopstock's door and that in a letter to Josiah Wedgwood he expressed his intention to write a study of Lessing's life and works: "What have I done in Germany?—I have learnt the language . . . . I have read & made collections for an history of the Belles Lettres in Germany before the time of Lessing . . . and very large collections for a Life of Lessing;—to which I was led by the miserably bald & unsatisfying Biographies that have been hitherto given, & by my personal acquaintance with two of Lessing's Friends [Klopstock and Heyne?]" in *Collected Letters of S. T. Coleridge*, ed. Earl Leslie Griggs (Oxford: The Clarendon Press, 1956), vol. 1, 518. Esteeming Kotzebue's energy and Schiller's accent on the sublime as primary literary values, Taylor cannot be blamed for missing the greater subtlety of Goethe's less spectacular qualities of naturalism and digression.

65   Antoine Berman, *The Experience of the Foreign: Culture and Translation in Romantic Germany* (Albany, New York: State University of New York Press, 1992), 4.

66   Goethe to Carlyle, 20 July 1827, *Correspondence between Goethe and Carlyle*, 25–27: "Whoever understands and studies German finds himself in the market, where all nations offer their wares; he plays the interpreter, while he enriches himself. And thus every translator is to be regarded as a middle-man in this spiritual commerce, and as making it his business to promote this exchange: for say what we may of the insufficiency of translation, yet the work is and will always be one of the weightiest and worthiest affairs in the general concerns of the world."

67   Goethe to Carlyle, 20 July 1827, *Correspondence between Goethe and Carlyle*, 16–18, 24–25: "It is obvious that the efforts of the best poets and aesthetic writers of all nations have now for some time been directed towards what is universal in humanity. In each special field, whether in history, mythology, or fiction, more or less arbitrarily conceived, one sees the traits which are universal always more clearly revealed and illumining what is merely national and personal. . . .Whatever in the poetry of any nation tends to this and contributes to it, the others should endeavor to appropriate. The peculiarities of each nation must be learned, and allowance made for them, in order by these very means to hold intercourse with it; for the special characteristics of a nation are like its language and its currency: they facilitate intercourse, nay they first make it completely possible . . . . A genuine, universal tolerance is most surely attained, if we do not quarrel with the peculiar characteristics of individual men and races, but only hold fast the conviction, that what is truly excellent is distinguished by its belonging to all mankind."

68   Berman, *The Experience of the Foreign*, 46.

Notes Chapter Two

1   11 April 1827, *Goethes Gespräche, 6. Band, 1827 und 1828*, ed. Woldemar Freiherr von Biedermann (Leipzig: F. W. von Biedermann, 1890), 100–101: "I asked Goethe which of the new philosophers he thought the best. 'Kant,' he said, 'beyond a doubt. He is the one whose doctrines still continue to work, and have penetrated most deeply into our German civilization. He has influenced even you, although you have never read him; now you need him no longer, for what he could give you you possess already.'"

2   Landmark studies in this tradition include the aforementioned *Confrontations* (1965) by Wellek and the following: Norman Fruman, *Coleridge, the Damaged Archangel* (New York: George Braziller, 1971), Geoffrey Hartmann, *Criticism in the Wilderness* (New Haven: Yale University Press, 1980), Rosemary Ashton, *The German Idea: Four English Writers and the Reception of German Thought, 1800–1860* (Cambridge: Cambridge University Press, 1980), Mark Kipperman, *Beyond Enchantment: German Idealism and English Romanticism* (Philadelphia: University of Pennsylvania Press, 1980), James Engell, *The Creative Imagination: Enlightenment to Romanticism* (Cambridge: Harvard University Press, 1981), Peter Edgerly Firchow, *The Death of the German Cousin* (London and Toronto: Associated University Presses, 1986), and Nicholas Boyle and John Guthrie, ed., *Goethe and the English-Speaking World: Essays from the Cambridge Symposium for His 250th Anniversary* (Rochester, New York: Camden House, 2002).

3   On the relationship between the reception of German culture in Britain and the rise of review criticism, see John Boening, "Pioneers and Precedents: The 'Importation of German' and the Emergence of Periodical Criticism in England," *Internationales Archiv für Sozialgeschicte der deutschen Literatur* VII (1982): 65–86.

4   On Taylor's engagement with German culture, see Merton A. Christensen, "Taylor of Norwich and the Higher Criticism," *Journal of the History of Ideas* 20: 179–194. A complete list of Taylor's articles and reviews is found in *A Memoir of the Life and Writings of the Late William Taylor of Norwich*, ed. J. W. Robberds (London: John Murray, 1843).

5   Concerning Taylor's impact on his younger contemporaries, see *The Correspondence of Henry Crabb Robinson with the Wordsworth Circle*, ed. Edith J. Morley (Oxford: The Clarendon Press, 1927), vol. 1, 497.

6   William Hazlitt, "Mr. Jeffrey," *The Complete Works of William Hazlitt*, ed. P.P. Howe after the edition of A.R. Waller and Arnold Glover (London: J.M. Dent, 1930–1934), vol. 11, 127. Cited by James M. Good, "William Taylor, Robert Southey, and the Word 'Autobiography'," *The Wordsworth Circle* 12 (Spring 1981): 2.

7   For the evolution of periodical criticism in the eighteenth century, see John Clive, *Scotch Reviewers: The Edinburgh Review, 1802–1815* (Cambridge: Harvard University Press, 1957); Derek Roper, *Reviewing before the Edinburgh, 1788–1802*

(Newark: The University of Delaware Press, 1978); and James G. Basker, *Tobias Smollett: Critic and Journalist* (Newark: The University of Delaware Press, 1988).

8   Saintsbury, vol. 3, 497.
9   *Monthly Review* 28: 62.
10 *Monthly Review* 28: 62. Eloa is a seraph and messenger of God in Canto I of Klopstock's *Messiah*.
11 *Monthly Review* 28: 63.
12 *Monthly Review* 28: 64–65.
13 *Monthly Review* 28: 65.
14 *Monthly Review* 11: 1072. Leslie Stephen, "Sir Walter Scott," *Dictionary of National Biography*, ed. Sidney Lee (London: Smith, Elder, and Co., 1897), vol. 51, 80–105. In the DNB entry on Matthew Gregory Lewis, D.L. Thomas relates what must have been one of the great formative influences of Lewis's youth: "In the summer of 1792, he went to Weimar where he was introduced to Goethe . . . . His taste for German literature either took him to Weimar or was acquired there. In any case, he became a good German scholar" (*Dictionary of National Biography*, ed. Sidney Lee (London: Smith, Elder, and Co., 1893), vol. 33, 192–194).
15 René Wellek, *Immanuel Kant in England* (Princeton: Princeton University Press, 1930), 139.
16 William Hazlitt, "Mme de Staël's Account of German Philosophy and Literature," *Morning Chronicle*, 3 and 17 February; 3 March; and 8 April 1814. Hazlitt's formula would, with only slight alterations, be appropriated by Carlyle to express his animus against Enlightenment utilitarianism. In Carlyle's admittedly idiosyncratic interpretation Kant's thought forms the "centre round which" German culture "turns." It has made "a Faith in Religion . . . again possible and inevitable for the scientific mind," and "for him that can read it, the beginning of a new revelation of the Godlike" ("Characteristics," *The Works of Thomas Carlyle*, vol. 26, 41).
17 *Edinburgh Review* 28 (August 1817): 488.
18 Wellek, *Immanuel Kant in England*, 169.
19 *The Collected Writings of Thomas De Quincey*, ed. David Masson (London: A.C. Black, 1897), vol. 11, 221.
20 De Quincey's translations do not compare favorably with Carlyle's skillful adaptations of "Quintus Fixlein" and "Feldprediger Schmelzle."
21 "On the English Notices of Kant," *London Magazine* (July 1823) is reprinted in *The Collected Writings of Thomas De Quincey*, vol. 10, 64ff.
22 *The Collected Writings of Thomas De Quincey*, vol. 10, 65.
23 *The Collected Writings of Thomas De Quincey*, vol. 10, 72.
24 *The Collected Writings of Thomas De Quincey*, vol. 10, 77.
25 *The Collected Writings of Thomas De Quincey*, vol. 10, 77.
26 *Tait's Magazine* (June 1836).
27 Wellek, *Immanuel Kant in England*, 180.

28 See Diana Behler, "Henry Crabb Robinson as a Mediator of Early German Romanticism to England," *Arcadia* 12 (1977): 117–155.
29 *Diary, Reminiscences, and Correspondence*, vol. 1, 87. See also Karl S. Gutke, "Destination Goethe: Travelling Englishmen in Weimar," in *Goethe and the English-Speaking World*, 111–142.
30 *Diary, Reminiscences, and Correspondence*, vol. 1, 87.
31 Wellek, *Immanuel Kant in England*, 159.
32 *The Works of Thomas Carlyle*, vol. 26, 41
33 Henry Crabb Robinson, "Letters on the Philosophy of Kant, No. 1. Introductory," *The Monthly Register and Encyclopedian Magazine* (August 1802). 102. Hereafter cited as Letter I.
34 Matthew Arnold, *Lectures and Essays in Criticism*, ed. R.H. Super (Ann Arbor: University of Michigan Press, 1962), vol. 2, 261–262.
35 Arnold, *Lectures and Essays in Criticism*, vol. 2, 262
36 Of relevance here is Saintbury's inversion of Goethe's comment that his entire oeuvre consisted of "fragments of a great confession": "the whole of Goethe's work . . . may be said to be a record of his criticism" (*A History of Criticism and Literary Taste in Europe*, vol. 3, 360–361).
37 Letter I: 411.
38 Letter I: 411.
39 *Diary, Reminiscences, and Correspondence*, vol. 1, 74. Crabb Robinson's remarks call to mind the essential arguments of Adam Smith's *Theory of Moral Sentiments* (1759) and Hazlitt's *Essay on the Principles of Human Action* (1805), in which sympathy rather than self-interest is demonstrated as the prime motive for human actions.
40 Letter I: 416.
41 Letter I: 412.
42 Letter I: 413.
43 *Sartor Resartus*, 140.
44 Letter I: 413.
45 Staël, *De l'Allemagne*, vol. 1, 46–47: "They occupy opposite ends of the moral chain, because the former considers external objects the prime mover of all ideas, and the latter considers ideas the prime mover of all sense impressions. These two nations nevertheless enjoy rather good social relations, but there are none more opposed in their literary and philosophical systems." Translation by April Alliston.
46 Crabb Robinson recalled his role in Staël's philosophical education in this way: "[S]he had a laudable anxiety to obtain a knowledge of the best German authors; and for this reason she sought my society, and I was not unwilling to be made use of by her" (*Diary, Reminiscences, and Correspondence*, vol. 1, 93). For Crabb Robinson's eyewitness account of Staël's sojourn in Weimar, see also vol. 1, 92–97.
47 Letter II (November 1802): 7.
48 Wellek, *Immanuel Kant in England*, 146.

49 Letter II: 8.
50 Letter II: 11.
51 *Diary, Reminiscences, and Correspondence*, vol. 1, 40.
52 Letter II: 11.
53 Letter II: 12.
54 Letter II: 12.
55 Letter II: 12.
56 Letter III (April 1803): 485.
57 Letter III: 485.
58 Letter III: 485.
59 Arthur Schopenhauer, *Die Welt als Wille und Vorstellung*, ed. Werner Brede (Munich and Vienna: Carl Hanser Verlag, 1977), Vol. 1, Par. I, 32: "The world is my representation . . . . Therefore no truth is more certain, more independent of all others and less in need of proof than this, namely, that everything exists for knowledge, and hence the whole of this world, is only object in relation to the subject, perception of the perceiver, in a word, representation."
60 The first published discussion of Schopenhauer in Britain was John Oxenford's influential review of the second edition of *Die Welt als Wille und Vorstellung* that appeared in *The Westminster Review* in April 1853: "We only wish we could see among the philosophers of modern Germany a writer of equal power, comprehensiveness, ingenuity and erudition, ranged on a side more in harmony with our own feelings and conviction, than that adopted by this misanthropic sage of Frankfort" (407).

Notes Chapter Three

1 Thomas Mann, *Freud und die Zukunft* in *Gesammelte Werke in dreizehn Bänden. Band 9: Reden und Aufsätze. Teil 1* (Frankfurt: Fischer, 1974), 478–501: "The bond with the father, the imitation of the father, the game of being the father, and the transference to father-substitute pictures of a higher and more developed type—how these infantile traits work upon the life of the individual to make and shape it. The *imitatio* Goethe, with its Werther and Wilhelm Meister stages, its old-age period of *Faust* and *Diwan*, can still shape and mythically mould the life of an artist–rising out of the unconscious, yet playing over—as is the artist way—into a smiling, childlike, and profound awareness." Translation by H. T. Lowe-Porter: Thomas Mann, "Freud and the Future," *Essays of Three Decades* (New York: Alfred A. Knopf, third printing, 1937), 426.
2 R. G. Alford, "Goethe's Earliest Critics in England," *Publications of the English Goethe Society* 7 (London: Printed for the Society by W. S. Maney and Son Ltd., 1893): 8–24. Alford cites the following translations and commentary that predated Crabb Robinson's translations: *Werther* (1790); *The Sister* (1792); William Taylor's *Iphigenia* (1793) and his article on *Faust* (1810); Benjamin Thompson's *Stella* (1798); the two versions of *Götz von Berlichingen* that appeared in 1799,

Walter Scott's and Miss Rose Laurence's; and Thomas Holcroft's *Hermann and Dorothea* (1801). The latter marks the end of the period covered by Alford who overlooked Crabb Robinson's translations in his survey: "But a period of apathy ensues that lasts at least ten years, during which, as far as I can ascertain, no new translations appeared and no criticisms" (13). Alford notes that while "Coleridge ... came very near to translating *Faust* ... the references that Coleridge makes to Goethe would hardly fill a page" (13). (Alford was not alone in not recognizing Coleridge's translation when it appeared.) Alford quotes a letter from Southey written in 1799 as remarking "it is only Klopstock that I long to read" (14). Alford credits the appearance of Staël's *De l'Allemagne* and the publication of Goethe's autobiography, (*Dichtung und Wahrheit*) in 1816 with sparking new interest in German culture on the part of the *Edinburgh Review* and, in 1817, the first number of *Blackwood's*, and the efforts of Wilson and Lockhart.

3   The relevant articles by Diana I. Behler are "Henry Crabb Crabb Robinson as a Mediator of Lessing and Herder to England," *Lessing Yearbook 7* (Detroit: Wayne State University Press, 1975): 105–126; "Henry Crabb Robinson as Mediator of Early German Romanticism to England," *Arcadia* 13 (Berlin and New York: De Gruyter, 1977): 117–155; "Henry Crabb Robinson: A British Acquaintance of Wieland and His Advocate in England," *Christoph Martin Wieland: Nordamerikanische Forschungsbeiträge zur 250. Wiederkehr seines Geburtstages 1983*, ed. Hansjörg Schelle (Tübingen: Max Niemeyer Verlag, 1984), 539–556; and "Goethezeit und westliche Denktradition: Der Gegensatz von Idealismus und Sensualismus im Spiegel Henry Crabb Robinsons," *Deutscher Literatur in der Weltliteratur: Kulturnation statt politischer Nation?* Ed. Franz Norbert Mennemeier and Conrad Wiedemann (Tübingen: Max Niemeyer Verlag, 1986), 21–26. Scholars associated with the Henry Crabb Robinson Project include Philipp Hunnekuhl, Eugene Stelzig, and Stefanie Stockhorst. See Hunnekuhl "Reconstructing the Voice of the Mediator: Henry Crabb Robinson's Literary Criticism." *Informal Romanticism*. Ed. James Vigus. Trier: Wissenschaftlicher Verlag Trier, 2012, 61–76; Hunnekuhl, "Hazlitt and Crabb Robinson: The Common Pursuit," *The Hazlitt Review* 6 (2013): 13–34; Hunnekuhl, "Beyond Whist Sobriety: the Lambs, Crabb Robinson, and their Discourse on Literature," *The Charles Lamb Bulletin*, New Series 158 (Autumn 2013): 126–138; Stelzig, *Henry Crabb Robinson in Germany: A Study in Nineteenth-Century Life Writing*. Lewisburg: Bucknell University Press, 2010; Stelzig, "Henry Crabb Robinson as Staël's Philosophical Informant," *Prism(s): Essays in Romanticism* 15 (2007): 113–128; Stelzig, "A Cultural Tourist in Romantic Germany: Henry Crabb Robinson as Nineteenth-Century Life Writer." *Biography* 28 (2005): 515–533; Stockhorst, "Gelehrte Geselligkeit und europäischer Kulturtransfer. Zur Deutung des produktiven Zusammentreffens von Henry Crabb Robinson und Mme de Staël in Weimar," "Weimar ist ja unser Athen." *Mit Seume in Weimar: Vorträge des Colloquiums zu Johann Gottfried Seume in Oßmannstedt 2007*. Ed. Jörg Drews and Gabi Pahnke (Bielefeld: Aisthesis, 2010), 119–140; Stockhorst, "Das klassische Weimar aus

englischer Sicht. Zum Funktionswandel des Reisens um 1800 am Beispiel von Charles Gore und Henry Crabb Robinson," *Reisen um 1800*. Ed. Helmut Peitsch. Munich: Peter Lang, 2012, 31–51; and Stockhorst, "Vermittlungstrategien und transnationale Kanonbildung. Zur britischen Kotzebue-Rezeption am Beispiel von William Taylor and Henry Crabb Robinson," *Angermion* 8, No. 1 (December 2015): 35–60.

4   Henry Crabb Robinson, "First Letter on German Literature," *The Monthly Register and Encyclopedian Magazine* (August 1802), 397.
5   First Letter, 398–399.
6   First Letter, 400. See also Diana I. Behler, "Goethezeit und westliche Denktradition: Der Gegensatz von Idealismus und Sensualismus im Spiegel Henry Crabb Robinsons," *Deutscher Literatur in der Weltliteratur: Kulturnation statt politischer Nation?* Ed. Franz Norbert Mennemeier und Conrad Wiedemann (Tübingen: Max Niemeyer Verlag, 1986), 21–26. Behler's central observation is extremely important: "Im verlauf [seiner] Studien ergab sich Crabb Robinson bald der Eindruck, 'that Germany is the only country at present which contains a great poet and a great philosopher,' womit er sich auf Goethe und Kant bezog. In der Literatur war er durch Kritiker wie Samuel Johnson und [William] Taylor geschult. Nun sah er sich in den Dichtungen Goethes mit einer Art von Poesie konfrontiert, die durch ihm 'evokativen' oder symbolischen Charakter über die von ihm gesehenen Möglichkeiten hinausging und die er durch mehrere Übersetzungen zu erschließen suchte" (24–25).
7   See especially Arnold, "A French Critic on Goethe," and George Santayana, *Three Philosophical Poets: Lucretius, Dante, and Goethe* (New York: Cooper Square Publishers, 1970 [1910]).
8   Carlyle, *Two Notebooks*, 92.
9   The poet Kenneth Rexroth made this point pithily: "All sensible men to whom English is native are distressed at the French enthusiasm for [Poe] . . . Nobody in France seems to be able to learn, ever, that his verse is dreadful doggerel and his ratiocinative fiction absurd . . . . The reason is, of course, that the French translate their whole culture into Poe before they even start to read him." Quoted by Jeffrey Meyers, *Edgar Allan Poe: His Life and Legacy* (New York: Cooper Square Press, 1992), 276.
10 First Letter, 398.
11 First Letter, 398.
12 First Letter, 398.
13 First Letter, 400.
14 First Letter, 401.
15 *Zahme Xenien*, Numbers 19, 27, 63, 101, 102, 209, 212, 213, 217.
16 The "Second Letter on German Literature," the briefest in the series, contains just two short translations. See Diana Behler, "Henry Crabb Robinson as a Mediator of Early German Romanticism in England," *Arcadia* 12 (1977): 117–155. In the following passage Behler attests to Crabb Robinson's facility as a translator of selected *Athenäum Fragmente*, suggesting the care and effort taken in other

translations: "A careful comparison of Crabb Robinson's renderings with the original German aphorisms reveals for the most part the English student's thorough familiarity with the German language at a level of comprehension not readily attained by many a native. Surely the fragments of the *Athenäum* count among the most difficult expressions of thought in German, and to translate them accurately and yet maintain a fluent, readable style of English required a deft facility of language and a sure understanding of the topics concerned. With few exceptions . . . Crabb Robinson was exceedingly accurate and complete in his translations." (152) Behler also observes that "Crabb Robinson seems to have striven to present them in the most original form possible. Yet he has not made the mistake of sacrificing good, readable English style for accuracy, and thus it is an aesthetic literary pleasure to read them without referring back to the original German. They are obviously the product of a literate man who had a distinct flair for witty and elegant forms of expression, and one can assume that it was the recognition of a kindred style that first stimulated Crabb Robinson to undertake these translations."

17 Third Letter, 205.
18 Third Letter, 207.
19 Third Letter, 207.
20 *The Complete Poetical Works of Samuel Taylor Coleridge*, 2 volumes, ed. E. H. Coleridge (Oxford: The Clarendon Press, 1912), vol. 2, 724.
21 Third Letter, 207.
22 Fourth Letter, 294.
23 Fourth Letter, 295.
24 Fourth Letter, 294.
25 Fourth Letter, 296.
26 Fourth Letter, 296.
27 Coleridge, *Biographia Literaria*, vol. 2, 23.
28 Fourth Letter, 297.
29 Fourth Letter, 297.
30 *Letters of Matthew Arnold to A. H. Clough*, ed. Howard Foster Lowry (London: Oxford University Press, 1932), 64–65, 124.
31 *The Letters of John Keats*, vol. 2, 102.
32 *Letters of Samuel Taylor Coleridge*, 2 volumes, ed. E.H. Coleridge (London: William Heinemann, 1895), vol. 1, 96–97.
33 Saintsbury, vol. 3, 229.
34 L. A. Willoughby, *The Romantic Movement in Germany* (Oxford: Oxford University Press, 1930), 1.
35 Coleridge's translation: "Little call as he may have to instruct others, he wishes nevertheless to open out his heart to such as he either knows or hopes to be of like mind with himself, but who are widely scattered in the world: he wishes to knit anew his connections with his oldest friends, to continue those recently formed, and to win other friends among the rising generation for the remaining

course of his life. He wishes to spare the young those circuitous paths, on which he himself had lost his way."
36   Fourth Letter, 297.
37   Fourth Letter, 297.
38   Cited in Norman, vol. 2, 48.

Notes Interlude One

1   Harold Bloom, *The Western Canon: The Books and School of the Ages* (New York: Harcourt Brace, 1994), 216.
2   George Eliot, *Middlemarch*, ed. Gregory Maertz (Peterborough: Broadview Editions, 2004), 19.
3   Novalis, *Fragmente des Jahres 1798, Gesammelte Werke*, ed. Carl Seelig (Herrliberg and Zürich: Bühl-Verlag, 1946), vol. 3, 24: "The artist stands above other human beings, like a statue on its pedestal."
4   Friedrich Schlegel, "Ideen, No. 43," *Werke in Zwei Bände*, ed. Wolfgang Hecht (Berlin and Weimar: Aufbau-Verlag, 1980), vol. 1, 268: "What humankind is to other life forms on earth, so the artist is in comparison to other human beings."
5   William Blake, "Letter to Dr. Trusler (23 August 1799)," *The Oxford Authors: William Blake*, ed. Michael Mason (Oxford and New York: Oxford University Press, 1988), 60–61.
6   William Wordsworth, "Preface," *Lyrical Ballads*, ed. R. I. Brett and A. R. Jones (London and New York: Routledge, 1968), 255–256.
7   Coleridge, *Biographia Literaria*, vol. 1, 15–16.
8   Shelley, Percy Bysshe, "A Defence of Poetry," *Shelley's Poetry and Prose*, ed. Neil Fraistat and Donald H. Reiman (New York and London: W.W. Norton, 2nd edition, 2002), 482.
9   *The Letters of John Keats*, vol. 2, 386–387.
10 Alfred de Vigny, *Stello, Oeuvres complètes*, ed. F. Baldensperger (Paris: Gallimard, Édition Pleïde, 1950), vol. 1, 679: "The poet seeks out in the stars which route the finger of God indicates to us."
11 Gottfried Keller, *Der grüne Heinrich*, ed. Peter Goldammer (Berlin and Weimar: Aufbau-Verlag, 1986), 178–179: "Why should it not be a grand and beautiful calling, always to be sitting in solitude before those works of God which have to this day kept their innocence and their complete beauty, to understand them and to honor them, and to worship Him by trying to reproduce them in their peacefulness? When one is drawing just a simple little bush, every branch fills one with reverence because it has grown thus and not otherwise, in accordance with the laws of the Creator; but when one becomes capable of painting, faithfully and truly, a whole wood or a wide field with its sky, and when at last one is able without a model to produce the like from one's imagination, forests, valleys and mountain chains, or just little nooks, freely and independently, and yet exactly as they are to be seen somewhere or other, then this art seems to me to

be kind of true participation in the joys of Creation." Translation by A.M. Holt. Gottfried Keller, *Green Henry* (London: John Calder, and New York: Riverrun Press, 1985), 155.

12 Staël, *De l'Allemagne*, vol. 1, 189.
13 *The Works of Thomas Carlyle*, vol. 26, 215.
14 *The Works of Thomas Carlyle*, vol. 26, 233.
15 *The Works of Thomas Carlyle*, vol. 26, 34.
16 *The Works of Thomas Carlyle*, vol. 27, 438.
17 See Mitchell Benjamin Frank, *Romantic Painting Redefined: Nazarene Tradition and the Narratives of Romanticism* (Farnham, UK: Ashgate Publishing, 2001) and Cordula Crewe, *The Nazarenes: Romantic Avant-Garde and the Art of the Concept* (University Park: Penn State University Press 2015).
18 Friedrich Schlegel, *Werke in Zwei Bände*, vol. 1, 204–205: "Romantic poetry is a progressive universal poetry. It is destined not merely to reunite the separate genres of poetry and to link poetry to philosophy and rhetoric. It would and should also mingle and fuse poetry and prose, genius and criticism, artistic poetry and natural poetry, make poetry lively and sociable, and life and society poetic, poeticize wit, fill and saturate the forms of art with worthy cultural matter of every kind, and animate them with a flow of humor. It embraces all that is poetic, from the greatest art system that enfolds further systems, down to the sigh, the kiss uttered in artless song by the child creating its own poetry . . . . Romantic poetry alone can, like the epic, become a mirror to the whole surrounding world, an image of its age." Translation by Lilian R. Furst, *European Romanticism: Self-Definition* (London and New York: Methuen, 1980), 4–5.
19 Wilhelm Heinrich Wackenroder and Ludwig Tieck, *Herzensergiessungen eines kunstliebenden Klosterbruders*, ed. A. Gillies (Oxford: Basil Blackwell, 1948), 51: "The language of words is a precious gift of Heaven, and it was to our everlasting benefit that the Creator loosed the tongue of our first ancestor so that he might name all the things which the Almighty had put in the world around him, and the spiritual images which He had implanted in his soul and so enrich his spirit by endlessly combining this wealth of names. By means of words we have dominion over all of nature; by means of words we acquire with ease all the treasures of the earth. Yet words cannot call down into our hearts the invisible spirit which reigns above us." Translation by Edward Mornin, *Outpourings of an Art-Loving Friar* (New York: Unger, 1975), 50.
20 Novalis, *Heinrich von Ofterdingen. Werke in einem Band*, ed. Hans-Joachim Mähl and Richard Samuel (Munich and Vienna: Carl Hanser Verlag, 1981), 255: "There is nothing of the art of poetry to be met with anywhere, externally. Nor does this art work with tools or hands; the eye and ear perceive nothing of it; for the mere hearing of words is not the real effect of this secret art. It is altogether a matter of the soul, and as those other artists delight the outer senses with pleasurable sensations, so the poet fills the inner sanctuary of the spirit with new, wonderful, and pleasing thoughts. He knows how to stir those secret powers in us at will, and by means of words he enables us to perceive a glorious

unknown world." Translation by Palmer Hilty, *Henry von Ofterdingen* (New York: Unger, 1964), 31.

21   Novalis, *Heinrich von Ofterdingen*, 335: "Language is really a little world in signs and sounds. As man is Lord over it, so he would also like to be lord over the great world. And be able to express himself freely in it. And precisely in this delight of revealing in the world what is beyond the world, of being able to do that which is really the original motive of our being here, therein lies the fountainhead of poesy." Translation by Hilty, *Henry von Ofterdingen*, 116.

22   William Godwin, *St. Leon: A Tale of the Sixteenth Century* (London: G. G. J. and J. Robinson, 1799), vol. 2, 9.

23   Arthur Schopenhauer, *Die Welt als Wille und Vorstellung*, ed. Julius Frauenstädt, 2 vols. (Leipzig: F.A. Brockhaus, 1877), vol. 2, 464: "Not merely philosophy but also the fine arts work at bottom towards the solution of the problem of existence.... Accordingly, every work of art really endeavors to show us life and things as they really are; but these cannot be grasped directly by everyone through the mist of objective and subjective contingencies. Art takes away this mist.... The works of poets, sculptors, and pictorial or graphic artists generally contain an acknowledged treasure of profound wisdom, just because the wisdom of the nature of things themselves speaks from them. They interpret the utterances of things merely by elucidation and purer repetition. Therefore everyone who reads the poem or contemplates the work of art must of course contribute from his own resources towards bringing that wisdom to light." Translation by R. F. J. Payne, *The World as Will and Representation* (New York: Dover, 1958), vol. 2, 406–407.

24   Friedrich Nietzsche, "Schopenhauer als Erzieher," *Unzeitgemässe Betrachtungen* (Leipzig: C. G. Naumann Verlag, 1899), vol. 2, 47: "The heroism of truth consists in ceasing one day to be time's plaything. In becoming, all is hollow, deceptive, superficial and contemptible; the riddle which man is to solve can only be solved in the unchangeable, in being, in being such-and-no-other." Translation by James W. Hillesheim and Malcolm R. Simpson, *Schopenhauer as Educator* (South Bend, Indiana: Regnery/Gateway, 1965), 47.

25   Schopenhauer, *Die Welt als Wille und Vorstellung*, vol. 1, 213: "Raised up by the power of the mind, relinquish the ordinary way of considering things, and cease to follow under the guidance of the forms of the principle of sufficient reason merely their relations to one another, whose final goal is always the relation of our will. Thus we no longer consider the where, the when, the why, and the whither in things, but simply and solely the *what*. We lose ourselves entirely in the object of contemplation.... We forget our individuality, our will, and continue to exist only as pure subject, as clear mirror of the object, so that it is as though the object alone existed without anyone to perceive it." Translation by Payne, vol. 1, 178.

26   Schopenhauer, *Die Welt als Wille und Vorstellung*, vol. 1, 213. Translation by Payne, vol. 1, 196: "... the painless state, prized by Epicurus as the highest good and as the state of the gods; for the moment we are delivered from the miserable

pressure of the will. We celebrate the Sabbath of the penal servitude of willing; the wheel of Ixion stands still."

27   Nietzsche, "Schopenhauer als Erzieher," *Unzeitgemässe Betrachtungen*, vol. 2, 43: "*Schopenhauerian man voluntarily takes the pain of truthfulness upon himself*, and this suffering serves to kill his individual will to prepare that complete revolution and reversal of his being, the attainment of which is the actual meaning of life." Translation by Hillesheim and Simpson, 43.

Notes Chapter Four

1   *The Poetical Works of Walter Savage Landor*, ed. Stephen Wheeler (Oxford: The Clarendon Press, 1937), vol. 3, 387; vol. 2, 264–271. During a conversation with Crabb Robinson Wordsworth called Goethe an "imposter." Crabb Robinson reported the remark to Walter Savage Landor, who then penned the comic verses cited above in the first epigraph. In a letter to Crabb Robinson Landor was forgiving of Wordsworth's blind spots: "What matters that he [Wordsworth] is insensible to the astonishing powers of Voltaire and Goethe? He has written a hundred poems the least excellent of which I would not sacrifice to give him that openness of heart you require. Productive power acts by means of concentration. With few exceptions those only love everything who, like me, can themselves do nothing." Cited in John Forster, *Walter Savage Landor* (Oxford: The Clarendon Press, 1875), 316.

2   Harold Bloom, *A Map of Misreading* (New York: Oxford University Press, 2nd edition, 2003 [1975]), 19.

3   Saintsbury, vol. 3, 230.

4   Saintsbury, vol. 3, 230.

5   T. S. Eliot, "Johnson as Critic and Poet," *On Poetry and Poets* (New York: Octagon Books, 1975 [1957]), 243; 243–244.

6   "State of German Literature," *The Works of Thomas Carlyle*, vol. 26, 53.

7   Noel Annan, *Leslie Stephen: The Godless Victorian* (New York: Random House, 1984), 172.

8   S. T. Coleridge, *Biographia Epistolaris*, ed. A. Turnbull (London: G. Bell and Sons, 1911), vol. 1. 93.

9   *The Monthly Review* (1800) XXXIII, 336.

10 Coleridge, *Complete Poetical Works*, vol. 2, 724.

11 *Collected Letters of Samuel Taylor Coleridge*, vol. 1, 96–97.

12 *Collected Letters of Samuel Taylor Coleridge*, vol. 1, 583, 587, 610.

13 Lilian R. Furst, "Two Versions of Schiller's *Wallenstein*," *The Contours of European Romanticism* (London: Macmillan, 1979), 105: "Coleridge's *Wallenstein* was first published in London by Pickering in 1828. Then it was reprinted separately in London by Moxon, and in 1842 by Smith before being included in Bohn's Standard Library in 1846, in the Universal Library (Ingram and Cooke) in 1853, and in the Masterpieces of Foreign Literature (Griffin) in 1866. . . . In the United

States, Coleridge's *The Piccolomini* was printed in New York by Longworth in 1805." Coleridge's translation appeared in successive American editions of Schiller's complete works published in Philadelphia in 1861 (Kohler) and 1883 (Barrie), in New York in 1884 (Williams's "Household Edition") and in 1915 in the German Publishing Society's series "German Classics of the Nineteenth and Twentieth Centuries."

14 Matthew Arnold, "Ecce, Convertimur and Gentes," *English Literature and Irish Politics*, ed. R. H. Super (Ann Arbor: University of Michigan Press, 1973), vol. 9, 5.

15 See, for example, George Henry Lewes, *Life and Works of Goethe, with Sketches of His Age and Contemporaries from Published and Unpublished Sources* (London: David Nutt, 1857), vol. 2, 217–218.

16 See E.S. Shaffer, "The 'Confessions' of Goethe and Coleridge: Goethe's 'Bekenntnisse einer Schönen Seele' and Coleridge's *Confessions of an Inquiring Spirit*," in *Goethe and the English-Speaking World*, 145–158.

17 See John Guillory, *Cultural Capital: The Problem of Literary Canon Formation* (Chicago: University of Chicago Press, 1993), xi: "If the 'middling sort' [of writers], especially those trained in the Dissenting Academies, embraced English literature as a politically empowering educational program, because it facilitated entrance into the relatively homogenized linguistic arena of the 'public sphere' . . . . Wordsworth and Coleridge responded to this crisis [the problem of assimilating new vernacular genres] with a programmatic attempt to reaffirm the High Cultural status of traditional canonical works in English against . . . popular novels [by mostly women authors and Jacobins] and narrative poetry [published by imitators of German poets] . . . . The effect of that program, which was of course shared by a literary culture much larger than the circle of Wordsworth and Coleridge, was to reserve the term 'literature' for High Canonical works, and in this way to maintain the cultural capital of those works."

18 See Norman Fruman, *Coleridge, the Damaged Archangel* (New York: George Braziller, 1971).

19 For a humorous and exhaustive account of the stream of visitors from Britain who came to Weimar and were welcomed by Goethe, see Karl S. Gutke, "Destination Goethe: Travelling Englishmen in Weimar," *Goethe and the English-Speaking World*, ed. Boyle and Guthrie, 111–142.

20 *Collected Letters of Coleridge*, vol. 1, 441. French troops had landed on the west coast of Ireland to support the Irish Rebellion of 1798. After a few stunning victories over British troops they were eventually defeated.

21 *Collected Letters of Coleridge*, vol. 1, 444.

22 James Simpson, "*The Authority of Culture*: Some Reflections on the Reception of a Classic," *Goethe and the English-Speaking World*, 189. Simpson's quotation from Wordsworth on Goethe is from Nowell C. Smith, ed., *Wordsworth's Literary Criticism* (London: Henry Frowde, 1905), 260.

23 Cited in Norman, vol. 2, 82.

24 *Collected Letters of Coleridge*, vol. 1, 454–455.

25 *Collected Letters of Coleridge*, vol. 1, 518.
26 *Diary, Reminiscences, and Correspondence*, vol. 1, 202.
27 *Diary, Reminiscences, and Correspondence*, vol. 1, 206–207.
28 *Diary, Reminiscences and Correspondence*, vol. 1, 214–215.
29 *Diary, Reminiscences, and Correspondence*, vol. 1, 214–215.
30 *Diary, Reminiscences, and Correspondence*, vol. 1, 207.
31 Cited in Norman, vol. 1, 75.
32 Coleridge famously claimed that the composition of "Kubla Khan" was interrupted by the arrival of a visitor.
33 Cited in Norman, vol. 1, 76.
34 Cited in Norman, vol. 1, 75.
35 Cited in Norman, vol. 1, 70.
36 James Simpson suggests that the case of the second generation of British Romantic poets "represents the first, and perhaps only, occasion, when Goethe as poet [as opposed to hero and object of a cult of personality] exercised a significant influence on the greatest poets, as poets." See *"The Authority of Culture*: Some Reflections on the Reception of a Classic," *Goethe and the English-Speaking World*, 189–190.
37 Harold Bloom, *The Western Canon*, 219–220: "Shelley's translation of parts of Part One is still the best in English, while the Byron-Goethe relationship is one of the crucial, only partly hidden centers of Part Two. The spirit of Byron appears as the Boy Charioteer and as the unfortunate Euphorion, child of the union between Faust and Helen. Even more weirdly, the Byronic essence of his personality rather than his work, which for Goethe is the same as the daemonic, works its way into the figure of the Homunculus, a much livelier being than either the Boy Charioteer or Euphorion . . . . [It is] not too much to say that Goethe developed a kind of infatuation for Byron, whom he weirdly ranked above Milton and just below Shakespeare . . . . Despite all of Goethe's classical yearnings, Faust, Part Two is the central work of European Romanticism, and Byronism inevitably had to play itself out in this German tragedy that is not a tragedy."
38 Arnold, "Heinrich Heine," *Lectures and Essays in Criticism*, ed. R. H. Super, vol. 3, 120–121.
39 Arnold, "Heinrich Heine," vol. 3, 122. The passage in Latin is a quotation from the Roman poet Lucan (39–65 CE) on the greatness of Pompeius Magnus, consul of the Roman Republic.
40 *Letters of P.B. Shelley*, ed. Roger Ingpen (London: Pitman and Sons, 1909), vol. 3, 882.
41 Frederick Burwick and James M. McCusick, ed., *Faustus. From the German of Goethe Translated by Samuel Taylor Coleridge* (Oxford: Oxford University Press, 2007).
42 *Letters of P. B. Shelley*, vol. 3, 931.
43 *Letters of P.B. Shelley*, vol. 3, 953–954.
44 *Letters of P.B. Shelley*, vol. 3, 977.

⁴⁵ Quoted in *Schriften zur Weltliteratur,* ed. Horst Günther (Frankfurt: Insel Verlag, 1987), 150–151: "This extraordinarily witty poet has fully internalized my Faust and fed his hypochondria on its bizarre nourishment. He so fully incorporated the motifs in his own way so that they are no longer the same, and that is why I cannot admire his brilliance enough. This transformation is so complete that one could offer highly interesting lectures on the similarity and difference between his poem and the original."
⁴⁶ *Byron's Letters and Journals,* ed. Leslie Marchand (Cambridge: Harvard University Press, 1975), vol. 7, 106.
⁴⁷ 7 June 1820, Marchand, vol. 7, 113.
⁴⁸ 22 July 1823, Marchand, vol. 10, 213.

Notes Chapter Five

¹ José Ortega y Gasset, "In Search of Goethe from Within," trans. Willard R. Trask, *The Dehumanization of Art and Other Essays on Art, Culture, and Literature* (Princeton: Princeton University Press, 1968 [1948]), 146.
² Marcuse fled to France in 1938 and emigrated to the United States in 1939. He taught literature and philosophy at the University of Southern California until he returned to (West) Germany in 1962 (*Encyclopedia of Contemporary German Culture,* ed. John Sandford (London and New York: Routledge, 1999, 397). His fellow German émigrés included the Mann family of writers—Thomas and Heinrich, Erika and Klaus—as well as Theodor Adorno, Hermann Broch, Siegfried Kracauer, Bertolt Brecht, Hannah Arendt, and Herbert Marcuse (no relation). Gerald D. Nash succinctly describes the impact of Marcuse and his colleagues on the cultural landscape of southern California: "Constituting the cream of the European intelligentsia, they brought an intellectual maturity and sophistication to cultural life in the West that it had previously lacked. Rarely had any such small group of western settlers had such for-reaching influence in so many different fields of cultural life as the European refugees who gathered in southern California during wartime" (*The American West Transformed: The Impact of the Second World War* (Lincoln and London: The University of Nebraska Press, 1985), 179). See also Anson Rabinbach, *In the Shadow of Catastrophe: German Intellectuals between Apocalypse and Enlightenment* (Berkeley: University of California Press, 1997) and Ehrhard Bahr, *Weimar on the Pacific: German Exile Culture in Los Angeles and the Crisis of Modernism* (Berkeley: University of California Press, 2007).
³ David Riede, "Transgression, Authority, and the Church of Literature in Carlyle," *Victorian Connections,* ed. Jerome J. McGann (Charlottesville: University Press of Virginia, 1989), 109.
⁴ Concerning Carlyle's transition from writing fiction to history, Chris R. Vanden Bossche argues that this involved "rejecting the transcendentalism of Goethe and the Germans in favor of his father's preference for the 'real'" (*Carlyle and*

the Search for Authority (Columbus: Ohio State University Press, 1991), 143. Vanden Bossche errs in lumping Goethe together with the German Romantics. For Carlyle the exemplary quality of Goethe's vision is his embrace of *reality*: "How has this man, to whom the world once offered nothing but blackness, denial, and despair, attained to that better vision which now shows it to him, not tolerable only, but full of solemnity and loveliness?" (*The Works of Thomas Carlyle*, vol. 26, 210–211).

5   Riede, Vanden Bossche, Kaplan, and LaValley are representative of the critics who have suggested this interpretation for the reciprocal attraction exerted in their relationship.

6   The controversy surrounding Coleridge's appropriation of German thought has been with us since Thomas De Quincey's article, "Goethe's *Wilhelm Meister's Apprenticeship*," *London Magazine* 10 (1824): 189–197; and a more scholarly article by James F. Ferrier, "The Plagiarisms of S. T. Coleridge," *Blackwood's Edinburgh Magazine* 47, No. 293 (March 1840), 287–299. More recent studies offering diametrically opposed views include the highly critical Norman Fruman, *Coleridge, the Damaged Archangel* (New York: George Braziller, 1971) and the more generous interpretations offered by Walter Jackson Bate, *Coleridge* (New York: Macmillan, 1968), Thomas McFarland, *Coleridge and the Pantheist Tradition* (Oxford: The Clarendon Press, 1969), and James Engell, "Coleridge and German Idealism: First Postulates, Final Causes" in *The Coleridge Connection: Essays for Thomas McFarland*, ed. Richard Gravil and Molly Lefebure (London: Macmillan, 1990), 153–177.

7   T. S. Eliot, "Johnson as Critic and Poet," *On Poetry and Poets* (New York: Farrar, Strauss and Giroux, 1957), 20.

8   Coleridge expressed ambivalence towards Goethe throughout his career. In August 1812 he confided to Crabb Robinson that he intended to write a new *Faust*: "Coleridge talks of writing a new Faust! He would never get out of a few barren, vague conceptions; he would lose himself in dreaming—his whole intellectual apparatus, employed by himself to no other purpose than to keep the different implements in exercise—I cannot say order" (*Henry Crabb Robinson on Books and their Writers*, ed. E. J. Morley (London: J.M. Dent and Sons, 1938), vol. 1, 108); quoted in Fruman, 85). Then, in August 1814, Coleridge agreed to translate *Faust* for John Murray but prevaricated and delayed and never actually applied himself to the task. Once again, in 1820, he considered writing an introductory essay to accompany Retzsch's celebrated illustrations for the play: "A preliminary Essay, stating *briefly* the peculiar character of Goethe, as man, philosopher, & poet; more at large, the specific character of his Faust, including its purposes, & the tone of mind presupposed in the Reader as well as it's form of Style, Humor of Pathos, Imagery, &c. Then to explain its *Nationality* as a German Poem, with its high merit on this very account—it is, perhaps, the only properly original work of German Poesy, & with the Louisa of Voss the most national—but from these very causes, especially the state of mind in those, whom Goethe had a right to calculate on as his readers, & the inclosed [sic]

number of those Readers, often most unfit, & in large portions uninteresting to the English Public" (*Collected Letters of Coleridge*, vol. 5, 43n). And yet, an anonymous author wound up supplying this essay. In a letter to John Gisborne Shelley expresses his frustration that Coleridge, the writer best equipped to mediate *Faust* for Britain, had not accepted the challenge: "We have just got the etchings of 'Faust,' the painter is worthy of Goethe.... The translations... are miserable. Ask Coleridge if their stupid misintelligence of the deep wisdom and harmony of the author does not spur him to action" (*Letters of P.B. Shelley*, vol. 2, 931). Ashton and Furst suggest that Coleridge's inaction may have been due to disagreeable associations left over from translating *Wallenstein*. See Ashton, *The German Idea*, 60; and Furst, "Two Versions of Schiller's *Wallenstein*," Furst, *The Contours of European Romanticism*, 96–99.

9 *Letters of Coleridge*, vol. 1, 96–97.

10 *The Works of Thomas Carlyle*, vol. 25, 78. The presence of such affinities supports Lovejoy's pioneering argument—which is given more nuance by Wellek, Furst, and Engell—for treating German and British Romanticisms as distinct but kindred cultural movements ("On the Discrimination of Romanticisms," *Essays in the History of Ideas* (Baltimore: The Johns Hopkins University Press, 1948); originally published in *PMLA*, vol. 39 (1924), 229–253). Moreover, the experience of Coleridge, Scott, and Carlyle (and that of Ticknor, Cogswell, Bancroft, and Emerson in America) attests to the productive fusion and cross-fertilization of these traditions.

11 Albert La Valley, *Carlyle and the Idea of the Modern* (New Haven: Yale University Press, 1968), 109.

12 Carlyle, *Two Notebooks*, 274.

13 Carlyle, *Two Notebooks*, 65.

14 Quoted in James Anthony Froude, *Thomas Carlyle: A History of His Life in London, 1833–1881* (London: Longmans, Green and Co., 1884), vol. 1, 96. Hereafter cited as *Life of Carlyle, 1833–1881*.

15 Chris R. Vanden Bossche, *Carlyle and the Search for Authority*, 3.

16 *Wilhelm Meister's Apprenticeship* (1824), *Wilhelm Meister's Travels* (1827), "Goethe's Helena" (*Foreign Review*, No. 2, 1828), "Goethe" (*Foreign Review*, No. 3, 1828), "Goethe's Portrait" (*Fraser's Magazine* 5, No. 26, 1832), "Death of Goethe" (*New Monthly Magazine* 34, No. 138, 1832), "Goethe's Works" (*Foreign Quarterly Review*, No. 19, 1832), "Novelle: Translated from Goethe" (*Fraser's Magazine* 6, No. 34, 1832), "The Tale: By Goethe" (*Fraser's Magazine* 6, No. 33, 1832). Albert LaValley describes how these essays form a special Carlylean genre: "Not primarily critical writings, they are autobiographical acts of self-discovery, closely analogous to Carlyle's mode of letter writing or notebook jotting.... But, unlike letter writing and notebook jotting, these articles are public acts. They enable Carlyle simultaneously to study his German heroes and to expound their vision to a sluggish and materialistically oriented British public. This is the literary origin of his principal creative role, that of the seer who quests, the prophet who is searching for the new vision" (21).

17   Carlyle, *Two Notebooks*, 205.
18   *The Works of Thomas Carlyle*, vol. 28, 25.
19   To Faust's questions about his identity Mephistopheles responds:
> Ein Teil von jener Kraft,
> Die stets Böse will, und stets das Gute schaft....
> Ich bin ein Teil des Teils, der anfangs alles war,
> Ein Teil der Finsternis, die sich das Licht gebar,
> Das stolze Licht, das nun der Mutter Nacht
> Den alten Rang, den Raum ihr streitig macht.

Faust I, Scene III, lines 1335–1336 and 1349–1352.
> Part of the Power, not understood,
> Which always wills the Bad, and always works the Good....
> Part of the Part am I, once All, in primal Night,—
> Part of the Darkness which brought forth the Light,
> The haughty Light, which now disputes the space,
> And claims of Mother Night her ancient place.

Faust: A Tragedy, Translated in the original metre by Bayard Taylor (Boston and New York: Houghton Mifflin Company, 1870), 54–55.
20   Translated by Carlyle respectively as "everlasting central Substance" and "transient superficial Semblance," *The Works of Thomas Carlyle*, vol. 27, 28.
21   Carlyle, *Two Notebooks*, 274
22   *The Works of Thomas Carlyle*, vol. 27, 28. The title of a novel by Chernyshevsky published in 1863.
23   Carlyle, *Two Notebooks*, 226
24   *The Works of Thomas Carlyle*, vol. 27, 24.
25   Carlyle, *Two Notebooks*, 227–228; 211.
26   Carlyle, *Two Notebooks*, 125.
27   Carlyle, *Two Notebooks*, 227–228.
28   Carlyle, *Two Notebooks*, 214, 71.
29   Carlyle, *Two Notebooks*, 230; and comment on Wordsworth quoted in *Life of Carlyle, 1833–1881*, vol. 1, 45.
30   Carlyle, *Two Notebooks*, 213.
31   Quoted in James Anthony Froude, *Thomas Carlyle: A History of the First Forty Years of His life, 1795–1835* (London: Longmans, Green and Co., 1882), vol. 1, 222. Hereafter cited as *Life of Carlyle, 1795–1835*.
32   *Collected Letters of Thomas and Jane Welsh Carlyle*, vol. 3, 234.
33   Quoted in *Life of Carlyle, 1795–1835*, vol. 1, 272, 274.
34   Carlyle, *Two Notebooks*, 180.
35   Carlyle, *Two Notebooks*, 151, 180. Saintsbury was one of Carlyle's first and most trenchant critics. He questions Carlyle's "position as a critic" (vol. 3, 496) based on this division in his career between the early period of enthusiastic engagement with literary criticism and the later period, in which "he draws away from the attitude of purely literary consideration, if he does not ... take up one actually hostile to this" (vol. 3, 497). He cites as particularly convincing evidence of

Carlyle's hostility to art "that invocation of the Devil . . . 'to fly away with the poor Fine Arts' that appears in the *Latter-Day Pamphlets*. Although he ascribes this remark to 'one of our most distinguished public men,' he 'avows sympathy with it. He even progresses from it to the Platonic view that 'Fiction,' at all 'is not quite a permissible thing" (vol. 3, 498–99). Saintsbury blames the influence of Carlyle's anti-aestheticism in the writings of "the most brilliant of his disciples—Ruskin, Froude, and Kingsley" for "the increasing disinclination to take the standpoint of pure literary criticism" and a "certain want of *interest* in literature as literature" (vol. 3, 537, 539). Despite Saintsbury's discomfort with Carlyle's distrust of art, he has good things to say about his mediation activities. He praises Carlyle's early essays on German writers as "sober and vigorous, fresh and well-disciplined" (vol. 3, 496). Even though he warns that "we may see already that the critic evidently prefers matter to form," he commends this body of work in the highest terms: "altogether there are few things in English criticism better worth reading, marking, and learning, by the novice" (vol. 3, 497).

36 Carlyle, *Two Notebooks*, 41.
37 Carlyle, *Two Notebooks*, 215.
38 Quoted in *Life of Carlyle, 1795–1835*, vol. 2, 371.
39 Vanden Bossche, viii.
40 Heinrich Heine, *Sämtliche Werke*, ed. Manfred Windfuhr (Hamburg: Hoffmann und Campe, 1979), vol. 1, 141.
41 Heine, *Sämtliche Werke*, vol. 1, 125.
42 Heine, *Sämtliche Werke*, vol. 1, 140, 144, 138, 184.
43 2 April 1829, *Goethes Gespräche, 7. Band, 1829 und 1830*. Ed. Woldemar Freiherr von Biedermann (Leipzig: F.W. von Biedermann, 1890), 40: "The classical I call healthy and the romantic sick. The most recent cultural developments are not romantic because they are new, but because they are weak, sickly, and diseased, while older cultural phenomena [such as *The Nibelungenlied* and Homer] are not classical simply because they are old, but because they are strong, fresh, happy, and healthy. If, according to such qualities, we distinguish between classical and romantic, we shall soon be in the clear."
44 Ludwig Marcuse, "Reaktionäre und progressive Romantik," *Monatshefte* 44, No. 4/5 (April–May 1952), 200: "Together the two counter-movements formed a rebellion against the present, which was perceived as increasingly unlikeable and colorless. Against this hated present both movements strove continuously, and because of this combined effort to this day we conflate the reactionary and the progressive Romantics. But they differentiate themselves according to the goals they strive for. Therefore, there are feudal, liberal, and socialist Romantics. Consider these words of Novalis: 'Everything becomes romantic when seen from a distance.' So that the past is just as romantic as the future. And that explains the ambiguity that has always been intrinsic to the concept of Romanticism."
45 *The Works of Thomas Carlyle*, vol. 5, 41.

46 Friedrich Nietzsche, *Die Geburt der Tragödie aus dem Geiste der Musik* (Stuttgart: Philipp Reclam Jun., 1979), 69–70.
47 Friedrich Nietzsche, *Umwertung aller Werte*, ed. Friedrich Würzbach (Munich: Deutscher Taschenbuch Verlag, 1977), No. 413, 758.
48 *The Works of Thomas Carlyle*, vol. 5, 13, 11.
49 *The Works of Thomas Carlyle*, vol. 5, 13. Nietzsche, *Jenseits von Gut und Böse, Werke* (Leipzig: C. G. Neumann, 1899), vol. 7, 117: "The essential thing, in heaven and on earth, seems to be, to say it once again, that there should be something to obey, over a long duration and in a single direction; given that, something always arises, and has developed, for whose sake it is worthwhile to live on earth; for example, virtue, art, music, dancing, reason, spirituality,—something transfiguring, subtle, made, and divine."
50 Friedrich Nietzsche, *Also Sprach Zarathustra* in *Werke* (Leipzig: Alfred Körner, 1910), vol. 6, 15.
51 Nietzsche, *Umwertung aller Werte*, No. 407, 757.
52 Søren Kierkegaard, *The Present Age: On the Death of Rebellion*, trans. Alexander Dru (New York: Harper Perennial Modern Classics, 2010 [1962]), 52.
53 Kierkegaard, *The Present Age*, 72.
54 Kierkegaard, *The Present Age*, 80.
55 Kierkegaard, *The Present Age*, 58.
56 Friedrich Schlegel, "Athenäum Fragment, No. 262," *Charakteristiken und Kritiken I* (1796–1801), ed. Hans Eichner (Munich: Ferdinand Schöningh, 1976), 210.
57 It is also possible that Nietzsche had Faust's creator in mind for the precursor of the *Übermensch*. By his own admission the most confessional of European writers, Goethe divested himself of intensely felt experiences by exercising the creative faculty and *Faust* contains among the most psychologically acute of Goethe's many self-portraits.
58 See, for example, Shelley's treatise "A Defence of Poetry" (1821).
59 Carlyle, *Two Notebooks*, 263, 264.
60 Wallace Stevens, "Two or Three Ideas," *Opus Posthumous*, ed. Milton J. Bates (New York: Vintage Books, 1989, [1957]), 206.
61 Novalis (Friedrich von Hardenberg), "Blütenstaub, No. 71" in *Gesammelte Werke*, vol. 2, 25: "In the beginning poets and priests were one. But the real poet is always a priest, just as the real priest has always remained a poet. And should not the future bring about the old state of things again?"
62 Pierre-Simon Ballanche, *Orphée* in *Oeuvres complètes* (Geneva: Slatkine, 1967), vol. 5, 96.
63 Friedrich Schlegel, "Athenäum Fragment, No. 64," in *Kritische Aufgabe*, vol. 2, 262.
64 Friedrich Schlegel, "Gespräch über die Poesie," *Kritische Schriften*, ed. Wolfdietrich Rasch (Munich: Paul Hauser, 1964), 497: "What I maintain is lacking at the heart of our poetry is a mythology such as that which the ancients knew, and all of the essential ways in which modern poetry is inferior to antiquity can be summed up in the words: We have no mythology."

65 Carlyle's efforts to "Germanize the public" are bound up with his mission to share the inspiration he received from Goethe. See Carlyle's letter to his brother John, 4 June 1827, *Letters of Thomas Carlyle, 1826–1836*, ed. Charles Eliot Norton (London and New York: Macmillan, 1889), 46.

66 See Robert Kiely, *The Romantic Novel in England* (Cambridge: Harvard University Press, 1972), 155–173.

67 Carlyle, *Two Notebooks*, 128. Carlyle's approach corresponds to Coleridge's definition of poetry, according to which everything depends on the identity of the poet and his poetry: "What is poetry? is so nearly the same question with, what is a poet? that the answer to the one is involved in the solution of the other. For it is a distinction resulting from the poetic genius itself" (*Biographia Literaria*, vol. 2, 12–13).

68 *The Works of Thomas Carlyle*, vol. 26, 216.

69 *The Works of Thomas Carlyle*, vol. 26, 260. Carlyle's concern with the personality, with ethics—one is reminded of James Boswell's phrase "ethic poetry" in referring to Johnson's poem "Vanity of Human Wishes" (1748/1749) in the *The Life of Samuel Johnson* (1791)—is yet another expression of his emulation of the German Romantics, whose "Bedeutung geht weit über das Ästhetische hinaus" [importance far exceeded merely aesthetic concerns] (Ferdinand Lion, cited in Klaus Doderer, "Das englische und französische Bild von der deutschen Romantik," 401).

70 *Sartor Resartus*, 55.

71 Friedrich Schlegel, *Kritische Aufgabe*, 497.

72 *The Works of Thomas Carlyle*, vol. 28, 109.

73 *The Works of Thomas Carlyle*, vol. 28, 108–109.

74 Friedrich Schiller, *Über naive und sentimentalische Dichtung*, *Schriften zur Philosophie und Kunst*, ed. Bernd Holger Bonsels (Munich: Wilhelm Goldmann, 1964), 197.

75 Kierkegaard, *The Present Age*, 35.

76 Saintsbury, vol. 3, 495; and Johann Gottfried von Herder, *Vom Erkennen und Empfinden der menschlichen Seele*, *Sämtliche Werke*, ed. B. Suphan, vol. 8, 208: "One should be able to regard every book as an imprint of a living human soul. . . . The life of an author is the best commentary on his writings, when he is faithful to himself, is at one with himself. . . . Every poem, especially a whole, great poem, is a venturing outward of the soul and of life, is a dangerous traitor to his author, often when he was least likely to betray himself." Milton makes this point just as emphatically: "a good book—the precious life blood of a master spirit" (*Areopagitica*, 1644).

77 Johann Casper Lavater, *Physiognomische Fragmente* (Leipzig: Winterthur, 1778), Erster Abschnitt, Zehntes Fragment, 83: "[H]uman gods! Creators! Destroyers! Revealers of the secrets of God and humankind! Interpreter of nature! Speaker of unspeakable things! Prophets! Priests! Kings of the world! Revealers of the majesty of all things! Geniuses."

78 Roy Pascal, *The Sturm und Drang* (Manchester: Manchester University Press, 1953), 138.
79 *The Works of Thomas Carlyle*, vol. 5, 90.
80 Paul Tillich, *The Courage to Be* (New Haven: Yale University Press, 2000 [1952]), 141.
81 Friedrich Schiller, *Über naive und sentimentalische Dichtung, Schriften zur Philosophie und Kunst*, 197.

Notes Interlude Two

1 John Milton, *History of Britain*, vol. III (1670), *The Prose Works of John Milton*, ed. R.W. Griswold (Philadelphia: John W. Moore, 1847), vol. 2, 245.
2 Letter of George Bancroft to J.T. Kirkland, President of Harvard College, 22 February 1819. Autograph File. The Houghton Library, Harvard University.
3 Russell Blaine Nye, *The Cultural Life of the New Nation, 1776–1830* (New York: Harper & Bros., 1960), 191: "Through such volumes as *Specimens of Foreign Standard Literature* (1838–1842), as well as by critical essays [in *The North American Review*], George Ripley was as zealous as Margaret Fuller in seeking to elevate American literature above its native sphere and to liberate it from English domination by infusing into the national mind the germinal strains of Continental thought." A remarkable cluster of studies of German literature and translations was published in New England over the next decade. More remarkable still, these works were written by members of the astonishing constellation of talent based in Concord, Cambridge, and Boston. These texts include John Sullivan Dwight's *Select Minor Poems of Goethe and Schiller* (1839), vol. 3 of *Specimens of Foreign Standard Literature*; Margaret Fuller's translation of Johann Peter Eckermann's *Conversations with Goethe* appeared in 1839 as volume 4 in Ripley's series (and then as a free-standing book in 1852); James Freeman Clarke's translation of De Wette's *Theodore: or the Sceptic's Conversion* (1841); Charles T. Brooks's anthology, *German Lyric Poetry* (1842); Theodore Parker's translation of De Wette's *Introduction to the Old Testament* (1843); Charles T. Brooks's *Life of Jean Paul Richter* (1845); Samuel Gray Ward's edition of Goethe's *Essay on Art* (1845); Frederic Henry Hedge's anthology *Prose Writers of Germany* (1849); and Ralph Waldo Emerson's essay on Goethe in *Representative Men* (1850), "Goethe, or The Writer."
4 Claude Lévi-Strauss, *Triste Tropiques* (New York: Atheneum Books, 1974), 326.
5 This bold move is comparable to similar efforts by the People's Republic of China, which began sending its best and brightest students to American universities in the early 1980s.
6 In an article in *The Atlantic Monthly* 79 (April 1897) Thomas Wentworth Higginson observed that "these young Americans who attended Göttingen took our whole educational system away from the English tradition, substituted

German models, and laid the foundation for non-English training not only in Boston but in America."

7   New textbooks introduced at Harvard include Edward Everett's translation of P.K. Buttmann's *Greek Grammar* (1837) and Everett's Greek reader, which was modeled on an anthology edited by C.F. Jacobs. Also influential were translations of such leading German theologians, philologists, Orientalists and linguists as Johann Gottfried Eichhorn (1752–1827), Karl Richard Lepsius (1810–1884), Johann Jakob Griesbach (1745–1812), Ernst Friedrich Karl Rosenmüller (1768–1835), Christian Gottlieb Kühnöl (1768–1841), Johann Benjamin Koppe (1750–1791), Georg Ludolf Dissen (1784–1837), and Georg Friedrich Benecke (1762–1844), many of whom were based at Göttingen University.

8   Concerning Joseph Cogswell's reform of the Harvard College library, George Ticknor commented in April 1822: "Cogswell is doing much good in the library, reforming it utterly." In February 1823 he wrote: "Cogswell has put the library in perfect order, and is now finishing his catalogue of it, but the Corporation neither comprehend what he has done, nor respect him enough for his great disinterested labor." Both passages are quoted in John A. Walz, *German Influence in American Education and Culture* (Philadelphia: Carl Schurz Memorial Foundation, 1936), 40.

9   See Nye, 90: "Despite their extensive rejection of Old World [read British] modes, proponents of a national literature in the ante-bellum decades were not blind to the fact that certain principles and literary developments currently dominant in Europe afforded a salient re-enforcement for their designs and aspirations. Between 1815 and 1830 Bancroft et al. were introduced to literary doctrines which were thoroughly congenial to the buoyant nationalism of America after the War of 1812 . . . . For in addition to the congenial doctrines which they found among the intellectuals, these students were impressed, as Ticknor enthusiastically reported, by the autochthonous expression of popular feelings in Germany and in Spain." For a survey of the German impact on American higher education see Anja Werner, *The Transatlantic World of Higher Education: Americans at German Universities, 1776–1914* (New York and Oxford: Berghahn Books, 2013).

10 See Nye, 166: Cousin's book "was widely read by American educators, who gained from it familiarity with Pestalozzian principles." Writing from Göttingen to John Thornton Kirkland, President of Harvard College, George Bancroft commented on the Prussian school system (Letter of George Bancroft to J. T. Kirkland, 3 November 1820. Autograph File. The Houghton Library, Harvard University): "I need not say, how fine the schools of Prussia are; they are acknowledged to be the finest in Germany. Here in Berlin a great many new ideas as going into application; and the indistinct forebodings of Pestalozzi, and the eloquent discourses of Fichte have not been without lasting fruits. I need not assure you how happy I am in having an opportunity subject of much discussion and where the Government have done so much, have done everything they could do, to realize the vast advantages about to result from the reform in

the institutions of instruction. No Government knows so well how to create Universities and high school as the Prussian. The new Academy at Bonn rivals already the oldest Universities."

11 Pestalozzi revolutionized pedagogy with his invention of the concept of *Kindheit* [childhood] as a separate phase of human development. In 1794 Pestalozzi visited Weimar where he met Goethe, Wieland, Herder, and Fichte. The latter encouraged him to put his revolutionary educational ideas into writing. The resulting text, *Meine Nachforschungen über den Gang der Natur in der Entwicklung des Menschengeschlechts* [*My Research on the Course of Nature in the Development of the Human Race*] (1821), galvanized the reform movement in education throughout Europe and North America.

12 Walz, *German Influence*, 42: "[The Round Hill School] forecast the various educational experiments by Bronson Alcott, the Brook Farmers, Elizabeth Peabody, and other Transcendentalists."

13 Both Frederic Henry Hedge and Margaret Fuller modeled their anthologies of German texts after Austin's. Moreover, Hedge's critical commentary in the head notes to *Prose Writers of Germany* (1849) incorporates extracts from Austin's *Fragments of German Prose Writers* and Carlyle's critical essays on German writers, which were originally published in the 1820s and 1830s.

14 *Conversations of Goethe in the Last Years of His Life. Translated from the German of Eckermann by Sarah Margaret Fuller* (1839) (Boston: James Munroe and Company, 1852), xvii.

15 *Correspondence of Fräulein Gunderode and Bettine von Arnim. Translated by Margaret Fuller and Minna Wesselhoft* (Boston: T. O. H. P. Burnham, 1861), x.

16 *Correspondence of Fräulein Gunderode and Bettine von Arnim*, xi.

17 Johann Wolfgang von Goethe, *Dichtung und Wahrheit*, ed. Walter Hettche (Stuttgart: Reclam, 1991), 303: "Alles, was daher von mir bekannt geworden, sind nur Bruchstücke einer großen Konfession, welche vollständig zu machen dieses Büchlein ein gewagter Versuch ist" [All the things that I have published, therefore, are only fragments of a great confession, which this daring little book seeks to clarify].

18 Margaret Fuller Ossoli, *Life Within and Without*, ed. Arthur B. Fuller (Boston: Brown, Taggard and Chase, 1860), 35.

19 John Sullivan Dwight, ed., *Select Minor Poems of Goethe and Schiller* (Boston: Hilliard, Gray, and Company, 1839), x.

20 Unpublished letter of Thomas Carlyle to John Sullivan Dwight, 14 March 1839. The Amy Lowell Autograph Collection. The Houghton Library, Harvard University.

21 Unpublished letter of George Ripley to Thomas Carlyle, 29 December 1836. Autograph File. The Houghton Library, Harvard University.

22 George Ripley to Thomas Carlyle, 29 December 1836.

23 Frederic Henry Hedge, *Prose Writers of Germany* (Philadelphia: Carey and Hart, 1849), 267.

24 The parallels between the reception of Goethe in New England in the first half of the nineteenth century and that of French theory in the final third of the twentieth century are revealed in the strategies of denigration practiced by Paul De Man's opponents in the conservative wing of the American professoriate. The assaults on his politics and conduct of his personal life are mirrored in the attacks on Goethe. For example, just as De Man's ideas were supposedly to be discredited because he had "abandoned" his first family when he left Belgium to study at Harvard in the late 1950s, Goethe could not be a "good poet" because he lived with a partner whom he had not yet married when she gave birth to his son. In addition, just as De Man supposedly "used" his benefactors, Goethe was deemed, in the language of his detractors, to be parasitically dependent on the patronage of Grand Duke Karl August and was therefore an immoral poet and infernal influence on his American readers. More seriously, however, De Man and Goethe were accused of reducing texts to mere aesthetic constructs, which drained them of moral content, authorial control, and secure reference points in the physical world.

25 Emerson's initial resistance to Goethe was based on the implications of Goethe's aristocratic sensibility for Concord intellectuals. Such ambivalence was ultimately overcome as evidenced by the publication of Emerson's "Goethe, or, the Writer," *Representative Men* in 1850 and, in 1886, of *The Life and Genius of Goethe: Lectures of the Concord School of Philosophy*, ed. F. B. Sanborn (Boston: Ticknor and Company, 1886), with contributions by Horatio Stevens White, John Albee, Thomas Davidson, Cyrus Augustus Bartol, Frederic Henry Hedge, William Ordway Partridge, Denton J. Snider, W. T. Harris, Ednah Dow Littlehale Cheney, Samuel Hopkins Emery, Caroline Kempton Sherman, and Julia Ward Howe.

Notes Chapter Six

1 Richard Wagner, "Religion und Kunst" [*Religion and Art*] (1880), *Gesammelte Schriften und Dichtungen,* Dritte Auflage, 9. Band (Leipzig: Verlag von E.W. Fritzsch, 1898), 211.

2 Oscar Wilde, "The Portrait of Mr. W.H.," *Blackwood's Edinburgh Magazine* 146 (July 1889): 1–21.

3 Letter to Dr. Joseph Frank Payne, 25 January 1876, *Selections from George Eliot's Letters*, ed. Gordon S. Haight (New Haven and London: Yale University Press, 1985), 466.

4 Carlyle published his translations of Johann Wolfgang von Goethe's *Wilhelm Meister's Apprenticeship* and *Wilhelm Meister's Travels* in 1824 and 1827, respectively. He also published an anthology of selections from German authors, *German Romance* (4 volumes) in 1827, and essays on Goethe, Schiller, Novalis, Fichte Jean Paul, and others throughout the 1820s and 1830s. In addition, his novel *Sartor Resartus* is a parody of German Romantic style and philosophical

idealism, while his posthumously published novel, *Wotton Reinfred*, is a *Bildungsroman* in the tradition of *Wilhelm Meister*. Through the influence and example of Carlyle's heroic efforts of cultural mediation a generation of Victorian writers put down their Byron and picked up their Goethe.

5 £20 in 1860 would be worth approximately £1,695 in 2017.

6 Arnold reproaches the Romantic poets for being "uncritical," seemingly untouched by the great revolutionary ideas coming out of Germany in the wake of Kant and Goethe.

7 See Chapter One and Interlude Two above.

8 Bloom, *The Anxiety of Influence*, 56.

9 Goethe to Carlyle, 20 July 1827, *Correspondence between Goethe and Carlyle*, 18.

10 Erich Heller's translation of *The Will to Power*, fragment number 822 (Friedrich Nietzsche, *Gesammelte Werke*, Musarion-Ausgabe (Munich, 1922–1929), vol. XIX, 229), *The Importance of Nietzsche* (Chicago: University of Chicago Press, 1988), 130.

11 Virginia Woolf, "George Eliot," *Times Literary Supplement* 18 (20 November 1919): 657–658.

12 George Eliot, "Recollections of Berlin 1854–1855," *The Journals of George Eliot*, ed. Margaret Harris and Judith Johnston (Cambridge: Cambridge University Press, 1998), 258.

13 Published in 1774 the slim narrative of Werther and Lotte's fervid but hopeless love made the 25-year old Goethe famous throughout Europe and caused a world-wide sensation, as evidenced by the fad for wearing blue waistcoats and yellow breeches, Werther's signature outfit, an epidemic of copy-cat suicides, and the world's first marketing tie-in as porcelain tea services with scenes from the novel painted on them were shipped as far away as China and North America. The influence of *Werther* has scarcely been equaled before or since. Napoleon Bonaparte never travelled anywhere without his copy and "Wertherism" was Carlyle's epithet for the spirit of passionate discontent that had seized modern Europe in the decades following the French Revolution (1789): "*Werther* is but the cry of that dim, rooted pain, under which all thoughtful men of a certain age were languishing."

14 Citing his many love affairs, the child he fathered out of wedlock with Christiane Vulpius, and the many actresses populating his fiction, conservative critics in Germany, Britain, and the United States vilified Goethe as an immoral man who, following Horace, therefore was a bad poet.

15 The Reform Acts of 1832 and 1867 extended the franchise to social and economic groups previously denied the right to vote. The combined impact of the two bills, which doubled the electorate to almost two million voters in England and Wales, is said to have achieved a redistribution of power equivalent to what was brought about by the French Revolution. In *Middlemarch* Eliot is thus giving voice to the anxiety that the new, more egalitarian political order undermined traditional sources of English identity and posed a threat to high culture.

16   See George Eliot's review of Wilhelm Riehl's *Die bürgerliche Gesellschaft* [*Middle-Class Society*] (1851) and *Land und Leute* [*Nation and People*] (1853), *Westminister Review* LXVI (July 1856): 28–44.
17   Richard Wagner, "Eine Mittheilung an meine Freunde" ["A Communiqué to My Friends"] (1851), *Gesammelte Schriften und Dichtungen, 4. Band* (Leipzig: Verlag von E.W. Fritzsch, 1872), 365.

Notes Postlude

1   Saintsbury, vol. 3, 373.
2   Dorothy Richardson Jones, *King of the Critics: George Saintsbury, 1845–1933* (Ann Arbor: University of Michigan Press, 1992). Another study that places Saintsbury in the broad context of Victorian criticism is Harold Orel's *Victorian Literary Critics: George Henry Lewes, Walter Bagehot, Richard Holt Hutton, Leslie Stephen, Andrew Lang, George Saintsbury and Edmund Gosse* (New York: St. Martin's, 1984).
3   At the end of his career Saintsbury estimated that his journalism would fill "at least a hundred volumes of the 'Every Gentleman's Library' type—and probably more" (*A Last Scrap Book* (London: Macmillan, 1924), vol. 1, x).
4   A partial list of Saintsbury's University of Edinburgh bibliography includes: *Sir Walter Scott* (1897), *The Flourishing of Romance and the Rise of Allegory* (1897), *A Short History of English Literature* (1898), *Matthew Arnold* (1899), *The Earlier Renaissance* (1901), *Loci Critici* (1903), *A History of English Prosody from the Twelfth Century to the Present Day* (3 volumes, 1906–1910), *The Later Nineteenth Century* (1907), *An Historical Manual of English Prosody* (1910), *A History of English Prose Rhythm* (1912), *The English Novel* (1913), and *The Peace of the Augustans: A Survey of Eighteenth-Century Literature as a Place of Rest and Refreshment* (1916). There are editions of Dryden (2 volumes, 1904), Shadwell (1912), and *Minor Poets of the Caroline Period* (3 volumes, 1905–1912). Saintsbury was also the leading contributor to the *Cambridge History of English Literature* (1907–1916) with 21 chapters.
5   D. Nichol Smith, "George Saintsbury," *Dictionary of National Biography, 1931–1940*, 5th Supplement, ed. L.G. Wickham Legg (Oxford: Oxford University Press, 1949), 776.
6   Over a decade Eliot produced a body of criticism that, in conjunction with H. J. C. Grierson's anthology, *Metaphysical Lyrics and Poems* (1921), altered the canon. Some of the most important essays include "Christopher Marlowe" (1918), "Hamlet" (1919), "Ben Jonson" (1919), "John Dryden" (1920), "Andrew Marvell" (1921), and "The Metaphysical Poets" (1921).
7   Matthew Arnold, "Ecce, Convertimur and Gentes," *English Literature and Irish Politics. Complete Prose Works of Matthew Arnold*, ed. R.H. Super (Ann Arbor: University of Michigan Press, 1973), vol. 9, 5
8   Saintsbury, vol. 3, 352.

9   The gist of Saintsbury's critique is anticipated in large part by Taylor, Coleridge, and De Quincey. These critics deplored Goethe's flaunting of conventional morality in such prose works as *Die Leiden des jungen Werthers, Die Wahlverwandschaften*, and, above all, *Wilhelm Meisters Lehrjahre* with its gallery of sexually available female characters. Saintsbury's reading of Goethe may also be extended to British critics who affiliated with Goethe's critical orientation, which combines pedagogy, psychology, and connoisseurship.
10 Saintsbury, vol. 3, 352.
11 Saintsbury, vol. 3, 495.
12 *Dichtung und Wahrheit*, Zweiter Teil, 7. Buch, *Goethes Werke, Band XI, Autobiographische Schriften I* (Munich: C.H. Beck, fourteenth printing, 2002 [1981]), 313: "Alles war daher von mir bekannt geworden, sind nur Bruchstücke einer großen Konfession, welche vollständig zu machen dieses Büchlein ein gewagter Versuch ist."
13 *The Works of Thomas Carlyle*, vol. 23, 225–226.
14 *Diary, Reminiscences, and Correspondence*, vol. 1, 49.
15 Indeed, Coleridge remarks how "little instructive any criticism can be which does not enter into minutiae" (*Biographia Literaria*, vol. 2, 19). Saintsbury's emphasis on textual analysis is paralleled in the following passage by Coleridge: "But I should call that investigation fair and philosophical, in which the critic announces and endeavors to establish the principles, which he holds for the foundation of poetry in general, which the specification of these in their application to the different classes of poetry. Having thus prepared his canons of criticism for praise and condemnation, he would proceed to particularize the most striking passages to which he deems them applicable, faithfully noticing the frequent or infrequent recurrence of similar merits or defects..." (*Biographia Literaria*, vol. 2, 107). Such parallels underscore why Saintsbury ranks Coleridge so highly; he considers him "the critical author to be turned over day and night." No critic can match his erudition and reading. By contrast, "Dryden is great, but he is not fully formed." Fontenelle, too, "is great," but he combines Dryden's limitations with "an almost, perhaps a quite, wilful eccentricity and capriciousness." Lessing is great in his way, but he has "fixed his main attention on the least literary parts of literature." Goethe is "great, but a great pedant" and Hazlitt may be great but in comparison with his "master," Coleridge, he is "insular and parochial in range and reading, if not in spirit." In Saint-Beuve's criticism "we want a little more theory; some more enthusiasm; a higher and more inspiring choice of subjects." In Arnold "the defects of Fontenelle reappear without Fontenelle's excuse of chronology" (Saintsbury, vol. 3, 230).
16 Saintsbury, vol. 3, 373.
17 Saintsbury, vol. 3, 361.
18 *The Works of Thomas Carlyle*, vol. 23, 225.
19 Saintsbury, vol. 3, 376.
20 Saintsbury, vol. 3, 361.

21 Johann Wolfgang von Goethe, "Zum Shäkespears Tag," *Schriften zur Weltliteratur*, ed. Horst Günther (Frankfurt: Insel Verlag, 1987), 19.
22 Goethe, "Zum Shäkespears Tag," 18.
23 Johann Wolfgang von Goethe, "Shakespeare und Kein Ende," *Schriften zur Weltliteratur*, 136, 138: "No one despised the outer costume of men more than he; but he understood well the inner man, and here all are similar. It is said that he has delineated the Romans with wonderful skill. I cannot see it. They are Englishmen to the bone; but they are human, thoroughly human, and thus the Roman toga presumably fits them."
24 Saintsbury, vol. 3, 362.
25 Saintsbury, vol. 3, 365.
26 Saintsbury, vol. 3, 369–370.
27 Saintsbury, vol. 3, 366.
28 Saintsbury, vol. 3, 375.
29 Saintsbury, vol. 3, 373.
30 Saintsbury, vol. 3, 377. In the *Edinburgh Review*, No. 92, "State of German Literature"; *Foreign Review*, No. 2, "Goethe's Helena"; *Foreign Review*, No. 3, "Goethe"; *Edinburgh Review*, No. 105, "Historic Survey of German Poetry"; *Fraser's Magazine*, No. 26, "Goethe's Portrait"; *New Monthly Magazine*, No. 138, "Death of Goethe"; *Foreign Quarterly Review*, No. 19, "Goethe's Works."
31 Saintsbury, vol. 1, 211.
32 Saintsbury, vol. 3, 375.
33 John Forster, *Walter Savage Landor* (Oxford: The Clarendon Press, 1874), 316.
34 *Goethes Gespräche, 7. Band 1829 und 1830*, ed. Woldemar Freiherr von Biedermann (Leipzig: F.W. von Biedermann, 1890), 277 (21 March 1830).
35 Friedrich von Schiller, *Über naïve und sentimentalische Dichtung*, ed. Karl-Maria Guth (Berlin: Verlag de Contumax, 2016), 12–13.
36 *Goethes Gespräche*, ed. Biedermann, 40: "I call the classic healthy and the romantic pathological . . . . Most modern art and literature is romantic—not because it is new but because it is weak, pathological, and diseased. And the antique classic—not because it is old but because it is strong, fresh, joyous, and healthy. If we distinguish 'classic' and 'romantic' by these qualities, it will be easy to find our way" (2 April 1829).
37 T.S. Eliot, "Goethe as Sage," *On Poetry and Poets* (New York: Octagon Books, 1975 [1957]), 243–244.
38 Eliot, "The Metaphysical Poets," originally published in the *Times Literary Supplement* 20 October 1921: "[a] thought to Donne was an experience; it modified his sensibility . . . . The poets of the seventeenth century . . . possessed a mechanism of sensibility which could devour any kind of experience . . . . In the seventeenth century a dissociation of sensibility set in, from which we have never recovered . . . " Hugo von Hofmannsthal, "Der Chandos-Brief," *Der Tag* (18 and 19 October 1902): "At that time, I was in a condition of constant intoxication and the whole of existence appeared to me as a great unity: the spiritual and physical world seemed to me no antithesis, just as life at court and

animal being, art and non-art, solitude and society. In everything I felt nature—in the aberrations of madness as well as in the utmost refinements of a Spanish ceremonial at the Habsburg Court; in the idioltic follies of young peasants, no less than in the sweetest allegories. And in all expressions of nature I felt myself. When I came into my hunting cabin and drank the warm, foaming milk which an unkempt wench milked from the burgeoning udder of a beautiful, soft-eyed cow into a wooden pail, it was no different from when I am sitting on the window seat in my studio and my mind abstorbed the sweet and foaming nourishment from a book. One was identical to the other: neither was superior to the other, whether in a dreamlike otherworldly quality or in physical intensity—and so it went on through the whole breadth of life in every direction; everywhere I was in the center of it, never suspecting anything to be mere appearance: or I guessed that all things were allegorical, and every creature was a key to the others, and I felt myself to be the only one in a position to seize one after the other by the horn and decipher as many of the others as were ready to be decoded."

39 Bloom, *The Anxiety of Influence*, 30.
40 Regine Otto, ed. Johann Peter Eckermann, *Gespräche mit Goethe in den letzten Jahren seines Lebens* (Munich: C.H. Beck, 1984), 387: "Certainly . . . in art and poetry personality is everything; yet there are many weaklings among modern critics who do not admit this, but consider a great personality in a work of poetry or art merely a kind of trifling appendage. . . . However, to empathize with and to respect a great personality one must be something onself" (12 February 1831).
41 Saintsbury, vol. 3, 388.
42 Saintsbury, vol. 1, 386–387.
43 Saintsbury, vol. 3, 382.
44 Saintsbury, vol. 3, 383.
45 Saintsbury, vol. 3, 383.
46 The discomfort with Schiller discloses a reaction against a tendency described by Erich Heller, "In Two Minds about Schiller," *The Artist's Journey into the Interior, and Other Essays* (New York: Harcourt, 1975), 47: "His work—a lifework of considerable genius, moving single-mindedness, and great moral integrity—is a striking instance of a European catastrophe of the spirit: the invasion and partial disruption of the aesthetic faculty by unemployed religious impulses. He is one of the most conspicuous and impressive figures among the host of theologically displaced persons who found a precarious refuge in the emergency camp of Art."
47 Herein lies a possible explanation for Carlyle's baroque, often parodied style. More than a mere imitation of Jean Paul and E.T.A. Hoffmann, Carlyle's bizarre intellectual topography, overheated tone, obsessive concern with interiority are representative symptoms of the unsteady and perhaps unnatural alliance of art and the quest for transcendental truths.

Index

A

Abel, Carl Friedrich 37
Adorno, Theodor 13
Age of Reason 21
Alcott, Louisa May 99
   The Modern Mephistopheles 99
American literature 99, 167
Analytical Review 38–39, 42
Anglo-American criticism 140, 171
Anglo-German literary relations 36, 191
Anglophilia 37
Anthropology 4, 151, 158, 186, 191, 200
Anti-Jacobin 14, 52, 54, 62, 78
Ariosto, Ludovico 202
Aristotle 49, 115, 196, 201
   Poetics 201
Armbruster, Johann Michael 41
Arnim, Bettina Brentano von 65, 96, 125, 129, 165–166
Arnold, Matthew 12–13, 18, 25, 35, 67, 77, 80, 92, 96, 116, 120–121, 130, 141, 154, 175, 185, 190–193, 226 n.38
   Culture and Anarchy 35
   „The Function of Criticism at the Present Time" 67, 175
   Hellenism and Hebraism 146, 185
Arnold, Thomas 121, 125
Atheism 68–70

Aufklärung 46
Austen, Jane 186
Austin, Sarah 9, 40, 46, 61, 164–165, 169, 175
   Characteristics of Goethe 164
   Fragments of German Prose Writers 165
   Germany from 1760 to 1814 165
   Report on the State of Public Instruction in Prussia 165
Avila, Saint Theresa of 181, 185

B

Bach, Johann Christian 37
Bach, Johann Sebastian 37
Bacon, Sir Francis 193, 199
Bakhtin, Mikhail 44
Ballanche, Pierre-Simon 155
Balzac, Honoré 186
Bancroft, George 65, 124, 133, 161–162, 165, 168–169, 171
Barnard, Henry 165
Barrow, George 46
Beaumarchais, Pierre 33–34
   The Marriage of Figaro 33–34, 42
Benjamin, Walter VII, 13
Bentham, Jeremy 143
Berlin 34, 106, 178, 179
Bildung IX, 56, 143, 154, 172, 193
Bildungsreise 110–111, 123, 125

Bildungsroman 99–100, 105, 108–109, 111, 120, 159, 181–182, 187
Biographical criticism 2–6, 14, 20, 49, 156, 197
Blake, William 37, 64, 101–102
Bloom, Harold IX, 14, 27, 99, 115, 175, 201
Bodmer, Johann Jakob 38
Bonneville, Nicholas 33
Bosanquet, Bernard 120
Boston University 169
Böttiger, Karl August 70–71, 96
Bradford, George 170
Bradley, F.H. 120
Brandes, Johann Christian 42
　The German Hotel 42
Brentano, Christian 65, 96, 125
Brentano, Clemens 65, 96, 125, 129
British Associationism 70
British literature X, 37, 95, 102, 127, 178
British Romanticism 37, 61, 70, 72, 93, 109, 131, 139, 160
British Romantics 92, 130, 140, 144–145, 147
Brontë, Anne 186
Brontë, Charlotte 186
Brontë, Emily 186
Brooks, Charles Timothy 168, 170
Büchner, Georg 149
Bürger, Gottfried August 50, 59
Burke, Edmund 35, 149

Reflections on the Revolution in France 35, 149
Byron, George Gordon Lord IX, 5, 17, 21–23, 61, 67, 79, 85, 90–93, 100–101, 130, 133–137, 144, 157, 181, 187–188, 190
　Childe Harold's Pilgrimage 188
　Goethe's *Faust* 133–137
　Manfred 92, 133–137, 188
　"Prometheus" 90–93
　Sardanapalus 133
　Werner 133, 147

C

Cabot, J. Elliot 170
Calderón, Pedro 132
　Magico Prodigioso 132
Calvert, George Henry 162
Canning, George 78
Carlyle, Thomas IX, 1–25, 36, 43, 46–47, 49, 50, 55, 58–59, 61–62, 64, 67–70, 75, 77, 80, 83, 88, 93–94, 96, 99–101, 104, 109–110, 117, 118, 120–122, 126, 128–130, 139–147, 149–160, 165, 168–169, 173, 175–176, 185, 191–194, 196, 200, 202–203, 263 n. 47
　"Characteristics" 142
　"Death of Goethe" 6
　German Romance 2, 94
　"Goethe" 3, 6
　Goethe's *Faust* 5, 18, 142
　"Goethe's Helena" 6
　"Goethe's Works" 3, 6, 23
　Life of Schiller 141

Oliver Cromwell's Letters and Speeches 6
On Heroes, Hero-Worship, and the Heroic in History 6, 88, 149
Past and Present 101, 143, 149
"Preface to *Meister's Apprenticeship*" 6
Sartor Resartus 21–22, 24, 67–68, 109, 120, 159–160
The Early Kings of Norway 149–150
Wilhelm Meister's Apprenticeship 4, 14, 23–24, 62, 100, 103–105, 129–130, 146
Wotton Reinfred 99, 105, 109–110
Cellini, Benvenuto 56
Channing, William Henry 168
Chapman, John 174, 180
Christianity 19, 23, 68, 88, 101, 120, 140, 150, 153, 155, 172–174, 177, 186, 201
Cibber, Colley 36
Clarke, James Freeman 168
Cogswell, Joseph Green 162, 165, 169, 171
Coleridge, Samuel Taylor X, 1, 4, 15–17, 20, 23, 38, 46–47, 54–56, 58, 61–66, 70, 75, 77, 79, 81, 84, 89, 93–94, 96, 100–102, 115–132, 135–137, 140–141, 144, 149, 190, 192, 202–203
  Biographia Literaria 20, 58, 62–63, 70, 75, 89, 94
  Goethe's *Faust* 15, 127, 128, 249 n. 8
  "Kubla Khan" 100
  "Life of Lessing" 125–126, 129
  On the Constitution of Church and State 101, 149

Schiller's *Wallenstein* 84, 93, 118–121
Goethe's *Zur Farbenlehre* 128–129
Collins, Wilkie 187
Concrete universal 49
Corneille, Pierre 56
Cornelius, Peter von 106
Cousin, Victor 67, 165
Covent Garden 34, 42
Crabb Robinson, Henry IX, 9, 15–16, 38, 43, 46, 49–50, 57–58, 64–97, 117–118, 122–129, 136, 149, 166, 192, 203
Cranch, Christopher Pearse 168
Cromwell, Oliver 146
Cult of personality IX–X, 11–12, 25, 49, 146, 160, 165
Cultural mediation 1, 5, 9, 13, 27–30, 37–38, 40, 53–54, 56–57, 71, 78, 94, 152, 161–164, 173–175
Culture war 57, 118, 165, 168, 172

D

Dante Alighieri 4, 14, 47, 202
Darwin, Charles 128, 152, 174–175, 177
de Cambon-van de Werken, Maria Geertruida 40
De kleine Grandison 40
de la Motte Fouqué, Caroline 165
De Man, Paul X, 115, 119, 258 n. 24
De Quincey, Thomas X, 23, 46–47, 57–58, 61–65, 74–75, 130, 202
de Voeux, Charles 13

Derrida, Jacques 119, 172
Dickens, Charles 185, 186
Diderot, Denis 31, 56
Dilthey, Wilhelm 2–3, 14, 46–47
   Das Erlebnis und die Dichtung [*Experience and Poetry*] 2–3, 14, 46–47
Dissenters IX, 9, 27–29, 38–39, 43, 71, 123–124, 143, 163
Dissociation of sensibility 199
Don Quixote 148
Dostoevsky, Fyodor 99–101, 176, 188
   Crime and Punishment 99, 188
   Notes from Underground 99, 101
Drury Lane 51
Dryden, John 13, 81, 116
Dwight, John Sullivan 163–165, 168–169, 171
   Select Minor Poems of Goethe and Schiller 168

E

Eckermann, Johann Peter 4–5, 57, 134, 148, 166–167, 179, 193, 198
Edinburgh Review 5, 16, 19, 47, 50, 58–59, 80, 96, 118
Ehret, Georg Dionysus 37
Eichhorn, Albert 121
Eliot, George IX, 9, 40, 99–101, 120, 164–165, 173–188, 191–192
   Adam Bede 121, 185–186
   Daniel Deronda 186
   Felix Holt 185
   Life of Jesus 185
   Middlemarch 99, 101, 173–188
   Romola 186
   Scenes of Clerical Life 121, 176, 180, 185–186
   Silas Marner 185, 186
   The Essence of Christianity 166, 174, 176
   The Mill on the Floss 184–186
Eliot, Thomas Stearns 13, 49, 116, 140, 190, 199–200, 202
   „Goethe as Sage" 199
Ellis, George 14, 78
Elyot, Sir Thomas 127
Emerson, Ralph Waldo 77, 80, 104, 143, 169, 172
   "Goethe or the Writer" 169
   Representative Men 169
Emerson, William 162
Enlightenment 7, 10, 28, 36–37, 46, 61, 67, 116, 109, 140
Eudaemonism 21
Euripides 56
European Union 36
Everett, Edward 65, 162, 169, 171

F

Fahrenheit, Daniel Gabriel 36
Feuerbach, Ludwig 120, 166, 174, 176, 184–185
   Das Wesen des Christentums 166, 174
Fichte, Johann Gottlieb 61, 65, 67, 74, 103, 107, 111, 121, 147, 159, 170

Über das Wesen des Gelehrten und seine Erscheinungen im Gebiete der Freiheit 159
Wissenschaftslehre 103, 159
Fielding, Henry 36, 186
Flaubert, Gustave 186
Franco-Prussian War 8, 177
Fraser's Magazine 8, 50
Frederick the Great 28, 146
French Classicism 194
French Revolution 10, 29–30, 32, 52, 103, 143, 191
Frere, John Hookam 14, 78
Freud, Sigmund 4, 13–14
Frothingham, Nathaniel Langdon 168
Froude, Anthony 9, 12, 22
  Life of Carlyle 22
Frühromantiker 201
Fuller, Margaret 40, 104, 163–164, 166–172, 175
  Art, Literature and the Drama 166
  "Goethe" 167
  Goethe's *Faust* 167
  Günderode 166
  Life Without and Life Within 167
Fuseli, Henry 27, 29, 37–42, 230 n 27

G

Galliard, John Ernest 36
Gay, John 36
Genlis, Madame de 33
George, Stefan 147

German Classicism 94, 104, 108, 133, 148, 197, 198
German Idealism 61–66, 70–75, 117, 120, 140
German literature IX, 5, 8–10, 13, 25, 27–28, 33, 38, 42, 46, 50, 53, 55, 57–59, 62–63, 77–80, 93–94, 109, 117, 120–121, 125–126, 142, 161, 163–164, 166, 168–171, 191, 202
German Pietism 37
German nationalism 147, 172, 201
German Romanticism 10, 71–72, 81, 101, 105, 123, 139, 146–148, 150, 178, 187, 201
Gesamtkunstwerk 106
Gillies, Robert Pearse 9, 45, 65, 78
Gillray, James 32
Gisborne, John and Maria 131, 132
Gladstone, William 189
Godwin, Mary Jane 32
Godwin, Parke 170
Godwin, William 27–32, 38–39, 42, 44, 53, 69, 99–100, 110, 140, 144, 149
  An Enquiry Concerning Political Justice 30, 32, 149
  Caleb Williams 31–32
  Cursory Strictures on the Charge Delivered by Lord Chief Justice Eyre to the Grand Jury 31–32
  St. Leon 32, 99, 101, 110–111
Goethe, Johann Wolfgang von IX, X, 1–7, 10–25, 27–29, 36, 38–39, 41, 43–50, 53–59, 61–71,

74, 77–80, 82–86, 88–96, 99–100, 103–105, 108–110, 115–136, 139–151, 153–162, 164, 166–169, 171–173, 175, 178–181, 183, 187–203

Clavigo 39

„Dauer im Wechsel" 86

„Der Wanderer" 84–86

Dichtung und Wahrheit 20, 48–49, 167, 170, 191

Die Leiden des jungen Werthers [*The Sufferings of Young Werther*] 3, 20–24, 39, 48, 77–78, 84–88, 104–105, 122, 136, 180, 199

Die Mitschuldigen 84

„Die neue Mesuline" 199

Die Wahlverwandschaften [*Elective Affinities*] 48, 170

Faust, Part I 3, 5, 15, 18, 23, 25, 77, 84, 89, 92, 110, 122, 127–128, 130–135, 142, 153, 158, 167, 188, 196, 199

Faust, Part II 92, 133, 189, 196

„Ganymed" 84, 89, 94–95

Götz von Berlichingen 20, 59, 61, 77, 84, 149

Hermann und Dorothea 43–44, 123

Iphigenie auf Tauris 25, 41, 47, 50, 59, 77, 197–198

„Kennst Du das Land" 130

Italienische Reise 199

„Mahotmetsgesang" 84, 88

„Prometheus" 84, 89, 93, 196

Propyläen 94

Römische Elegien 198

„Shakespeare und kein Ende" 193–195

Sprüche in Prosa: Maximen und Reflexionen 195

Stella 39

Torquato Tasso 3, 13, 15, 84, 127, 166

Über Kunst und Altertum 133

Venetianische Epigramme 25, 79, 82

„Von deutscher Baukunst" 199

West-östlicher Divan 22–23, 77

Wilhelm Meisters Lehrjahre 4, 14, 22–24, 48, 77, 80, 89, 100, 103–105, 109, 120, 125, 130, 146, 170, 181–183, 187, 192, 200

Winckelmann und sein Jahrhundert 198–199

Zahme Xenien 79, 82, 195

„Zum Schäkespears Tag" 199

Zur Farbenlehre 128, 129

Goethe, Ottilie von 179

Goethezeit 126, 190

Goldsmith, Oliver 66

Göttingen 65, 122, 136, 162–163, 165, 171

Grand Tour 123

Green, T.H. 120

Günderode, Karoline von 166

H

Haak, Theodor 36

Habermas, Jürgen 13

Hahn-Hahn, Ida Gräfin von 165

Haller, Albrecht von 36

Hamsun, Knut 99–101, 114, 188

Sult [*Hunger*] 99–100, 101, 188

Händel, Georg Friedrich 36

Hardy, Thomas (the Jacobin) 31–32

Hardy, Thomas (the novelist) 185
Hare, Julius 121
Hartley, David 67
Hartmann, Eduard von 170
Harvard College 65, 136, 162–165, 169–171
Harvard Corporation 162
Hawthorne, Nathaniel 99
Haydon, Benjamin Robert 64
Hazlitt, William X, 17–18, 31, 45–47, 57–59, 61–62, 64–65, 73, 75, 116, 130, 144, 158
Hedge, Frederic Henry 162, 168–172
Hegel, Georg Wilhelm Friedrich 49, 67, 111, 121, 146, 184, 199
  Vorlesungen über die Ästhetik 121
Heidegger, John James 36
Heidegger, Martin 13, 120
Heine, Heinrich 2, 5, 8–11, 18, 131, 139, 146–149
  Die Romantische Schule [The Romantic School] 2, 9–10, 147
Heller, Erich 27
Herder, Johann Gottfried 39, 59, 81, 129, 147, 158, 193–194
  Vom Erkennen und Empfinden der Menschlichen Seele 158
  Von deutscher Art und Kunst 193–194
Hero worship 6, 10, 144, 150–153, 159
Herschel, William 36
Heyne, Christian Gottlob 122, 126

Higher Criticism 162, 166
Hoffmann, E.T.A. 94, 99, 100
Hofmannsthal, Hugo 199
  „Chandos–Brief" 199–200
Holcroft, Thomas IX, 9, 27, 29–35, 38–45, 53, 56, 78, 121, 123, 136, 159, 203
  Alwyn 34
  Anna St. Ives 30, 34
  Follies of the Day 42
  Hermann and Dorothea 43–45, 123
  He's Much to Blame 34
  Life of Baron Frederic Trenck 42–43, 231 n 36
  Love's Frailties 33
  Memoirs of Bryan Perdue 34
  Physiognomical Fragments 28, 40, 159
  The Deserted Daughter 34
  The German Hotel 42
  The Marriage of Figaro 33–34
  The Posthumous Works of Frederick the Great 28, 33
  The Road to Ruin 34
  The School for Arrogance 34
  Travels from Hamburg 43
  Travels through Germany 43
Hölderlin, Friedrich 81, 149, 160
  „Brot und Wein" 160
Humbolt, Alexander von 174
Humbolt, Wilhelm von 165
Hume, David 69, 73
  An Enquiry Concerning Human Understanding 73
Hunt, Thornton Leigh 174
Hunter, Henry 40–41

I

Iffland, August Wilhelm 79
Inchbald, Elizabeth 51
   Lover's Vows 51
Irving, Edward 129
Ivanov, Vyacheslav 114

J

Jacobi, Friedrich Heinrich 69
Jacobinism 27, 34, 42–43, 68, 163
Jacobsen, Jens Peter 99–101
   Niels Lyhne 99–101
Jena 65, 71, 107, 140, 171
Johnson, Joseph 27, 38, 143
Johnson, Samuel 13, 81, 83, 116, 156, 180, 195–196
   Lives of the Most Eminent English Poets 13, 156
   "Preface to Shakespeare" 195
Jonson, Ben 127
Joyce, James 188
Jungdeutschland [Young Germany] 5

K

Kant, Immanuel 57–75, 77, 82, 111, 117, 118, 121, 124–125, 167, 170
Karl August, Grand Duke 65, 124
Keats, John 24, 45, 81, 93, 101, 103, 131, 140, 154, 180
   „Ode on a Grecian Urn" 154
Keller, Gottfried 99, 100, 103, 188
   Der grüne Heinrich 99, 188

Kierkegaard, Søren 69, 151–153, 155, 158–159
Kingsley, Charles 12
Kirkland, John Thornton 162
Klopstock, Friedrich Gottlieb 33, 46, 50, 54–55, 59, 81, 122–126, 136
   Der Messias 81, 123
Knebel, Karl Ludwig von 96, 133
Kneller, Sir Godfrey 37
Kotzebue, August von 7, 11, 38, 47, 50–55, 59, 78–81, 104, 117
   Das Kind der Liebe 51
   Die Spanier in Peru, oder Rollas Tod 50
   Menschenhaß und Reue 50
   Kulturträger 162

L

LaFontaine, August 79
Lamb, Charles 129
Lampe, Johann Friedrich 37
Landor, Walter Savage 59, 115, 197
Lavater, Johann Kaspar 28, 38–42, 159
   Physiognomische Fragmente zur Beförderung der Menschenkenntnis und Menschenliebe 28, 40–42, 159
Leibniz, Gottfried Wilhelm 36, 74, 170
Lessing, Johann Gottfried 51, 54, 59, 116, 125, 126, 129, 147
   Emilia Galotti 51
   Nathan der Weise 59

Lévi-Strauss, Claude 161
Lewes, George Henry 25, 77, 96, 104, 120, 128, 141, 167, 173–174, 176, 178–180, 191–193
  Life of Goethe 167, 178
Lewis, Matthew Gregory 30, 40, 46, 61, 65, 124, 134, 231 n 31
  The Monk 30
Liszt, Franz 179
Locke, John 61, 67–68, 70–73
Lockhart, John Gibson 9, 45–46, 156
London Corresponding Society 31
Longfellow, Henry Wadsworth 65, 162
Louisa Queen of Prussia 165
Loyola, Saint Ignatius of 69
Lukasbund [Nazarenes] 105–106, 178

M

Maaß, Johann Gebhard Ehrenreich 70
  Versuch über die Einbildungskraft 70
Mackenzie, Henry 117
Malraux, André 29–30
Mann, Horace 165
Mann, Thomas 77, 100, 114, 188
  Buddenbrooks 100
  Der Zauberberg 187
  Der Tod in Venedig 100, 187–188
  Doktor Faustus 188
  „Tonio Kröger" 100, 187

Marcuse, Ludwig 139, 146, 148–151
Marx, Karl 13
Materialism 67–71, 173
Maurice, Frederick Denison 25, 120
McTaggert, John McTaggert Ellis 120
Menzel, Adolf 47
Mephistopheles 16, 89, 127
Mercier, Louis-Sébastien 31, 33
Methodism 37
Michaelis, Johann David 59
Mill, John Stuart 143, 176, 185
Milman, Henry 121
Milton, John 81, 89, 93, 119, 140–141, 154, 161, 183, 200, 202
Modernism IX, 15, 114, 191, 199
Molière 202
Montesquieu, Charles-Louis 66
More, Hannah 53
  Strictures on the Modern System of Female Education 53
Moritz, Karl Philipp 34, 106
Motley, John Lothrop 162
Mozart, Wolfgang Amadeus 37
Muhammad {Mahomet} 88–89
Müller, Adam von 147, 149, 164
Munch, Edvard 114
Murray, John 61, 134

N

New Criticism 203
New England IX, 103, 161–172

Newman, John Henry 176
Newton, Isaac 175
Niebuhr, Berthold Georg 121
Nietzsche, Friedrich 13, 25, 112–117, 120, 149–155, 159, 170, 175–177, 185
  Also Sprach Zarathustra 101, 151
  Die fröhliche Wissenschaft 177
  Die Geburt der Tragödie aus dem Geiste der Musik 150
  Goethean *Bildung* 154
  Jenseits von Gut und Böse 151–153
  Umwertung aller Werte 150, 152
Novalis (Hardenberg, Georg Philipp Friedrich von) 2, 13–14, 23, 81, 99–102, 107–109, 121, 129, 147–149, 154, 157, 200–202
  Christenheit oder Europa 101, 201
  Heinrich von Ofterdingen 99, 101, 107–109

O

Objective correlative 49
Oldenburg, Heinrich 36
Ortega y Gasset, José 139
Overbeck, Friedrich 106

P

Paganism 25, 149–150
Paine, Thomas 31–33
  The Rights of Man 33
Palingenesia 143
Parr, Samuel 32
Pascal, Blaise 183

Pater, Walter 25, 114, 117, 120–121, 150, 177, 186
  Studies in the History of the Renaissance 150, 186
Paulus, Heinrich E.G. 59
Pepusch, Johann Christoph 36
Perkins, Samuel 119
Pestalozzi, Johann Heinrich 165
Pforr, Franz 106
Phi Beta Kappa 171
Platonism 60
Poe, Edgar Allan 80
Pope, Alexander 37, 82
  The Dunciad 82
Poststructuralism 118–119, 171
Practical criticism 201
Pre-Raphaelitism 178
Presbyterianism 164
Prévost, Antoine François 31
Primitivism 146–148
Progressive Romanticism 148
Puritanism 164, 172
Pushkin, Alexander 85
Pye, Henry James 50

Q

Quintilian 127
  Institutio Oratoria 127

R

Rabelais, François 202
Racine, Jean 56
Radcliffe, Ann 30
  The Mysteries of Udolpho 30

Raphael, Alice 164
Rationalism 140, 150
Reactionary Romanticism 117, 147, 149
Realism 16, 18–19, 23–24, 48, 89, 96, 105, 108, 144, 173, 195, 198
Reform Bill of 1832 142, 185
Reform Bill of 1867 185
Retsch, Friedrich Moritz 131
Richardson, Samuel 40
Richter, Jean Paul Friedrich 8, 11, 13–14, 62, 94, 118, 120–121, 140, 170
  „Army Chaplain Schmelze's Journey to Flätz" 94
  „Life of Quintus Fixlein" 94
  Titan 170
Riehl, Wilhelm 165, 186
Ripley, George 161, 163–164, 166, 168–169, 171–172
  Specimens of Foreign Standard Literature 161, 166, 168
Roman Catholicism 60, 69, 105, 107, 164, 178, 201
Romanticism 8, 10, 15, 27, 45, 56, 58, 61, 69, 71, 78, 90, 94, 99, 101, 103, 106–108, 116, 133–134, 139, 146–147, 150, 153–155, 157, 160, 173, 191, 197–199, 201
Romantik 11, 148
Round Hill School 165
Rousseau, Jean-Jacques 31, 39, 140
Royal Academy of Music 36
Royal Society 36

Ruskin, John 176

S

Said, Edward 35
Saint-Aubin, Stéphanie Félicité du Crest de 42
Sainte-Beuve, Charles Augustin 116
Saintsbury, George X, 4, 15, 49, 59, 94, 96, 115–116, 158, 189–203
  A History of Criticism and Literary Taste in Europe 115, 190–191, 203
Salzmann, Christian Gotthilf 39
  Moralisches Elementarbuch 39
Santayana, George 80
Saturday Review 189
Sauvigny, Marie-Jules César 42
Savary, Claude-Étienne 42
Schauerroman 40
Schelling, Friedrich Wilhelm 61, 65, 71, 74–75, 96, 117, 121, 125, 147, 167, 170
Schicksalsdramen 117, 179
Schiller, Friedrich von 1, 7, 11, 13–14, 16, 18, 38, 47, 50, 54, 59, 61, 65, 77, 79, 81–82, 84, 93–95, 104, 107–108, 117–120, 122, 124–125, 129, 135, 140–141, 145, 147, 149, 157, 168, 170, 197–199, 201–202
  „Das Genie" 83
  Die Räuber [*The Robbers*] 18, 54, 93, 141, 202

Über naive und sentimentalische Dichtung 157–158, 197–199, 201–202
Wallenstein 77, 84, 93, 118–119, 121
Schlegel, August Wilhelm 11, 59, 65, 70, 96, 107, 108, 139, 147, 149, 193, 201
Schlegel, Friedrich 11, 13, 102–103, 106–109, 117, 139, 147, 149, 153, 155, 157, 201
„Athenäum Fragment, No. 116" 106–107
Schleiermacher, Friedrich 165, 170
Schopenhauer, Arthur 49, 65, 73–75, 111–113, 149, 152, 170
Die Welt als Wille und Vorstellung 49, 73–75, 112–113
Schopenhauer, Johanna 165
Scott, Sir Walter 1, 9, 16, 43, 46, 48, 50, 59, 61, 77, 130–131, 144, 149, 156
Goethe's *Götz von Berlichingen* 59
Sehnsucht 85
Shakespeare, William 5, 14, 18, 22, 24, 47, 50, 52, 140, 149, 156, 175, 178, 191–195, 201–202
Hamlet 191–193
Shaw, Samuel 41
Shelley, Mary Wollstonecraft 99, 110–111, 149, 187, 190
Frankenstein 99, 110–111
Shelley, Percy Bysshe IX, 23, 61, 79, 90–91, 130–132, 135–136, 144, 149, 181, 187, 190
"A Defence of Poetry" 102

"Scenes from the *Faust* of Goethe" 130–133
Prometheus Unbound 90, 149
Sheridan, Richard Brinsley 50
Pizarro 50, 52
The Stranger 50
Sidney, Sir Philip 49, 154
Solger, Karl Wilhelm Ferdinand 121
Vorlesungen über Ästhetik 121
Southey, Robert 46, 54, 58–59, 93, 119, 129, 141
Spencer, Herbert 174, 180
Spengler, Oswald 154
Der Untergang des Abendlandes 154
Spenser, Edmund 23
The Faerie Queene 23
Spinoza, Baruch 74
Staël, Germaine de 2, 5, 7–10, 19, 61, 63, 66, 70, 79, 96, 99, 104, 169
Corinne, ou Italie 99, 101, 104
De l'Allemagne [*On Germany*] 2, 7–10, 14, 19, 61, 63, 66, 70–71, 79, 104
Stanley, Arthur 121
Stephen, Leslie 12, 61
Stevens, Wallace 154
Stewart, Dugald 62–63
Stolberg-Stolberg, Friedrich Leopold Graf zu 28, 42, 232 n. 41
Strauß, David Friedrich 166, 173–174, 185
Das Leben Jesu 166, 173–174

Index 277

Sturm und Drang 10, 93–94, 159, 193–194

T

Tacitus 8
Taine, Hyppolyte 5, 14
Tasso, Torquato 82
   Gerusalemme liberata 82
Taylor, William X, 9, 14, 27, 29, 38, 40, 43, 46–50, 53–62, 65, 69, 72–73, 75, 77–80, 96, 121–125, 129–130, 202–203
   An Historical Survey of German Literature 80, 130
   English Synonyms Discriminated 58
   Iphigenie in Tauris 40, 47, 77
   "Leonore" 50
Thackeray, William Makepeace 65, 185, 186
The Anti-Jacobin Review X, 49, 52, 54, 57, 60, 62, 78, 118, 128, 130, 233 n 62
The Christian Examiner 171
The Critical Review 41, 53, 58, 79
The European Magazine 41
The Ladies Monthly Museum 51
The Leader 174, 178
The Monthly Mirror 53
The Monthly Register and Encyclopedian Magazine 64–66, 75, 77, 96
The Monthly Review 53, 55, 58–59, 69, 79, 118
The North American Review 171
Thirwall, Connop 121
Thoreau, Henry David 128

Ticknor, George 65, 162, 169, 171
Tieck, Ludwig 83, 94, 99, 105, 107–109, 149, 193, 201
   Altenglisches Theater 193
   Briefe über Shakespeare 193
   „Die Zeichen im Walde" 83
   Herzensergiessungen eines kunstliebenden Klosterbruders 99, 105–107
   Shakespeares Vorschule 193
Tillich, Paul 160
Tolstoy, Leo 114
Tooke, John Horne 31–32
Transcendentalism 161, 172
Translation 27–56, 77–97, 118–119, 164–172, 203

U

Übermensch 151–153, 155, 177
Unitarian Church 164, 170
University of Edinburgh 189
University of Göttingen 65, 162–163
University of Jena 65, 125, 149

V

Varnhagen von Ense, Karl 179
Varnhagen, Rahel 165, 179
Veit, Philipp 106
Ventriloquism 29, 35–36
Victorian Britain 104, 176, 183, 193, 202
Voltaire 31, 56
Voss, Johann Heinrich 34
Vulpius, Christiane 179

W

Wackenroder, Heinrich Wilhelm 99, 105–108, 147, 149
- *Herzensergiessungen eines kunstliebenden Klosterbruders* 99, 105–107

Wagner, Richard 100, 106, 114, 117, 173, 188
- *Der fliegende Holländer* 100, 188
- *Der Ring des Nibelungen* 106
- *Lohengrin* 188
- *Parsifal* 106
- *Tristan und Isolde* 106

Wallace, Alfred Russell 152

Weber, Max 186

Wedgwood, Josiah 119, 126

Weimar 7, 11, 46, 65, 71, 74, 122–125, 129, 133, 135–136, 146, 159, 162, 171, 178–181, 186, 201

Weltliteratur 1, 13, 36, 55

Werner, Zacharias 133, 147

Wesley, John 37
- *A Collection of German Hymns* 37

Westminster Review 174, 178

Wharton, Edith 164

Wieland, Christoph Martin 7, 13, 31, 38, 50, 59, 65, 80, 104, 124, 129, 193

Wilde, Oscar 114, 173, 177

Williams, Helen Maria 122
- *Julia* 122

Willich, A.F.M. 59–60, 62
- *Elements of the Critical Philosophy* 59

Wilson, Thomas 127

Winckelmann, Johann Joachim 38, 122, 198–199
- *Geschichte der Kunst des Alterthums* 38

Wolff, Christian 36

Wollstonecraft, Mary 9, 27, 29, 38–41, 43, 56, 100, 164, 175
- *A Short Residence in Sweden, Norway, and Denmark* 43
- *A Vindication of the Rights of Woman* 40
- *Elements of Morality for the use of children* 39
- *Original Stories from Real Life* 39–40
- *The Confidential Letters of Albert* 39
- *The Female Reader* 39
- *The Wrongs of Woman, or Maria* 40
- *Thoughts on the Education of Daughters* 39
- *Young Grandison* 40

Woolf, Virginia 179

Wordsworth, Dorothy 122

Wordsworth, William X, 12, 15, 17, 18, 46, 54–55, 79, 81, 101–102, 115, 122–125, 127, 130–131, 136, 140, 144, 149, 190
- *Lyrical Ballads* 149

Z

Zinzendorf und Puttendorf, Nikolaus Ludwig Reichsgraf, 37

Zollmann, Philipp Heinrich 36

Zwinglianism 39

ibidem-Verlag

Melchiorstr. 15

D-70439 Stuttgart

info@ibidem-verlag.de

www.ibidem-verlag.de
www.ibidem.eu
www.edition-noema.de
www.autorenbetreuung.de